Introduction to SPSS® in Psychology

Visit the *Introduction to SPSS in Psychology, third edition* Companion Website at **www.pearsoned.co.uk/howitt** to find valuable **student** learning material including:

- Learning objectives for each chapter
- Dataset
- Annotated links to relevant sites on the web

PEARSON
Education

We work with leading authors to develop the
strongest educational materials in psychology,
bringing cutting-edge thinking and best
learning practice to a global market.

Under a range of well-known imprints, including
Prentice Hall, we craft high quality print and
electronic publications which help readers to
understand and apply their content,
whether studying or at work.

To find out about the complete range of our
publishing please visit us on the World Wide Web at:
www.pearsoned.co.uk

Introduction to SPSS® in Psychology

With supplements for Releases 10, 11, 12 and 13

Third edition

Dennis Howitt

Duncan Cramer

PEARSON
Prentice
Hall

Harlow, England • London • New York • Boston • San Francisco • Toronto • Sydney • Singapore • Hong Kong
Tokyo • Seoul • Taipei • New Delhi • Cape Town • Madrid • Mexico City • Amsterdam • Munich • Paris • Milan

Pearson Education Limited
Edinburgh Gate
Harlow
Essex CM20 2JE
England

and Associated Companies throughout the world

Visit us on the World Wide Web at:
www.pearsoned.co.uk

First published 1997
Second edition published 2000
Second (revised) edition published 2002
Third edition published 2005

ISBN 0 131 39986 1

British Library Cataloguing-in-Publication Data
A catalogue record for this book is available from the British Library

Library of Congress Cataloging-in-Publication Data
Howitt, Dennis.
　　Introduction to SPSS in psychology : with supplements for releases 10, 11, and 12 /
Dennis Howitt and Duncan Cramer.
　　　p.　cm.
　　Includes bibliographical references and index.
　　ISBN-10: 0-13-139986-1
　　ISBN-13: 978-0-13-139986-0

　　　1. Psychometrics.　2. SPSS for Windows.　3. Psychometrics–Computer programs.
　I. Cramer, Duncan, 1948-　II. Title.

BF39.H72 2005
150′.1′5195–dc21
　　　　　　　　　　　　　　　　　　　　　　　　　　　　　　　　2004060177

10　9　8　7　6　5　4　3　2
10　09　08　07　06　05

Typeset in 10/12pt Times by 35
Printed by Ashford Colour Press Ltd., Gosport

The publisher's policy is to use paper manufactured from sustainable forests.

Summary of contents

Companion Website resources

Visit **www.pearsoned.co.uk/howitt** to find valuable online resources

For students
- Learning objectives for each chapter
- Dataset
- Annotated links to relevant sites on the web

For more information please contact your local Pearson Education sales representative or visit **www.pearsoned.co.uk/howitt**

Contents

7   Correlation coefficients: Pearson's correlation and Spearman's rho   56

8   Regression: Prediction with precision   64

9   Samples and populations: Generating a random sample   72

15 Missing values 106

16 Recoding values 112

17 Computing new variables 117

Introduction

Statistical Package for the Social Sciences (SPSS) was initially developed in 1965 at Stanford University in California. It is the leading data analysis package in the field and available all over the world in universities and elsewhere. Modern computing developments have enabled its use on home computers. Because of its popularity and universality, using SPSS is one of the most readily transferable of all research skills. Once SPSS has been learnt it can be used practically anywhere. Furthermore, SPSS is constantly being updated so that up-to-date statistical methods are included in each new version.

This book is a stand-alone step-by-step approach to statistical analysis using SPSS for Windows and is applicable to Releases 10, 11, 12 and 13. It is suitable for students and researchers wishing to analyse psychological, sociological, criminological, health and similar data.

It updates the approach of *A Guide to Computing Statistics with SPSS 11 for Windows* to ensure even faster access to computerised data analysis using SPSS. Each statistical technique is carefully described step-by-step using screenshots of SPSS data analysis and output. The user's attention is now focused directly on the screenshots, what each of them signifies, and why they are important. In other words, it is as close as is possible in a textbook to face-to-face individual instruction. Users with little or no previous computer skills will be able to quickly analyse quite complex data and appreciate what the output means.

Most chapters have a common pattern. The computer steps (which keys to press) are given in exact sequence. However, this is not the end of any data analysis, and so there are also explanations of how to interpret and report the SPSS output. The common structure is:

- An overview explains the important features of the statistical analyses contained in the chapter. This will be sufficient in most cases for a user to get a clear idea of where and when to use the techniques.
- There is a short introduction to the chapter and the data to be analysed.
- Simple examples are given of the appropriate sorts of data for each statistical technique. These examples allow the user to work through our computations, and to gain confidence before moving on to their own data.
- Data entry for a particular statistical analysis is presented visually and explained in adjacent text.
- This is followed by a step-by-step, screenshot-by-screenshot, description of how a particular statistical analysis is done using SPSS for Windows.
- The SPSS statistical output is included exactly as it appears on the monitor screen and in printouts of the analysis. This is crucial – SPSS output can be confusing and unclear at first.

■ The key features of the statistical output are highlighted on the output itself together with simple explanations of what the important parts of the output mean – SPSS output is infamous for its overinclusiveness.

■ Suggestions are made on reporting the statistical findings in reports, theses and publications. These includes samples of how to describe research findings and present tables clearly.

This book is based on the latest versions of *SPSS for Windows* (that is, Releases 12 and 13); but remains suitable for Releases 9, 10 and 11 because of their similarity. Notes after this Introduction describe the main differences between these releases. Although SPSS is updated every few years, usually there is little difficulty in adapting knowledge gained on the older versions to the new version.

Introduction to SPSS in Psychology is an excellent single source for data analysis. It is complete in itself and contains many features not available elsewhere. Unlike other SPSS books, it meets the needs of students and researchers at all levels. However, it is also part of a package of methodology books by the same authors designed to be comprehensive, authoritative and exhaustive. The three volumes in this series are closely tied to each other. The other two are:

■ *Introduction to Statistics in Psychology* (3rd edn, Pearson Education: Harlow, 2005): This is a thorough introduction to statistics for all students. It consists of a basic introduction to key psychological statistics and, although maintaining its accessibility to students, it also covers many intermediate and advanced techniques in detail. It contains chapters on topics, such as meta-analysis, which are seldom covered in other statistics texts. Importantly, the structure of the statistics textbook is closely linked to this book. Thus, anyone following a chapter in the statistics book will, where appropriate, find an equivalent chapter in this book with details of how to do the analysis using SPSS. Similarly, anyone using this book will be able to find a detailed account of the technique in the statistics textbook.

■ *Introduction to Research Methods in Psychology* (Pearson Education: Harlow, 2005): This is a major textbook on research methods in psychology. It covers both quantitative and qualitative methods. There are major chapters on report writing, ethics in psychology and searching the literature. All aspects of experimental, field study, survey and questionnaire construction are covered, and guidance is given on qualitative data collection and analysis. There are numerous cross-references to this book and *Introduction to Statistics in Psychology*.

In other words, the three books offer a comprehensive introduction to conducting research in psychology. They may be used independently or in any combination.

Introduction to SPSS in Psychology can be used alongside virtually any statistics textbook to support a wide variety of statistics and practical courses. The range of statistical techniques covered is large and includes the simplest as well as the most important advanced statistical techniques. The variety of techniques described and the relative ease of using SPSS for Windows ensure that this guide can be used at introductory, intermediate and advanced levels of statistics teaching. The structure of the book is such that statistical procedures are described more-or-less in order of conceptual difficulty. Generally speaking, computing with SPSS is as easy for advanced statistical techniques as it is for simple ones.

Chapter 1 is essential reading, as it explains data entry and basic computer operating. However, the remaining chapters can be used on a stand-alone basis if desired. Users with insufficient time to work chapter-by-chapter through the guide should find enough detail in the relevant chapters to complete an SPSS analysis successfully. Table 1.1, at the end of Chapter 1, states which chapter is most appropriate for which purpose, thereby enabling the reader to move directly to that part of the book.

Those who work steadily through the book will profit by doing so. They will have a much better overview of SPSS computing procedures. For most readers, this is possible in a matter of hours, especially if they have prior knowledge of statistics.

SPSS has an extensive catalogue of statistical procedures – far more than could be included. We have selected those suitable for most purposes when the range of possibilities is likely to confuse the average reader. The quickness and ease of SPSS mean that more advanced users can explore the alternatives by using the menus and dialogue boxes. Most users will find our coverage more than sufficient.

> The data and statistical analyses carried out in this book correspond almost always to those in the authors' accompanying statistics text, *Introduction to Statistics in Psychology* (3rd edn, Pearson Education: Harlow, 2005). This book is referred to as *ISP*, followed by the corresponding chapter or table number.

We wish to thank the typesetter for laying out the screenshots and the accompanying textboxes and arrows so much more clearly than we could have done.

Dennis Howitt
Duncan Cramer

Key differences between SPSS 13 and earlier versions

SPSS 12

The major differences between SPSS 12 and SPSS 13 for the topics covered in this book are to 'Compute Variable . . .', 'Scatter/Dot . . .' and the 'Chart Editor'. Also the plots in the output of SPSS 13 are now shaded.

In SPSS 12 the 'Compute Variable' dialogue screen has a single 'Functions' screen from which options can be chosen. 'Scatter/Dot . . .' is called 'Scatter . . .', the 'Scatter/Dot' dialogue screen is called 'Scatterplot' and there is no 'Dot' option.

In SPSS 12, to label the slices of a pie diagram and add the percentages of cases in each, double click anywhere in the 'Chart Editor', double click on the pie diagram (to open the 'Properties' dialogue screen), select 'Data Value Labels' (in the 'Properties' dialogue screen), select 'Count' in the 'Contents' screen, select the red 'X' (to put 'Count' in the 'Available' screen), select the variable name (e.g. 'Occupation'), select the curved upward arrow (to put 'Occupation' in the 'Contents' screen), select 'Percent' and the curved upward arrow (to put 'Percent' in the 'Contents' screen), select 'Apply' and then 'Close'.

To fit a regression line to a scatterplot, click on a dot in the chart of the 'Chart Editor' so that the circles in the plot become highlighted, select 'Chart', select 'Add Chart Element', select 'Fit Line at Total' (which opens the 'Properties' dialogue screen). Assuming that the 'Fit Line' tab is active, select 'Linear' (this is usually the default) and then 'Close'.

SPSS 11

The major differences between SPSS 12 and SPSS 11 also apply to SPSS 10. They are relatively few. In SPSS 11 and 10 variable names cannot begin with a capital letter and are restricted to eight characters. The 'Data' and 'Transform' options are not available in the 'Viewer' or 'Output' window. Some output, such as partial correlation and reliability, is not organised into tables. The 'Chart Editor' works differently. To fit a regression line to a scatterplot, double click anywhere in the scatterplot to open the 'Chart Editor', select 'Chart', select 'Options . . .' (which opens the 'Scatterplot Options' dialogue screen), select 'Total' under 'Fit Line' and then 'OK'.

SPSS 10

Differences between SPSS 10 and SPSS 11 are very minor and hardly noticeable.

1 Basics of SPSS data entry and statistical analysis

Overview

- This chapter gives the basics of operating SPSS on a personal computer. It includes data entry as well as saving files. There will be small variations in how SPSS is accessed from location to location. The basics are fairly obvious and quickly learnt.
- A few essential statistical concepts are included to help researchers plan appropriate statistical analyses.

1.1 Introduction

SPSS Releases 12 and 13, or earlier versions such as Releases 10 and 11, are commonly available on university and college computers. Most users will access SPSS from these locations. It is by far the most widely used computer package for statistical analysis throughout the world. As such, learning to use SPSS is a transferable skill, often valuable in the job market. The program is used at all levels from students to specialist researchers, and in a great many academic fields and practical settings. One big advantage is that once the basics are learnt, SPSS is just as easy to use for simple analyses as for complex ones. The purpose of this guide is to enable beginners quickly to take advantage of the facilities of SPSS.

Most people nowadays are familiar with the basic operation of personal computers (PCs). The total novice though will not be at too much of a disadvantage since the elements of SPSS are quickly learnt. Users who have familiarity with, say, word processing will find much of this relevant to using SPSS – opening programs, opening files and saving files, for instance. Do not be afraid to experiment.

Since SPSS is commonly used in universities and colleges, many users will require a user name and a password that is obtained from their institution. Documentation is often available on registration at the college or university. If not, such documentation is usually easily available.

SPSS may be found as a shortcut among the on-screen icons or it may be found in the list of programs on Windows. Each institution has its own idiosyncrasies as to where SPSS can be found. This book is based on Releases 12 and 13 of SPSS. Although they are slightly different from Releases 10 and 11, the instructions apply almost universally to those releases too.

1.2 To access SPSS

SPSS for Windows is generally accessed using buttons and menus in conjunction with clicks of the mouse. Consequently the quickest way of learning is simply to follow our steps and screenshots on a computer. The following sequence of screenshots is annotated with instructions labelled Step 1, Step 2, etc.

Step 1:

Double left click on the SPSS icon with the mouse if it appears anywhere in the window – otherwise click the 'Start' button to find the list of programs, open the list of programs, and click on SPSS.

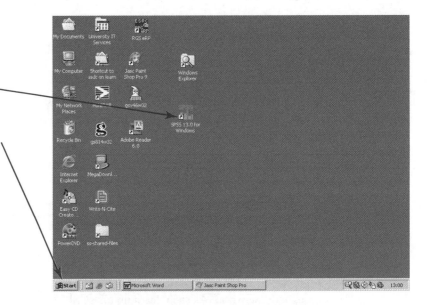

Step 2:

This screen appears after a few moments. You could choose any of the options in the window. However, it is best to close down the superimposed menu by clicking on the close-down button. The superimposed menu may not appear, as it can be permanently closed down.

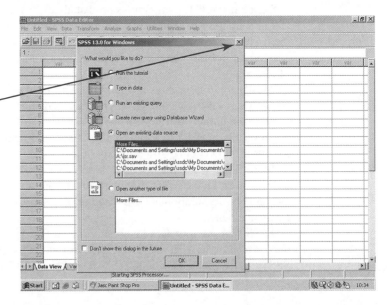

1.3 To enter data

Step 3:

The SPSS Data Editor can now be seen unobstructed by the window. The Data Editor is a spreadsheet into which data are entered.

The columns are used to represent different variables.

The rows are the different cases or individuals for which you have data.

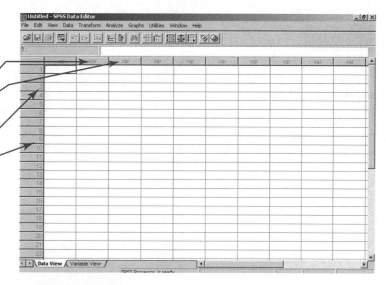

Step 4:

To enter data into SPSS simply highlight one of the cells by clicking on that cell – SPSS always has one cell highlighted.

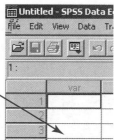

Step 5:

Then type a number using the computer keyboard. On pressing return on the keyboard or selecting another cell with the mouse this number will be entered into the spreadsheet as shown here. The value 6.00 is the entry for the first row (first case) of the variable VAR00001.

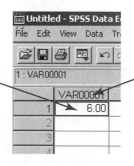

Notice that the variable has been given a standard name automatically. It can be changed – just click on variable name and make the change.

Step 6:

Correcting errors – using your mouse simply highlight the cell where the error is and type in the correction. On pressing return or moving to another cell, the correction will be entered.

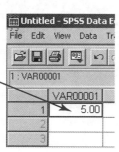

1.4 Moving within a window with the mouse

Step 7:

One can move a row or column at a time by clicking on the arrowhead buttons near the vertical and horizontal scroll bars.

For major movements, drag the vertical and horizontal scroll bars to move around the page.

The relative position of the scroll bar indicates the relative position in the file.

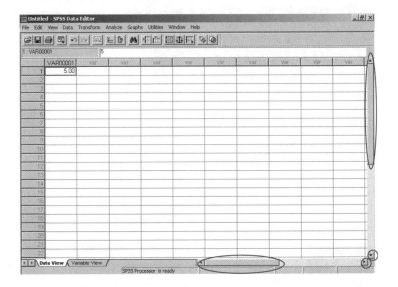

1.5 Moving within a window using the keyboard keys with the mouse

Step 8:

One can move one page up or down on the screen by pressing the 'Pg Up' and 'Pg Dn' keyboard keys.

The cursor keys on the keyboard move the cursor one space or character according to the direction of the arrow.

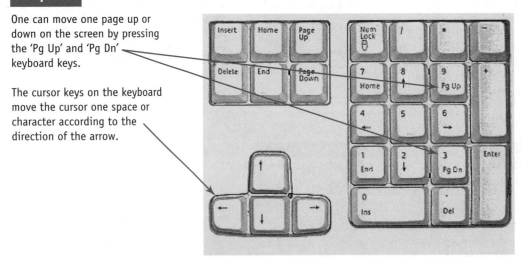

1.6 Saving data

Step 9:

By selecting 'File' then
'Save As . . .' it is possible to
save the data as a file. The saved
data file is automatically given
the extension '.sav' by SPSS.
A distinctive file name is helpful,
such as 'eg1', so that its contents
are clear.

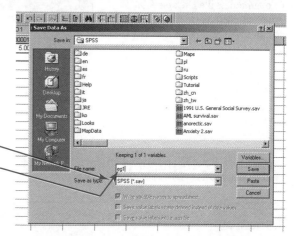

Step 10:

To choose the place where the
data file will be saved, indicate
this place in the 'Save in:' box.
Use the arrow to browse to
the selected location.

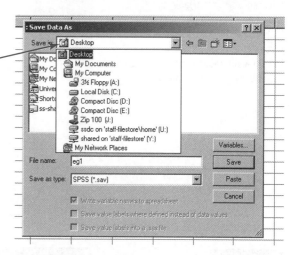

1.7 Opening up a data file

Step 11:

To open an existing file, click on
'File', 'Open', 'Data', 'Look in:'
if the file is not in the 'Open File'
box (which it will be if you have
just saved it), type in the file
name ('eg1') and then 'Open'.

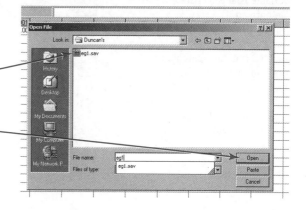

Step 12:

To open a new file click on 'File', 'New' and then 'Data'. This file can be saved as in Step 9.

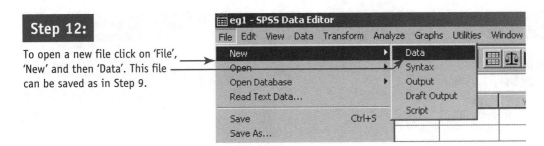

1.8 Using Variable View to create and label variables

Step 13:

Clicking on the 'Variable View' tab at the bottom changes the 'Data View' (the data spreadsheet) screen to one in which information about your variables may be entered conveniently.

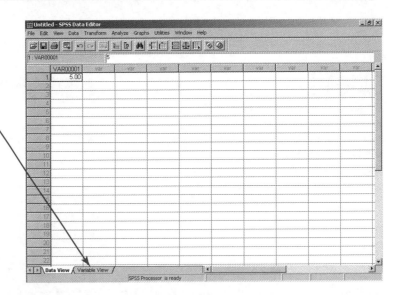

Step 14:

This is the 'Variable View' spreadsheet. In this case one variable is already listed. We entered it in Step 5. But we can rename it and add extra variables quite simply by highlighting the appropriate cell and typing in a new or further variable names.

Change the width of the data column here.

Change the number of decimals here.

Step 15:

There is no practical limit to the length of variable names in Releases 12 and 13 compared to earlier SPSS versions. Earlier releases were limited to eight characters. Highlight one of the cells under 'Name' and type in a distinct Variable name. The rest of the columns are given default values but may be changed. These renamed and newly defined variables will appear on the 'Data View' screen when this is selected.

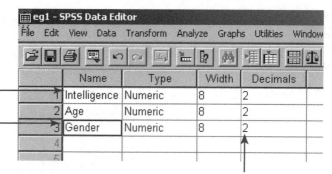

This is the number of decimals which will appear on screen – the calculation uses the actual decimal value.

Step 16:

It is important to note that other columns are easily changed too.

Label allows one to give the variable a longer name than is possible using the Variable name column. Simply type in a longer name in the cells. This is no longer so important now that Release 12 variable names can be much longer.

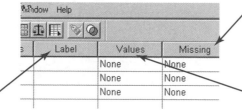

Missing values are dealt with in Chapter 15.

Values allows one to name the different categories or values of a nominal (category or categorical) variable such as gender. See Step 17 for details. It is recommended that 'Values' are given for all nominal variables.

Step 17:

This 'button' appears. Click on it.

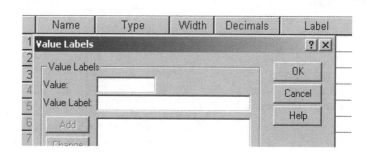

Step 18:

This small window appears. Follow the next few steps. They show how male and female would be entered using the codes '1' for male and '2' for female.

Step 19:

Type in '1' next to 'Value:' and 'male' next to 'Value Label:'.

Then click 'Add'.

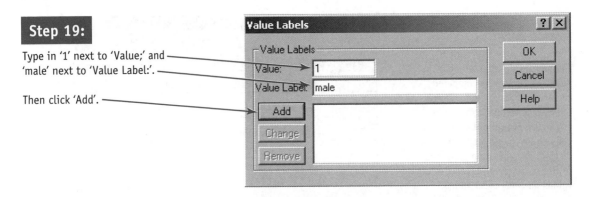

Step 20:

This transfers the information into the large box.

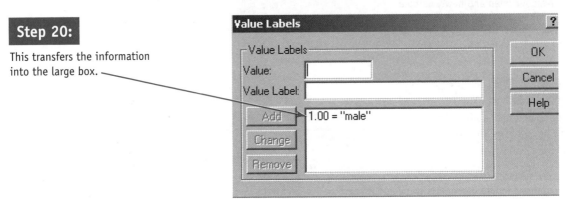

Step 21:

Now type in '2' next to 'Value:' and 'female' next to 'Value Label:'.

Then click 'Add'.

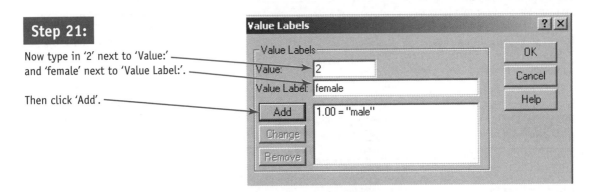

Step 22:

This transfers the information into the large box.

It is bad practice *not* to label values in this way.

Click OK to close Window.

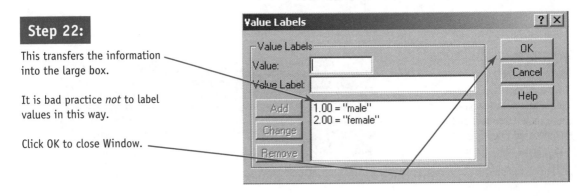

1.9   More on Data View

Step 23:

To return to 'Data View'
click on this tab at the
bottom left of the screen.

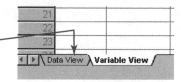

Step 24:

This is how 'Data View' looks now.
The data can be entered for all of
the variables and cases. Remember
that the value 5.00 was entered
earlier along with the variable
names. We can start entering the
data in full now.

To enter data, simply highlight a
cell, enter the number, then press
return. You will be in the next cell
down which will be highlighted.

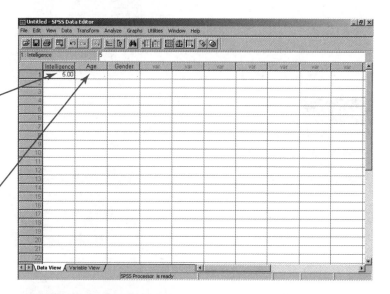

Step 25:

This shows how a typical data
spreadsheet looks. Notice how
the values for gender are coded
as 1.00 and 2.00. It is possible
to reveal their value labels
instead. Click on 'View' on
the task bar at the top.

	Intelligence	Age	Gender
1	5.00	27.00	1.00
2	8.00	22.00	1.00
3	5.00	20.00	2.00
4	4.00	19.00	2.00
5	3.00	18.00	2.00
6	5.00	19.00	1.00
7	2.00	21.00	1.00
8	3.00	22.00	2.00
9	2.00	19.00	1.00
10	1.00	18.00	2.00
11	2.00	18.00	1.00
12	4.00	20.00	2.00
13			
14			

Step 26:

Then click on 'Value Labels'.

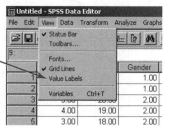

Step 27:

Now the values are given as male and female – just as we coded them in Steps 19 to 21.

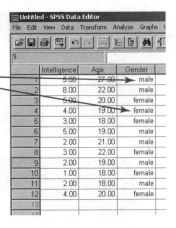

Step 28:

There are many options available to you – including statistical analyses. Some of these options are shown here.

Select 'Data' to insert extra variables, extra cases, select cases and other data manipulations.

Select 'Window' to switch between the data spreadsheet and any output calculated on the data.

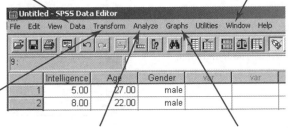

Select 'Transform' for a range of things that can be done with the data – such as recoding the values and computing combinations of variables.

Select 'Analyze' to access the full range of statistical calculations that SPSS calculates.

Select 'Graphs' for bar charts, scatterplots and many other graphical representation methods.

1.10 A simple statistical calculation

Step 29:

To calculate the average (i.e. mean) age follow the following stages:

Click 'Analyze'.

Select 'Descriptive Statistics'.

Select 'Descriptives'.

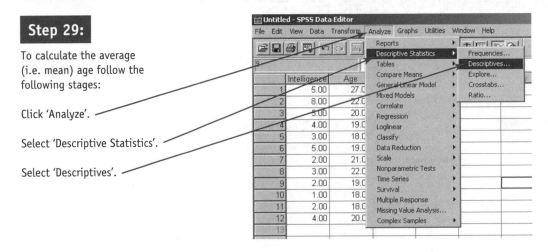

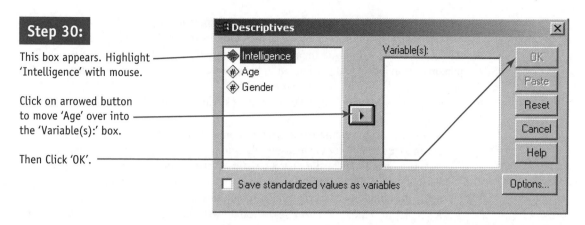

Step 30:

This box appears. Highlight 'Intelligence' with mouse.

Click on arrowed button to move 'Age' over into the 'Variable(s):' box.

Then Click 'OK'.

1.11 SPSS output

Step 31:

The Data Editor window is replaced in view by the SPSS output. This table appears for the analysis just completed.

The average (mean) intelligence score is encircled.

Descriptive Statistics

	N	Minimum	Maximum	Mean	Std. Deviation
Intelligence	12	1.00	8.00	3.6667	1.92275
Valid N (listwise)	12				

The good news is that anyone who can follow the above steps should have no difficulty in carrying out the vast majority of statistical analyses available on SPSS with the help of this book. It is worthwhile spending an hour or so simply practising with SPSS. You will find that this is the quickest way to learn.

1.12 Basic statistical concepts essential in SPSS analyses

The elements of statistics are quite simple. The problem is in putting the elements together. Nobody can become expert in statistical analysis overnight but, with a very small amount of knowledge, quite sophisticated analyses can be carried out by inexperienced researchers. Mathematical ability has very little role to play in data analysis.

There are just a few basic concepts which the researcher needs to understand before proceeding to SPSS analyses. These include:

■ *Variable*   A variable is any concept that can be measured and which varies. Variables are largely inventions of the researcher and they vary enormously from study to study. There are a few fairly standard variables, such as age and gender, that are very commonly measured. Typically, variables are specific to particular topics of study. Variables appear in SPSS analyses as the columns of the data spreadsheet.

■ *Cases*   A case is simply a member of the sample. In psychology a case is usually a person (i.e. an individual participant in the research). Cases (normally) appear in SPSS analyses as the rows of the data spreadsheet.

■ *Types of variable*   For all practical purposes, variables can be classified as being of *two* types:

– *Score variables*   Some variables are scores. A score is when a numerical value is given to a variable for each case in the sample. This numerical value indicates the quantity or amount of the characteristic (variable) in question. So age is a score variable since the numerical value indicates an increasing amount of the variable age. One could also describe this as quantitative.

– *Nominal or category variables*   Some variables are measured by classifying cases into one of several named categories. These are also known as nominal, categorical or category variables. For example, gender has two named categories – male and female. Nationality is another example: English, Welsh, Irish and Scottish are the nationalities of people of Britain. They have *no* numerical implications as such. To say that a person is Scottish is simply to put them into that named category. One could also describe this as qualitative. There is one risk of confusion – categories such as gender are entered into SPSS using different numbers to represent the different categories. For example, the variable gender has two categories – males could be represented by the number 1 and females by the number 2 (or vice versa). The numbers used are arbitrary. It is vital not to confuse these numbers which merely represent different coding categories with scores. For this reason, it is important to label the different values of nominal variables in full in the SPSS data spreadsheet. This is easily done as was shown on pages 7–8.

Sometimes variables are classified as nominal, ordinal, interval and ratio. This is of conceptual interest but of little practical significance in selecting appropriate statistics.

■ It is important to decide for each of your variables whether it is a nominal (category) variable or a score variable. Write a list of your variables and classify each of them if you are a beginner. Eventually you will do it without much thought. The statistical techniques which are appropriate for score variables are often inappropriate for qualitative variables (and vice versa). So, for example, it is appropriate to calculate the mean (numerical average) of any variable which is a score (e.g. average age). On the other hand, it is totally inappropriate to calculate the mean (average) for variables which consist of categories. It would be nonsense to say that the average nationality is 1.7 since nationality is not a score. The problem is that SPSS works with the numbers in the data spreadsheet and does not know whether they are scores or numerical codes for different categories.

■ There are two main types of statistical techniques – *descriptive* and *inferential* statistics:

– Descriptive statistics chiefly describe the main features of individual variables. So to calculate the average age of a sample of people is an example of descriptive statistics. Counting the number of English people would be another example of descriptive statistics. If one variable is considered at a time this is known as univariate statistics. Bivariate statistics are used when the relationship between two (or more) variables is being described.

– Inferential statistics is a totally distinct aspect of statistics. It only addresses the question of whether one can rely on the findings based on a *sample* of cases rather than *all* cases. The use of samples is characteristic of nearly all modern research.

The problem with samples is that some of them are not similar to the populations from which they are taken. The phrases 'statistically significant' and 'not statistically significant' simply indicate that any trends in the data can be accepted as substantial (i.e. statistically significant) or not substantial enough to rely on (i.e. not statistically significant). A statistically significant finding is one which is unlikely to be the result of chance factors determining the results in a particular sample. See the authors' accompanying statistics text, D. Howitt and D. Cramer, *Introduction to Statistics in Psychology* (3rd edn, Pearson Education: Harlow, 2005), for a detailed discussion of the meaning of statistical significance since it is difficult to explain accurately in a few words.

– Every descriptive statistic has a corresponding inferential statistic. For example, the correlation coefficient is a descriptive statistic indicating the direction and the strength of the relationship between two variables. Associated with it is the inferential statistic – the significance of the correlation coefficient. The descriptive statistic is important for understanding the trends in the data – the inferential statistic simply deals with the reliance that can be placed on the finding.

■ Researchers should be aware also of *two* different types of research design – that which uses *related measures* and that which uses *unrelated measures*. Related measures may also be called correlated measures or paired measures. Unrelated measures may also be called uncorrelated measures or unpaired measures. The terms are mostly used when the mean or averages of scores are being compared for two or more samples of data:

– Where the means of a single sample of individuals are compared on two (or more) measures of the same variable (e.g. taken at different points in time) then this is a related measures design.

– Where the means of two quite different samples of participants are compared on a variable, this is an unrelated design.

– Where two (or more) groups of participants have been carefully matched so that *sets* of participants in the two (or more) conditions are similar in some respects, then this is a related design too. In this case, members of each set are treated as if they were the same person. Normally, a researcher would know if the participants were matched in sets because it requires effort on the part of the researcher. For example, the researcher has to decide what characteristics to match of sets on, then choose individuals for the sets on the basis of their similarity on these characteristics, and (often) has to allocate participants to the different samples (conditions) especially in experimental research.

The main point of using related designs is that variability due to sampling is reduced.

Almost without exception, the researcher will be using a variety of these techniques with the same data. Fortunately, once the data are entered, in many cases, data analysis may take just a minute or so.

1.13 Which test to use

One common heartfelt plea is the demand to know how to choose appropriate statistical techniques for data. Over the years, writers of statistics textbooks have laboured to simplify the process of choosing. This is done largely by producing spreadsheets which indicate what sorts of statistics are appropriate for different sorts of data. If you want that sort of approach then there are a number of web sites which take you through the decision-making process:

http://www.orthoteers.co.uk/Nrujp~ij33lm/Orthstatstests.htm
http://www.wtc.edu/online/bcanada/choose2.htm
http://www.members.aol.com/statware/pubpage.htm
http://www.socialresearchmethods.net/selstat/ssstart.htm
http://www.graphpad.com/www/Book/Choose.htm
http://www.whichtest.info/
http://www.google.com/search?q=choosing+statistical+tests&hl=en&lr=&ie=UTF-8&safe=off&start=10&sa=N
http://www.google.com/search?q=choosing+statistical+tests&hl=en&lr=&ie=UTF-8&safe=off&start=20&sa=N

For basic statistics this is probably a useful approach. The difficulty increasingly is that research designs, even for student projects, are very varied and quite complex. Once psychology was almost a purely laboratory-based subject which concentrated on randomised experiments. Psychologists still use this sort of experimentation, but their methods have extended greatly, so extending the demands on their statistical knowledge. Therefore, there is a distinct limit to the extent to which a simple spreadsheet or flow diagram can help the researcher select appropriate statistical analyses.

One fundamental mistake that novice researchers make is to assume that data analysis is primarily driven by statistics. It is more accurate to regard statistics as being largely a tool which adds a little finesse to the basic task of research – to answer the researcher's research questions. Only the researcher can fully know what they want their research to achieve – what issues they want resolving through collecting research data and analysing it. Unless the researcher clearly understands what they want the research to achieve, statistics can be of little help. Very often when approached for statistical advice we find that we have to clarify the objectives of the research first of all – and then try to unravel how the researcher thought that the data collected would help them. These are *not* statistical matters but issues to do with developing research ideas and planning appropriate data collection. So the first thing is to list the questions that the data were intended to answer. Too often sight of the purpose of the research is lost in the forest of the research practicalities. The following may help clarify the role of statistics in research:

■ Much of the most important aspects of data analysis need little other than an understanding of averages and frequency counts. These are common in SPSS output. Many research questions may be answered simply by examining differences in means between samples or crosstabulation tables or scattergrams. It is useful to ask oneself how one could answer the research questions just using such basic approaches. Too often, the complexities of statistical output become the focus of attention which can lead to confusion about how the data relate to the research question. It is not easy to focus on the research issues and avoid being drawn in unhelpful directions.

■ Statistical analyses are actively constructed by the researcher. There is usually no single correct statistical analysis for any data but probably a range of equally acceptable alternatives. The researcher may need to make many decisions in the process of carrying out data analysis – some of these may have to be carefully justified but others are fairly arbitrary. The researcher is in charge of the data analysis – statistics is the researcher's tool. The analysis should not be a statistical tour de force, but led by the questions which necessitated data collection in the first place. There is no excuse – if you collected the data then you ought to know why you collected it.

■ The more research you read in its entirety the better you will understand how statistics can be used in a particular field of research. Very little research is carried out which is not related to other research. What are the typical statistical methods used by researchers in your chosen field? Knowing what techniques are generally used is often the best guide to what ought to be considered.

Table 1.1 gives some insight into the styles of analysis which researchers may wish to apply to their data and what sections of this book describe these statistical techniques in detail.

Table 1.1   Major types of analysis and suggested SPSS procedures

Type/purpose of analysis	Suggested procedures	Chapter
All types of study	Descriptive statistics, tables and diagrams	2–6
Assessing the relationship between two variables	Correlation coefficient	7
	Regression	8
Comparing two sets of scores for differences	Unrelated *t*-test	13
	F-ratio test	19
	Related *t*-test	12
	Unrelated ANOVA	20
	Related ANOVA	21
	Mann–Whitney	18
	Wilcoxon matched pairs	18
Comparing the means of two or more sets of scores	Unrelated ANOVA	20
	Related ANOVA	21
	Multiple comparisons	23
Complex experiments etc. with *two* or more independent variables and *one* dependent variable	Two (or more)-way ANOVA	22
– if you have related *and* unrelated measures	Mixed-design ANOVA	24
– if other variables may be affecting scores on dependent variable	Analysis of covariance	24
Eliminating third variables which may be affecting a correlation coefficient	Partial correlation	26
Finding predictors for a score variable	Simple regression	8
	Stepwise multiple regression	28
	Hierarchical multiple regression	29
	Log-linear analysis	31
Finding predictors for a category variable	Multinomial logistic regression	32
	Binomial logistic regression	33
Analysing a questionnaire	Factor analysis	27
	Alpha reliability	30
	Split-half reliability	30
	Recoding	16
	Computing new variables	17
Comparing frequency data	Chi-square	14
	Fisher test	14
	McNemar test	14
	Log-linear analysis	31
Coding open-ended data using raters	Kappa coefficient	30

2 Describing variables
Tables and diagrams

Overview

■ Tables and diagrams should quickly and effectively communicate important features of one's data. Complexity, for its own sake, is not a helpful characteristic of good tables and diagrams.

■ Clear and meaningful tables and diagrams are crucial in statistical analysis and report writing. Virtually every analysis of data uses them in order to allow the distributions of variables to be examined. In this chapter we provide the basic computer techniques to allow the construction of tables and diagrams to describe the distributions of individual variables presented one at a time.

■ All tables and diagrams should be clearly titled and labelled. Depending on the table or diagram in question, horizontal and vertical axes should be labelled, bars identified, scales marked and so forth. Great care should be taken with this. Generally speaking, SPSS tables and diagrams require considerable work to make them optimally effective.

■ Frequency tables merely count the number of times the different values of the variable appear in the data. A simple example would be a count of the number of males and the number of females in the research. Tables need to be relatively simple and this usually requires that the variable only has a small number of values or, if not, that a number of different values of the variable are grouped together.

■ Pie diagrams are effective and simple ways of presenting frequency counts. However, they are only useful when the variable being illustrated only has a small number of different values. Pie diagrams are relatively uncommon in publications because they consume space, although they are good for conference presentations and lectures.

■ A bar chart can be used in similar circumstances to the pie chart but can cope with a larger number of values of variables before becoming too cluttered. Frequencies of the different values of the variable are represented as physically separated bars of heights which vary according to the frequency in that category.

■ A histogram looks similar to a bar chart but is used for numerical scores rather than categories. Thus the bars in a histogram are presented in size order of the scores that they represent. The bars in histograms are *not* separated by spaces. Often a histogram will need the ranges of scores covered by each bar to be changed in order to maximise the usefulness and clarity of the diagram. This can be done by recoding variables (Chapter 16) but SPSS also allows this to be done in the 'Chart Editor'. Producing charts like these is one of the harder tasks on SPSS.

Table 2.1   Occupational status of participants in the research expressed as frequencies and percentage frequencies

Occupation	Frequency	Percentage frequency
Nuns	17	21.25
Nursery teachers	3	3.75
Television presenters	23	28.75
Students	20	25.00
Other	17	21.25

SPSS is generally used to summarise raw data but it can use data which have already been summarised such as those shown in Table 2.1 (*ISP*, Table 2.1).

In other words, since the data in Table 2.1 are based on 80 people, the data would occupy 80 cells of one column in the 'Data Editor' window and each occupation would be coded with a separate number, so that nuns might be coded 1, nursery teachers 2 and so on. Thus, one would need 17 rows containing 1 to represent nuns, 3 rows containing 2 to represent nursery teachers and so on. However, it is possible to carry out certain analyses on summarised data provided that we appropriately weight the categories by the number or frequency of cases in them.

2.1 Entering summarised categorical or frequency data by weighting

It seems better practice to define your variables in 'Variable View' of the 'Data Editor' before entering the data in 'Data View' because we can remove the decimal places where they are not necessary. So we always do this first. If you prefer to enter the data first then do so.

For this table we need two columns in 'Data View'. One to say what the categories are. The other to give the frequencies for these categories. In 'Variable View' variables are presented as rows. As we will be entering the data into columns we will refer to these rows as columns.

Step 1:

Select 'Variable View' in 'Data Editor'.

Name the first two columns 'Occupation' and 'Freq'.
Remove the two decimal places.

Select the right side of the cell for the 'Values' of 'Occupation'.

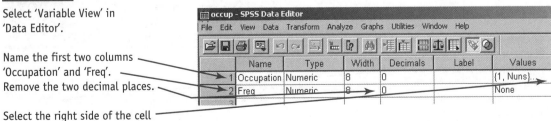

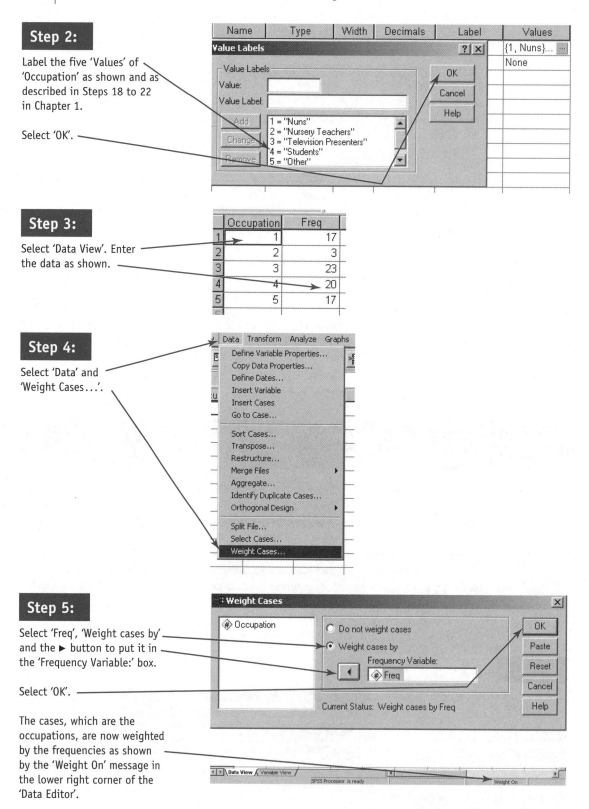

Step 2:

Label the five 'Values' of 'Occupation' as shown and as described in Steps 18 to 22 in Chapter 1.

Select 'OK'.

Step 3:

Select 'Data View'. Enter the data as shown.

Step 4:

Select 'Data' and 'Weight Cases...'.

Step 5:

Select 'Freq', 'Weight cases by' and the ► button to put it in the 'Frequency Variable:' box.

Select 'OK'.

The cases, which are the occupations, are now weighted by the frequencies as shown by the 'Weight On' message in the lower right corner of the 'Data Editor'.

2.2 Percentage frequencies

Step 1:

Select 'Analyze', 'Descriptive Statistics' and 'Frequencies...'.

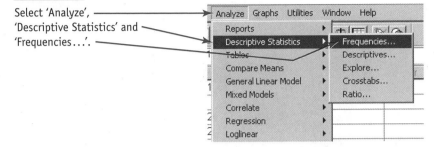

Step 2:

Select 'Occupation' and the ► button to put 'Occupation' in the 'Variables(s):' box.

Select 'OK'.

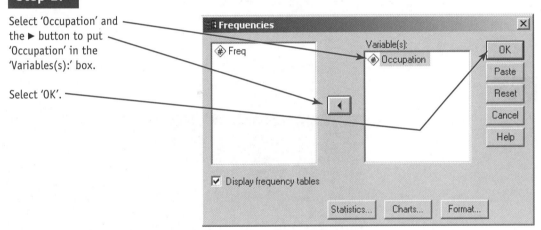

2.3 Interpreting the output

The first column of this table gives the value of the five categories. To change these to labels, which is more meaningful, carry out the following three steps and rerun the analysis as described.

Occupation

		Frequency	Percent	Valid Percent	Cumulative Percent
Valid	1	17	21.3	21.3	21.3
	2	3	3.8	3.8	25.0
	3	23	28.8	28.8	53.8
	4	20	25.0	25.0	78.8
	5	17	21.3	21.3	100.0
	Total	80	100.0	100.0	

2.4 Labelling the values

Step 1:

Select 'Edit' and then 'Options...'.

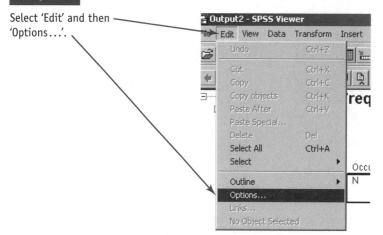

Step 2:

Select 'Output Labels'.

Step 3:

Select the ▼ button below 'Variable values in labels shown as:' and 'Labels' from the drop-down menu.

Select 'OK'.

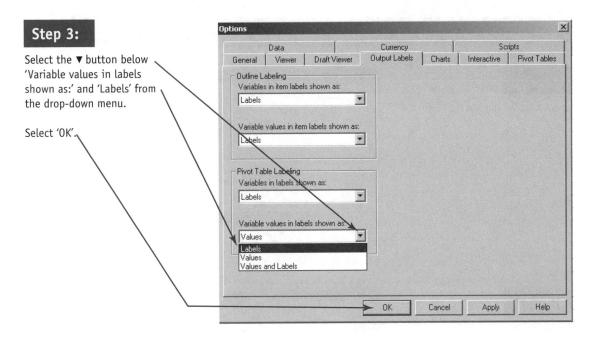

The labels are now given.

The third column gives the percentage frequency for each category, including any missing values of which there are none.

So 17 is 21.3% of a total of 80.

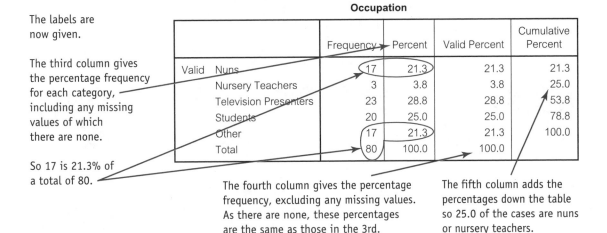

Occupation

		Frequency	Percent	Valid Percent	Cumulative Percent
Valid	Nuns	17	21.3	21.3	21.3
	Nursery Teachers	3	3.8	3.8	25.0
	Television Presenters	23	28.8	28.8	53.8
	Students	20	25.0	25.0	78.8
	Other	17	21.3	21.3	100.0
	Total	80	100.0	100.0	

The fourth column gives the percentage frequency, excluding any missing values. As there are none, these percentages are the same as those in the 3rd.

The fifth column adds the percentages down the table so 25.0 of the cases are nuns or nursery teachers.

2.5 Reporting the results

Only the category labels, the frequency and the percentage frequency need be reported. Consequently you need to simplify this table if you are going to present it. If the occupation was missing for some of the cases you would need to decide whether you would present percentages including or excluding them. There is no need to present both sets of figures. Also omit the term 'Valid' in the first column as its meaning may only be familiar to SPSS users.

2.6 Pie diagram of category data

Step 1:

Select 'Graphs' and 'Pie...'.

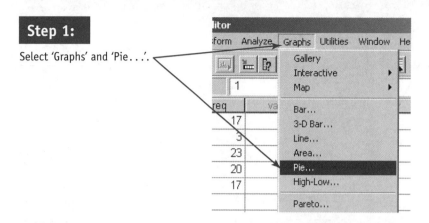

Step 2:

Select 'Define'.

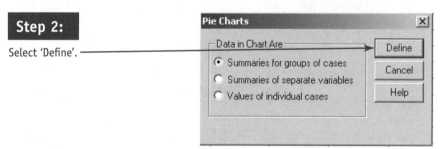

Step 3:

Select 'Occupation' and the ▶ button next to 'Define Slices by:' to put 'Occupation' there.

Select 'OK'.

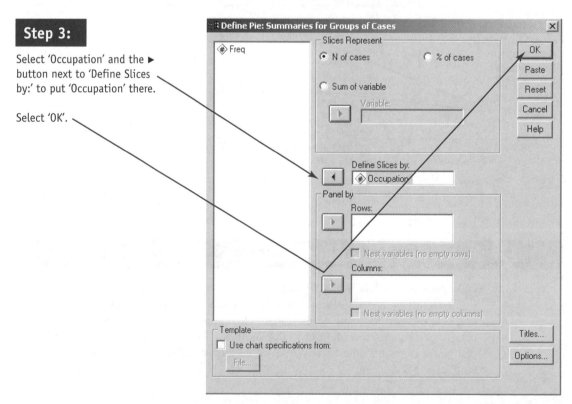

This is the way the pie diagram appears if the default options in SPSS have not been altered. The slices are colour coded. The colours have not been reproduced here.

Features in this diagram may be altered with the 'Chart Editor'. We will show how to label each slice so that the reader does not have to refer to the colour code and how to change the colours to monochrome patterns.

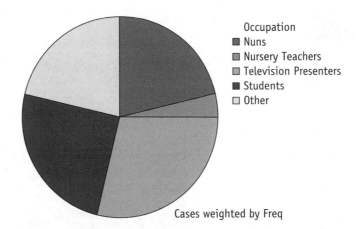

Occupation
■ Nuns
■ Nursery Teachers
□ Television Presenters
■ Students
□ Other

Cases weighted by Freq

2.7 Adding labels to the pie diagram and removing the legend and label

Step 1:

Double click anywhere in the rectangle containing the diagram to select the 'Chart Editor'.

Select 'Elements' and 'Show Data Labels'.

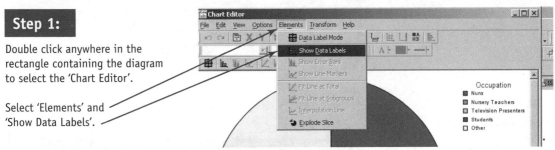

Step 2:

Select 'Count' and the red '✗' to not display it.

Select 'Occupation' and the curved upward green arrow to display the names of the occupations.

Do the same for 'Percent' to display the percentage of each occupation.

Select 'Apply' and 'Close' if you do not want to make further changes to the properties of the pie diagram.

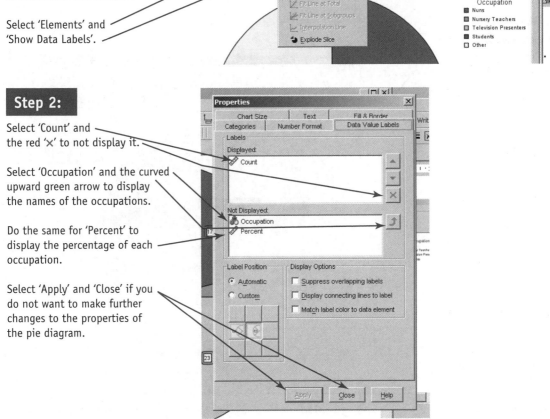

Step 3:

Select 'Text' if you want to change aspects of the text such as making it bold and increasing its font size.

To make it bold, select the ▼ button next to 'Style' and 'Bold' from the dropdown menu.
To increase the font size to 14, select the ▼ button next to 'Size' and '14' from the dropdown menu.

If you do not want to make further changes to the properties of the pie diagram, select 'Apply' and 'Close' ('Cancel' changes to 'Close').

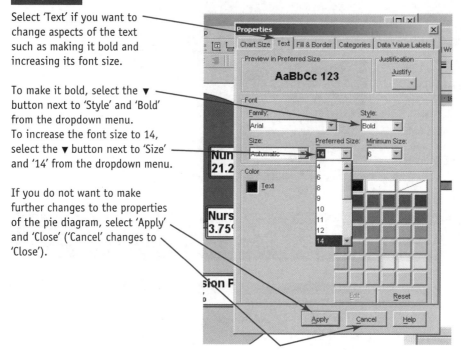

Step 4:

To remove the legend, select 'Options' and 'Hide Legend'.

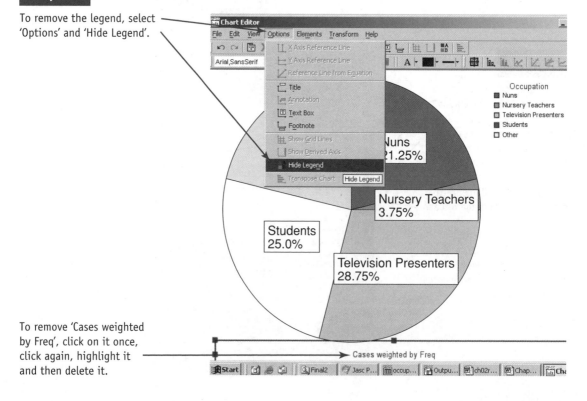

To remove 'Cases weighted by Freq', click on it once, click again, highlight it and then delete it.

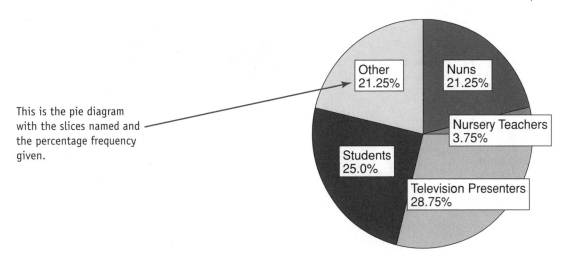

This is the pie diagram with the slices named and the percentage frequency given.

2.8 Changing the colour of a pie diagram slice to a black and white pattern

Step 1:

In the 'Chart Editor', click on the slice you want to change and then click again when the border has a double line.

Step 2:

Select 'Edit' and 'Properties'.

Select 'Fill' and the colour white.

To add a black border, select 'Border' and the colour black. To add a pattern, select the ▼ button beside 'Pattern' and the pattern you want.

Select 'Apply' and then 'Close'. Apply this same procedure to the other four slices.

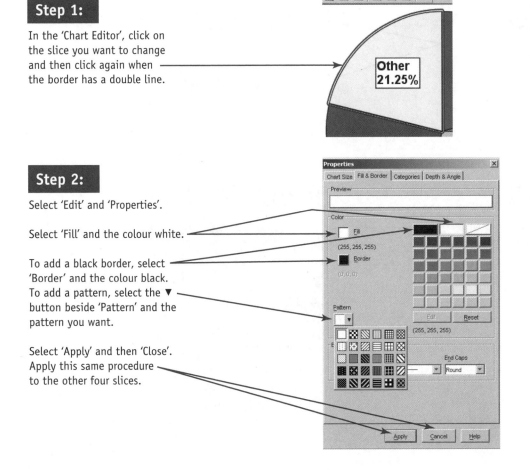

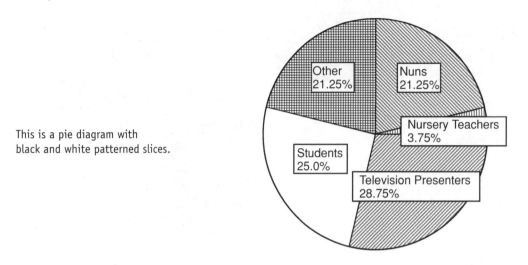

This is a pie diagram with
black and white patterned slices.

2.9 Bar chart of category data

Step 1:

Select 'Graphs' and 'Bar . . .'.

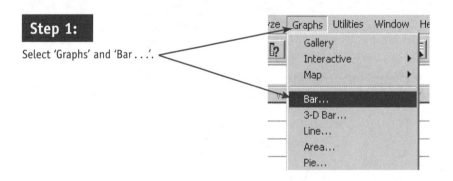

Step 2:

Select 'Define', as 'Simple'
has been pre-selected.

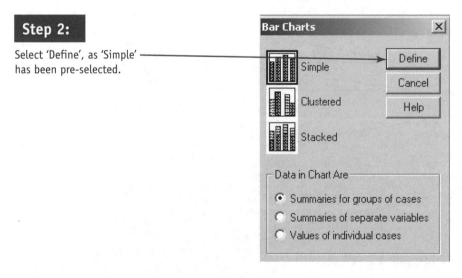

Step 3:

Select 'Occupation' and the ►
button beside 'Category Axis:'
to put 'Occupation' in there.

Select '% of cases'.

Select 'OK'.

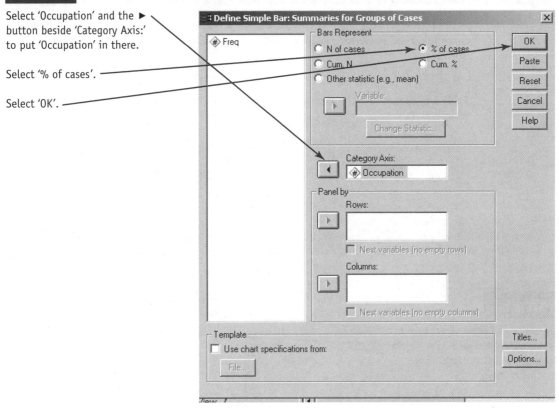

This is the bar chart. You can
edit it with the 'Chart Editor'
if you wish.

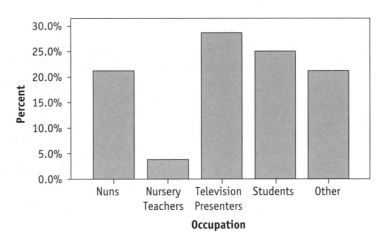

2.10 Histograms

We will illustrate the making of a histogram with the data in Table 2.2 which shows the distribution of students' attitudes towards statistics. We have labelled this variable 'Response'.

Table 2.2 Distribution of students' replies to the statement 'Statistics is my favourite university subject'

Response category	Value	Frequency
Strongly agree	1	17
Agree	2	14
Neither agree nor disagree	3	6
Disagree	4	2
Strongly disagree	5	1

Step 1:

In the 'Data Editor' enter the data, weight and label them as described at the beginning of this chapter.

Step 2:

Select 'Graphs' and 'Histogram . . .'.

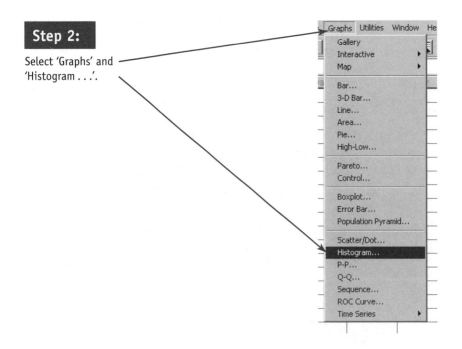

Step 3:

Select 'Response' and the ▶ button beside 'Variable:' to put 'Response' in that box.

Select 'OK'.

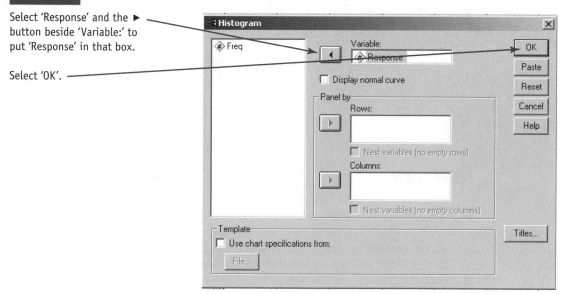

This is the histogram which you can edit with the 'Chart Editor'.

To remove the statistics, click on them and delete.

To change the titles of the axes, click on them and edit them.

To remove 'Cases weighted by Freq', click on it, highlight it and delete it.

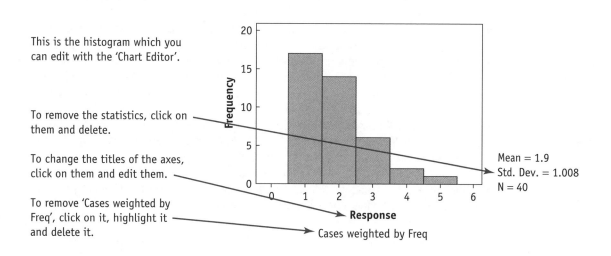

3 Describing variables numerically

Averages, variation and spread

Overview

- In this chapter we describe the computation of a number of statistics which summarise and describe the essential characteristics of each important variable. The techniques presented in this chapter involve individual variables taken one at a time. In other words they are single variable or univariate statistical techniques.

- Each of them generates a numerical index to describe the characteristics of the data.

- With the exception of the mode which can be used for any type of data, the other techniques are for data in the form of numerical scores.

- The mean is the everyday or numerical average of a set of scores. It is obtained by summing the scores and dividing by the number of scores.

- The mode is simply the most frequently occurring score. A set of scores can have more than one mode if two or more scores occur equally frequently. The mode is the value of the score occurring most frequently – it is *not* the frequency with which the most frequent score occurs.

- The median is the score in the middle of the distribution if the scores are ordered in size from the smallest to the largest. For various reasons, sometimes the median is an estimate of the score in the middle – for example, where the number of scores is equal, and so that there is no exact middle.

- The procedures described in this chapter can readily be modified to produce measures of variance, kurtosis and other descriptive statistics.

We will illustrate the computation of the mean, median and mode on the ages of university students – see Table 3.1 (*ISP*, Table 3.7).

Table 3.1 Ages of 12 students

| 18 | 21 | 23 | 18 | 19 | 19 | 19 | 33 | 18 | 19 | 19 | 20 |

3.1 Entering the data

Step 1:

In 'Variable View' of the
'Data Editor' name the first
column 'Age'. ————————

Remove the two decimal places. ————————

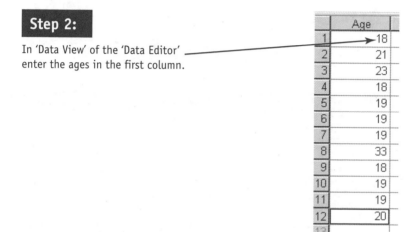

Step 2:

In 'Data View' of the 'Data Editor' ————————
enter the ages in the first column.

3.2 Conducting the analysis

Step 3:

Select 'Analyze', ————————
'Descriptive Statistics' and ————————
'Frequencies...'. ————————

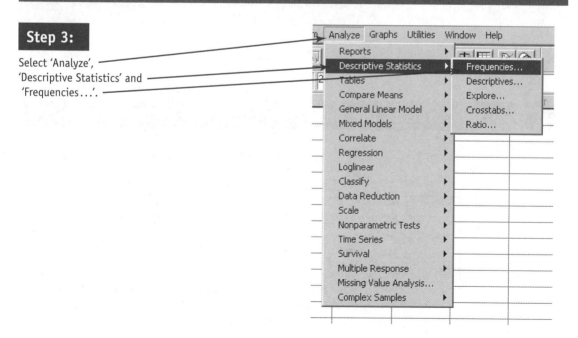

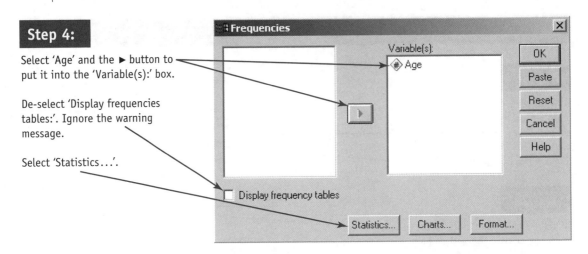

Step 4:

Select 'Age' and the ▶ button to put it into the 'Variable(s):' box.

De-select 'Display frequencies tables:'. Ignore the warning message.

Select 'Statistics…'.

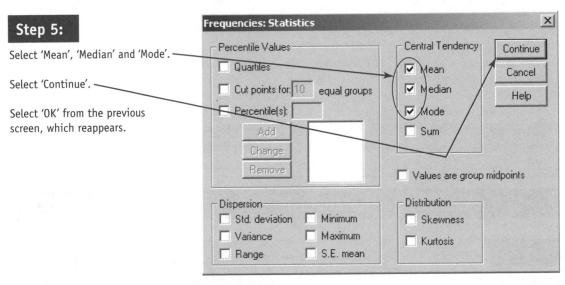

Step 5:

Select 'Mean', 'Median' and 'Mode'.

Select 'Continue'.

Select 'OK' from the previous screen, which reappears.

3.3 Interpreting the output

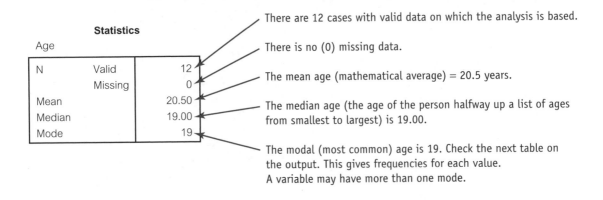

Statistics

Age

N	Valid	12
	Missing	0
Mean		20.50
Median		19.00
Mode		19

There are 12 cases with valid data on which the analysis is based.

There is no (0) missing data.

The mean age (mathematical average) = 20.5 years.

The median age (the age of the person halfway up a list of ages from smallest to largest) is 19.00.

The modal (most common) age is 19. Check the next table on the output. This gives frequencies for each value.
A variable may have more than one mode.

3.4 Reporting the output

- The mean, median and mode can be presented as a table such as Table 3.2.
- Two decimal places are more than enough for most data. Most measurement is approximate, and the use of several decimal places tends to imply an unwarranted degree of precision.
- For the median, it is probably less confusing if you do not report values as 19.00 but as 19. However, if the decimal places were anything other than .00 then this should be reported since it indicates that the median is estimated and does not correspond to any actual scores.

Table 3.2   Mean, median and mode of age

Ages of students ($N = 12$)	
Mean	20.50 years
Median	19 years
Mode	19 years

3.5 Other features

You will see from the dialogue box in Step 5 there are many additional statistical values which may be calculated. You should have little difficulty obtaining these by adapting the steps already described.

Percentiles   These indicate the cut-off points for percentages of scores. Thus the 90th percentile is the score which cuts off the bottom 90% of scores in terms of size.

Quartiles   The values of a distribution that indicate the cut-off points for the lowest 25%, lowest 50% and lowest 75% of scores.

Sum   The total of the scores on a variable.

Skewness   Frequency distributions are not always symmetrical about the mean. Skewness is an index of the asymmetry or lopsidedness of the distribution of scores on a variable. It takes a positive value if the values are skewed to the left and a negative value if they are skewed to the right.

Kurtosis   This is an index of how much steeper or flatter the distribution of scores on the variable is compared to the normal distribution. It takes a '+' sign for steep frequency curves and a '−' sign for flat curves.

Standard deviation (estimate)   This is a measure of the amount by which scores differ on average from the mean of the scores on a particular variable. In SPSS the standard deviation is calculated as an estimate of the population standard deviation. It is an index of the variability of scores around the mean of a variable. Some authors call this the sample standard deviation.

Variance (estimate)   This is a measure of the amount by which scores on average vary around the mean of the scores on that variable. It is the square of the standard deviation and is obviously therefore closely related to it. It is also always an estimate of the population variance in SPSS. Some authors call this the sample variance. Like standard deviation, it is an index of the variability of scores around the mean of a variable, but also has other uses in statistics. In particular, it is the standard unit of measurement in statistics.

Range The numerical difference between the largest and the smallest scores obtained on a variable. It is a single number.

Minimum (score) The value of the lowest score in the data for a particular variable.

Maximum (score) The value of the highest score in the data for a particular variable.

Standard error (SE mean) The average amount by which the means of samples drawn from a population differ from the population mean. Standard error can be used much like standard deviation and variance as an index of how much variability there is in the scores on a variable.

4 Shapes of distributions of scores

Overview

- It is important to study the shape of the distribution of scores on a variable. Ideally for most statistical techniques, a distribution should be symmetrical and normally distributed (bell-shaped).

- Some statistical techniques are at their most powerful when the distributions of the variables involved are normally distributed. Major deviations from normality should be avoided but, for relatively small sample sizes, visual inspection of frequency diagrams is the only practical way to assess this. The effects of failure to meet this criterion can be overstated. Sometimes it is possible to transform one's scores statistically to approximate a normal distribution but this is largely a matter of trial and error, using, for example, logarithmic scales.

- Nevertheless, researchers should be wary of very asymmetrical (skewed) distributions and distributions that contain a few unusually high or low scores (outliers). Histograms, for example, can be used to detect asymmetry and outliers.

- The researcher should consider combining ranges of scores together (as opposed to tabulating each individual possible score) in order to clarify the distribution of the data. Small sample sizes, typical of much work in psychology and other social sciences, can lead to a sparse figure or diagram in which trends are not clear.

We will compute a frequency table and histogram of the extraversion scores of the 50 airline pilots shown in Table 4.1 (*ISP*, Table 4.1).

Table 4.1 Extraversion scores of 50 airline pilots

3	5	5	4	4	5	5	3	5	2
1	2	5	3	2	1	2	3	3	3
4	2	5	5	4	2	4	5	1	5
5	3	3	4	1	4	2	5	1	2
3	2	5	4	2	1	2	3	4	1

4.1 Entering the data

Step 1:

In 'Variable View' of the 'Data Editor' name the 1st column 'Extrav'.

Remove the two decimal places.

Save this data as a file to use for Chapter 9.

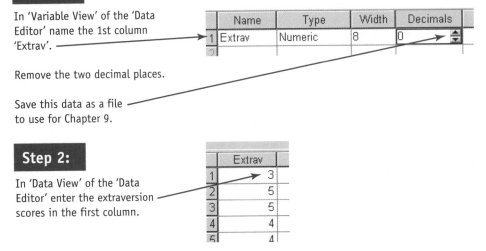

Step 2:

In 'Data View' of the 'Data Editor' enter the extraversion scores in the first column.

4.2 Frequency tables

Step 3:

Select 'Analyze', 'Descriptive Statistics' and 'Frequencies...'.

Step 4:

Select 'Extrav' and the ▶ button to put it in the 'Variable(s):' box.

Select 'OK'.

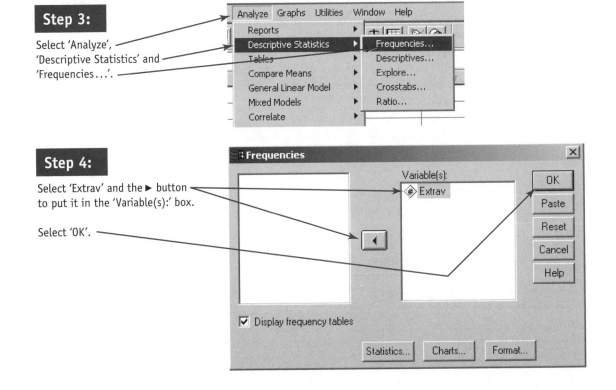

4.3 Interpreting the output

The first column shows the five values of extraversion which are 1 to 5.

The second column shows the frequency of these values. There are seven cases with a value of one.

The third column expresses these frequencies as a percentage of the total number including missing data. Of all cases, 14% have a value of 1.

Extrav

		Frequency	Percent	Valid Percent	Cumulative Percent
Valid	1	7	14.0	14.0	14.0
	2	11	22.0	22.0	36.0
	3	10	20.0	20.0	56.0
	4	9	18.0	18.0	74.0
	5	13	26.0	26.0	100.0
	Total	50	100.0	100.0	

The fourth column expresses these frequencies as a percentage of the total number excluding missing data. As there are no missing cases the percentages are the same as in the third column.

The fifth column adds these percentages together cumulatively down the table. So 56% of the cases have values of 3 or less.

4.4 Reporting the output

Notice that in Table 4.2 we omitted some of the confusion of detail in the output. Tables and diagrams should clarify the results.

Table 4.2   One style of reporting output from SPSS

Extraversion score	Frequency	Percentage frequency	Cumulative percentage frequency
1	7	14.0	14.0
2	11	22.0	36.0
3	10	20.0	56.0
4	9	18.0	74.0
5	13	26.0	100.0

4.5 Histograms

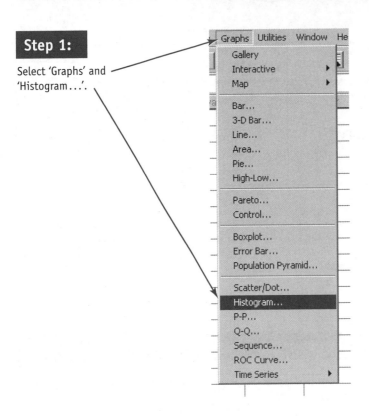

Step 1:

Select 'Graphs' and
'Histogram...'.

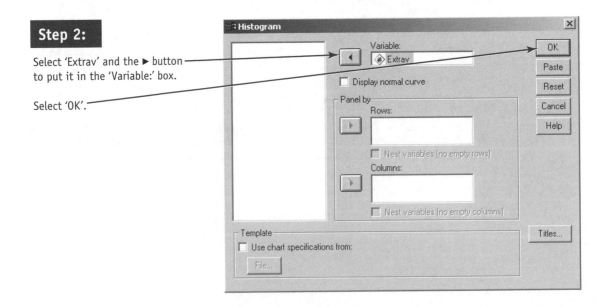

Step 2:

Select 'Extrav' and the ► button
to put it in the 'Variable:' box.

Select 'OK'.

4.6 Interpreting the output

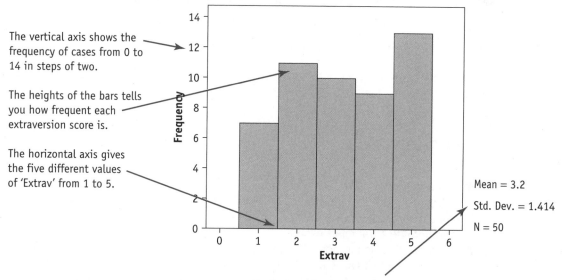

The vertical axis shows the frequency of cases from 0 to 14 in steps of two.

The heights of the bars tells you how frequent each extraversion score is.

The horizontal axis gives the five different values of 'Extrav' from 1 to 5.

Mean = 3.2
Std. Dev. = 1.414
N = 50

The mean extraversion score is 3.2.

The standard deviation is 1.414.

The number of cases is 50.

4.7 Reporting histograms

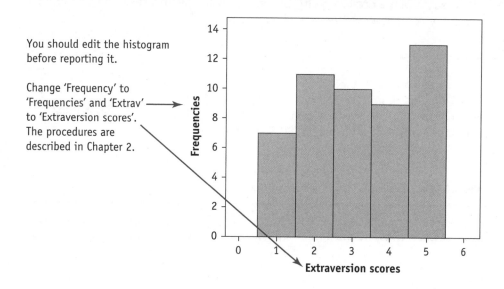

You should edit the histogram before reporting it.

Change 'Frequency' to 'Frequencies' and 'Extrav' to 'Extraversion scores'. The procedures are described in Chapter 2.

5   Standard deviation

The standard unit of measurement in statistics

Overview

- Basically, standard deviation is an index of how much scores deviate (differ) 'on average' from the average of the set of scores of which they are members. In other words, standard deviation is an index of the amount of variability of scores around the mean of the scores.

- Standard deviation can also be used in order to turn scores on very different variables into z or 'standard scores' that are easily compared and summed since they are on the same scale of measurement. This standard scale always has a mean of zero and a standard deviation of 1.0 irrespective of the variable in question.

- Standard scores occur in a variety of ways in statistics although not always in an obvious form. For example, beta weights in multiple regression are based on standard scores. z-scores are easily computed in SPSS but a conceptual understanding of them is helpful in many contexts.

- Standard deviation itself always takes a positive value, *but* researchers write of a number of standard deviations above the mean (i.e. '+' relative to the mean) or a number of standard deviations below the mean (i.e. '−' relative to the mean). That is, scores above the mean of the sample will always convert to a z-score or standard score with a positive prefix. Scores below the mean will always convert to a z-score or standard score with a negative prefix.

The computation of the standard deviation and z-scores is illustrated with the nine age scores shown in Table 5.1 (based on *ISP*, Table 5.1).

Table 5.1   Data for the calculation of standard deviation

Age	20	25	19	35	19	17	15	30	27

5.1 Entering the data

Step 1:

In 'Variable View' of the 'Data Editor' name the first column 'Age'.

Remove the two decimal places.

Name	Type	Width	Decimals
Age	Numeric	8	0

Step 2:

In 'Data View' of the 'Data Editor' enter age in the first column.

	Age
1	20
2	25
3	19
4	35
5	19
6	17
7	15
8	30
9	27
10	

5.2 Standard deviation

Step 3:

Select 'Analyze', 'Descriptive Statistics' and 'Descriptives...'.

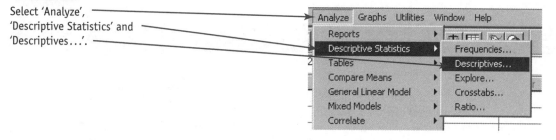

Step 4:

Select 'Age' and the ▶ button to put it in the 'Variable(s):' box.

Select 'Options...'.

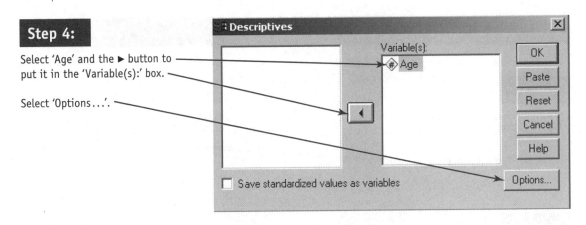

Step 5:

De-select 'Mean', 'Minimum' and 'Maximum'.

Select 'Continue'.

Select 'OK' from the previous screen, which reappears.

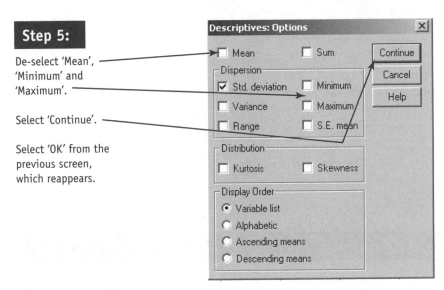

5.3 Interpreting the output

The number of cases is 9.

The standard deviation of 'Age' is 6.652.

Descriptive Statistics

	N	Std. Deviation
Age	9	6.652
Valid N (listwise)	9	

5.4 z-scores

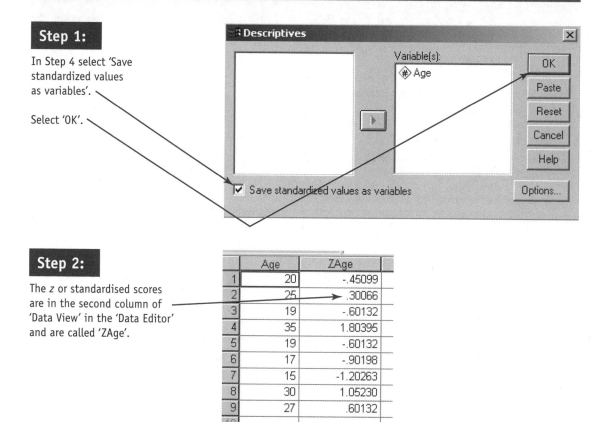

Step 1:

In Step 4 select 'Save standardized values as variables'.

Select 'OK'.

Step 2:

The *z* or standardised scores are in the second column of 'Data View' in the 'Data Editor' and are called 'ZAge'.

5.5 Reporting the output

The standard deviation of just one variable can easily be mentioned in the text of your report: 'It was found that the standard deviation of age was 6.65 years ($N = 9$).'

However, it is more likely that you would wish to record the standard deviation alongside other statistics such as the mean and range, as illustrated in Table 5.2. You would probably wish to include these statistics for other numerical score variables that you have data on.

Table 5.2   The sample size, mean, range and standard deviations of age, IQ and verbal fluency

	N	Mean	Range	Standard deviation
Age	9	23.00	20.00	6.65
IQ	9	122.17	17.42	14.38
Verbal fluency	9	18.23	4.91	2.36

5.6 Other features

'Descriptives . . .' contains a number of statistical calculations which can easily be selected:

Mean
Sum
Standard deviation (estimate)
Range
Minimum (score)
Maximum (score)
Standard error (S.E. mean)
Kurtosis
Skewness

These different statistical concepts are briefly explained at the end of Chapter 3.

6 Relationships between two or more variables

Diagrams and tables

Overview

- A great deal of research explores the relationship between two or more variables. The univariate (single-variable) statistical procedures described so far have their place in the analysis of practically any data. Neverthless, most research questions also require the interrelationships or correlations between different variables to be addressed.

- As with univariate statistics, a thorough bivariate statistical analysis of data requires an exploration of the basic trends in the data using tables and diagrams. Methods of presenting bivariate relationships include cross-tabulation tables, compound histograms (clustered bar charts) and scattergrams. Most of these will be familiar to you already, but nevertheless can cause difficulties.

- Care has to be taken to make sure that the tables and diagrams you obtain are useful and communicate well. In particular, ensure that your data for cross-tabulation tables and compound histograms (clustered bar charts) only contain a small number of different data values. If they do not, SPSS will produce massive tables and dense unreadable graphs and diagrams.

- Labelling tables and diagrams in full is a basic essential, along with a clear title.

- Scattergrams, on the other hand, also work well when you have many different values for the scores on your variables.

- The type of table or diagram which is most effective at communicating relationships in your data depends very much on the types of data involved. Two score variables will generally be most effectively presented as a scattergram whereas two nominal variables are generally presented in terms of a cross-tabulation table.

- Remember that the effective presentation of basic descriptive statistics requires that researchers consider their tables and diagrams carefully. Often researchers will have to 'tweak' things to make the finished tables and graphs effective forms of communication. That this can be done quickly is one of the advantages of using SPSS. It is recommended that the temptation to simply cut and paste tables and diagrams from SPSS output into reports is avoided. There is virtually no SPSS output which cannot be improved upon and made clearer. The basic options of SPSS are not always ideal in this respect. Often the editing procedures available for SPSS charts can improve things enormously.

- Producing charts like those discussed in this chapter is one of the harder tasks on SPSS.

We will illustrate the drawing up of a cross-tabulation table and compound bar chart with the data shown in Table 6.1 (*ISP*, Table 6.4). This shows the number of men and women in a study who have or have not been previously hospitalised. If your data are already entered into SPSS then Steps 1 to 5 may be ignored.

Table 6.1   Cross-tabulation table of sex against hospitalisation

	Male	**Female**
Previously hospitalised	$f = 20$	$f = 25$
Not previously hospitalised	$f = 30$	$f = 14$

6.1   Entering the data

Step 1:

The quickest way to enter the data in Table 6.1 is to create the four cells as four rows.

To do this we need three variables.

In 'Variable View' of the 'Data Editor' name the first column 'Hospitalisation', the second column 'Gender' and the third column 'Freq'.

Remove the two decimal places.

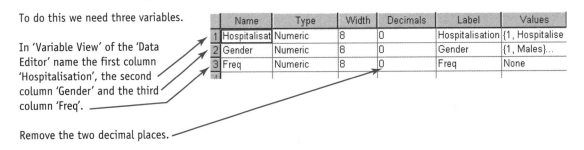

	Name	Type	Width	Decimals	Label	Values
1	Hospitalisat	Numeric	8	0	Hospitalisation	{1, Hospitalise
2	Gender	Numeric	8	0	Gender	{1, Males}...
3	Freq	Numeric	8	0	Freq	None
4						

Step 2:

Label the two values of 'Hospitalisation' (1 = 'Hospitalised'; 2 = 'Not hospitalised') and 'Gender' (1 = 'Males'; 2 = 'Females').

How to do this was explained in Chapter 1.

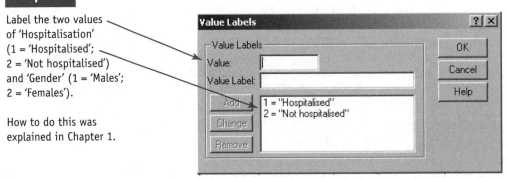

Step 3:

Enter these numbers in 'Data View' of the 'Data Editor'.

The first row refers to 'Hospitalised' 'Males' of whom there are 20.

The second row to 'Hospitalised' 'Females' of whom there are 25.

The third row to 'Not hospitalised' 'Males' of whom there are 30.

The fourth row to 'Not hospitalised' 'Females' of whom there are 14.

	Hospitalisation	Gender	Freq
1	1	1	20
2	1	2	25
3	2	1	30
4	2	2	14

6.2 Weighting the data

Step 4:

To weight the data so that the four cells have the appropriate number of cases in them, select 'Data' and 'Weight Cases...'.

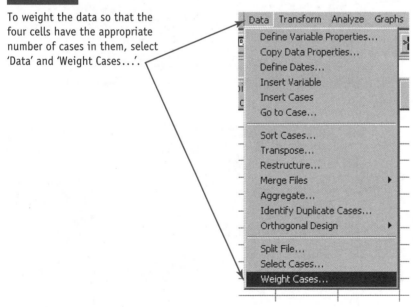

Step 5:

Select 'Freq', 'Weight cases by' and the ► button to put it in the 'Frequency Variable:' box.

Select 'OK'.

The cases are now weighted as shown by the 'Weight On' message in the lower right corner of the 'Data Editor'.

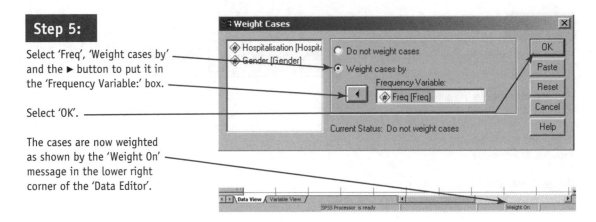

6.3   Cross-tabulation with frequencies

Step 6:

Select 'Analyze', 'Tables' and 'Basic Tables...'.

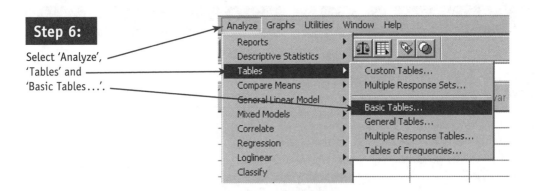

Step 7:

To put 'Hospitalisation' in the rows of the table, select it and the ► button near 'Down:'.

To put 'Gender' in the columns of the table, select it and the ► button near 'Across'.

Select 'OK'.

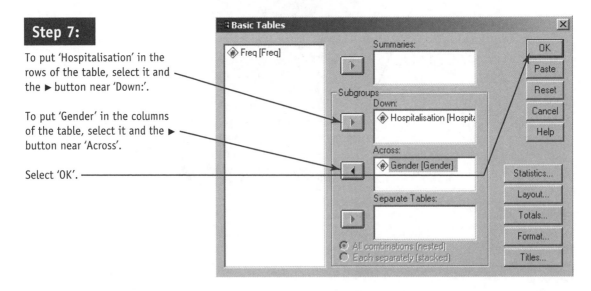

Step 8:

The table in the output is laid out like Table 6.1 except that the two values for each variable are not labelled. If necessary, label these values using Steps 9, 10 and 11 and rerun the analysis.

		Gender	
		1	2
Hospitalisation	1	20	25
	2	30	14

Step 9:

Select 'Edit' and 'Options'.

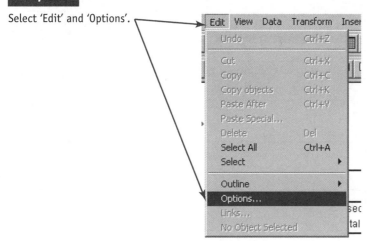

Step 10:

Select 'Output Labels'.

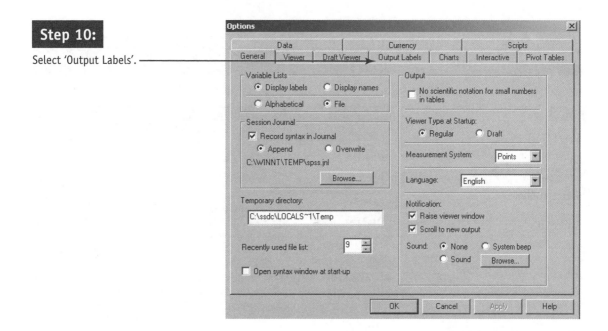

Step 11:

Select the ▼ button below 'Variable values in labels shown as:' and 'Labels' from the drop-down menu.

Select 'OK'.

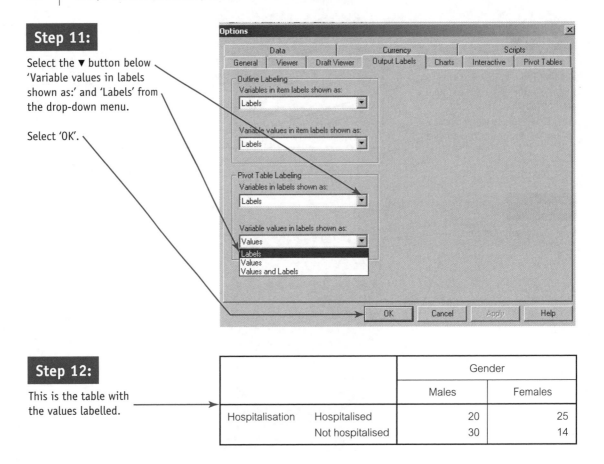

Step 12:

This is the table with the values labelled.

		Gender	
		Males	Females
Hospitalisation	Hospitalised	20	25
	Not hospitalised	30	14

6.4 Displaying frequencies as a percentage of the total number

In Step 7 Select 'Statistics…'.

Select 'Tables%'.

Then select 'Add'.

Select 'Continue'.

Select 'OK'.

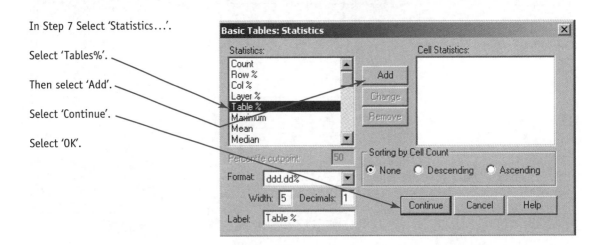

		Gender	
		1	2
		Table %	Table %
Hospitalisation	1	22.5%	28.1%
	2	33.7%	15.7%

If you add the percentages in each of the four cells they total 100.

6.5 Displaying frequencies as a percentage of the column total

Select 'Col%' and 'Add'.

Select 'Continue'.

Select 'OK' from the previous screen, which reappears.

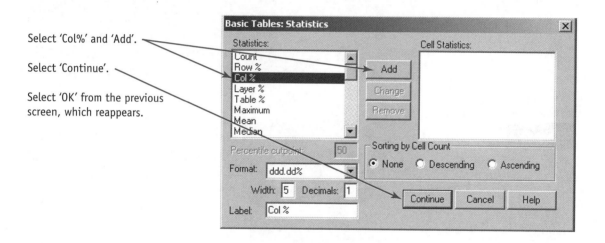

		Gender	
		1	2
		Col %	Col %
Hospitalisation	1	40.0%	64.1%
	2	60.0%	35.9%

If you add the % in each column they total 100.

6.6 Compound (stacked) percentage bar chart

Step 1:

To obtain a compound (stacked) percentage bar chart in which the bars represent 100% you need to enter the percentage figures (called 'ColPerCent') for the two bars and weight them.

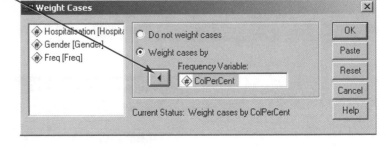

	Hospitalisation	Gender	Freq	ColPerCent
1	1	1	20	40.00
2	1	2	25	60.00
3	2	1	30	64.10
4	2	2	14	35.90

Weight Cases

- Hospitalisation [Hospita
- Gender [Gender]
- Freq [Freq]

○ Do not weight cases
● Weight cases by
   Frequency Variable:
   ColPerCent

Current Status: Weight cases by ColPerCent

OK
Paste
Reset
Cancel
Help

Step 2:

Select 'Graphs' and 'Bar...'.

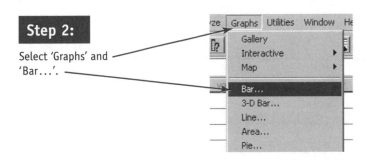

Graphs   Utilities   Window   He

- Gallery
- Interactive ▶
- Map ▶
- Bar...
- 3-D Bar...
- Line...
- Area...
- Pie...

Step 3:

Select 'Stacked'.

Select 'Define'.

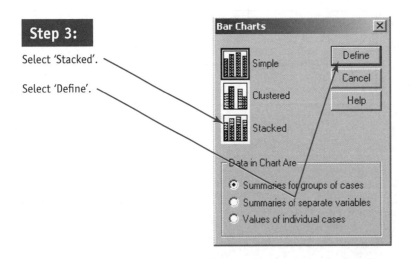

Bar Charts

- Simple
- Clustered
- Stacked

Define
Cancel
Help

Data in Chart Are
● Summaries for groups of cases
○ Summaries of separate variables
○ Values of individual cases

Step 4:

Select 'Hospitalisation' and the ▶ button next to 'Category Axis:'.

Select 'Gender' and the ▶ button next to 'Define Stacks by:'.

Select 'OK'.

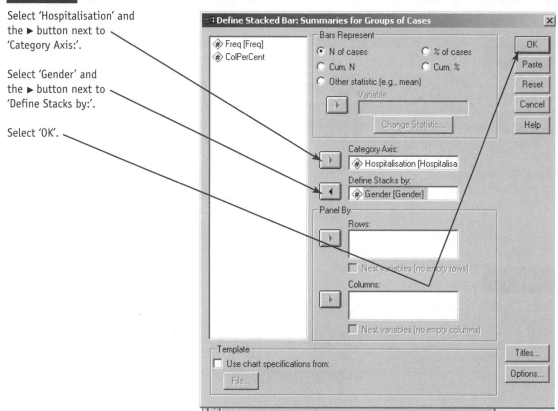

Step 5:

'Count' refers to 'Per cent' which you could change with the Chart Editor (see Chapter 2).

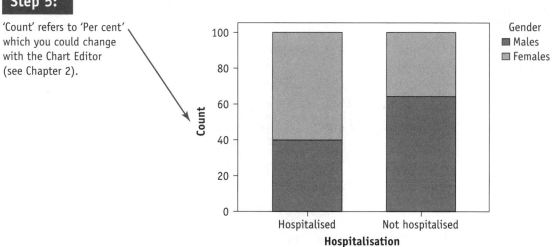

6.7 Compound histogram (clustered bar chart)

Step 1:

Weight cases by 'Freq' instead of 'ColPerCent' by selecting 'Data', 'Weight Cases...', 'Freq', 'Weight cases by' and the ▶ button to put it in the 'Frequency Variable:' box.

Select 'OK'.

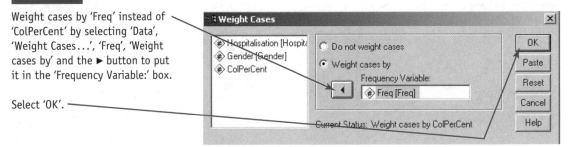

Step 2:

Select 'Graphs' then 'Bar...'.

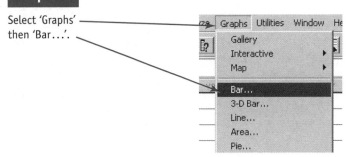

Step 3:

Select 'Clustered' then 'Define'.

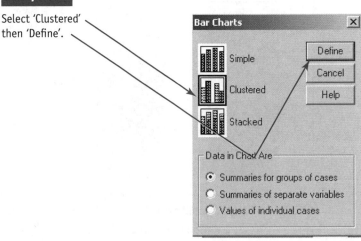

Step 4:

Select 'Hospitalisation' and the ▶ button next to 'Category Axis:'.

Select 'Gender' and the ▶ button next to 'Define Stacks by:'.

Select '% of cases'.

Select 'OK'.

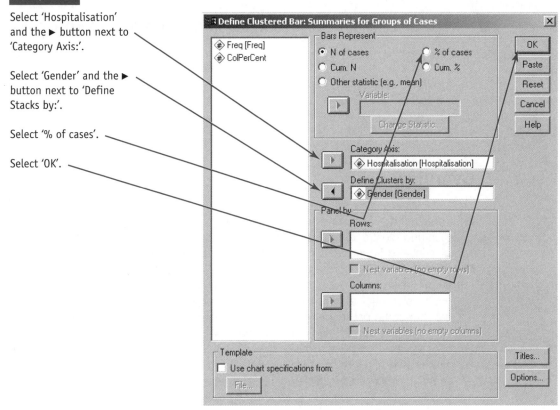

Step 5:

This is the bar chart produced.

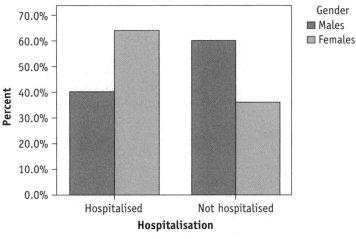

Cases weighted by Freq

7 Correlation coefficients
Pearson's correlation and Spearman's rho

Overview

■ There are a number of different correlation coefficients. In general, the most common and most useful by far is the Pearson correlation coefficient. The phi, point biserial and Spearman's rho correlation coefficients are all merely variants of it.

■ It is good practice to draw a scattergram as this represents the data included in a correlation coefficient. Not only will this give you a visual representation of the relationship but it also helps identify a number of problems such as a curved relationship or the presence of outliers. The Pearson correlation coefficient assumes a straight-line relationship between two variables. It is misleading if a curved relationship exists between the two variables. Outliers are extreme and unusual scores which distort the size of the correlation coefficient. Remedies include examining the relationship if the outliers are omitted. Alternatively, a Spearman correlation coefficient is less affected by outliers, and so one could examine the size of the Spearman correlation for the same data.

■ A correlation coefficient is a numerical measure or index of the amount of association between two sets of scores. It ranges in size from a maximum of +1.00 through 0.00 to −1.00.

■ The '+' sign indicates a positive correlation – that is, the scores on one variable increase as the scores on the other variable increase. A '−' sign indicates a negative correlation – that is, as the scores on one variable increase, the scores on the other variable decrease.

■ A correlation of 1.00 indicates a perfect association between the two variables. In other words, a scattergram of the two variables will show that *all* of the points fit a straight line exactly. A value of 0.00 indicates that the points of the scattergram are essentially scattered randomly around any straight line drawn through the data or are arranged in a curvilinear manner. A correlation coefficient of −0.5 would indicate a moderate negative relationship between the two variables.

■ Spearman's rho is the Pearson correlation coefficient applied to the scores after they have been ranked from the smallest to the largest on the two variables separately. It is used when the basic assumptions of the Pearson correlation coefficient have not been met by the data – that is especially when the scores are markedly asymmetrical (skewed) on a variable.

■ Since correlation coefficients are usually based on samples of data, it is usual to include a statement of the statistical significance of the correlation coefficient.

Statistical significance is a statement of the likelihood of obtaining a particular correlation coefficient for a sample of data *if* there is no correlation (i.e. a correlation of 0.00) in the population from which the sample was drawn. SPSS can give statistical significance as an exact value or as one of the conventional critical significance levels (for example 0.05 and 0.01).

We will illustrate the computation of Pearson's correlation, a scatter diagram and Spearman's rho for the data in Table 7.1 (*ISP*, Table 7.1), which gives scores for the musical ability and mathematical ability of 10 children.

Table 7.1 Scores on musical ability and mathematical ability for 10 children

Music score	Mathematics score
2	8
6	3
4	9
5	7
7	2
7	3
2	9
3	8
5	6
4	7

7.1 Entering the data

Step 1:

In 'Variable View' of the 'Data Editor' name the first row 'Music' and the second column 'Maths'.

Remove the two decimal places by changing the figure already here to zero.

	Name	Type	Width	Decimals
1	Music	Numeric	8	0
2	Maths	Numeric	8	0

Step 2:

In 'Data View' of the 'Data Editor' enter the music data in the first column and the maths data in the second column.

Save the data as a file to use for Chapter 8.

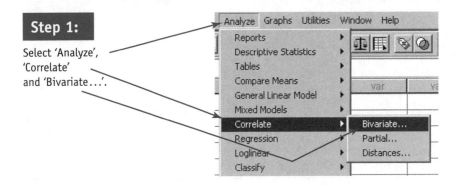

	Music	Maths
1	2	8
2	6	3
3	4	9
4	5	7
5	7	2
6	7	3
7	2	9
8	3	8
9	5	6
10	4	7
11		

7.2 Pearson's correlation

Step 1:

Select 'Analyze', 'Correlate' and 'Bivariate...'.

Step 2:

Select 'Music' and 'Maths' either singly or together and use the ▶ button to put them in the 'Variables' box as shown here.

Select 'OK'.

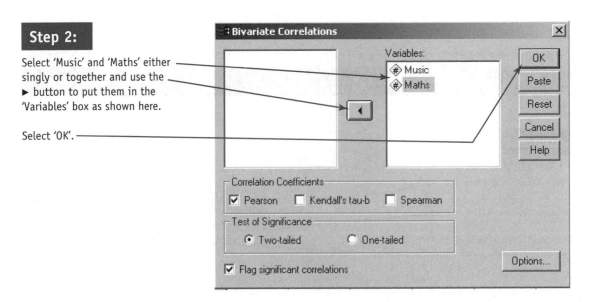

7.3 Interpreting the output

Correlations

The correlation between 'Maths' and 'Music' is –0.900. The two-tailed significance or probability level is 0.001 or less, so the correlation is statistically significant.

The number of cases on which this correlation is based is 10. This information is also given in this cell.

		Music	Maths
Music	Pearson Correlation	1	–.900**
	Sig. (2-tailed)	.	.000
	N	10	10
Maths	Pearson Correlation	–.900**	1
	Sig. (2-tailed)	.000	.
	N	10	10

**. Correlation is significant at the 0.01 level

7.4 Reporting the output

■ The correlation between musical ability and mathematical ability is −0.900. It is usual to round correlations to two decimal places, which would make it −0.90. This is more than precise enough for most psychological measurements.

■ The exact significance level to three decimal places is 0.000. This means that the significance level is less than 0.001. We would suggest that you do not use a string of zeros, as these confuse people. Always change the last zero to a 1. This means that the significance level can be reported as being $p < 0.001$.

■ It is customary to present the degrees of freedom (DF) rather than the number of cases when presenting correlations. The degrees of freedom are the number of cases minus 2, which makes them 8 for this correlation. There is nothing wrong with reporting the number of cases instead.

■ In a report, we would write 'There is a significant negative relationship between musical ability and mathematical ability ($r = -0.90, DF = 8, p < 0.001$). Children with more musical ability have lower mathematical ability.' Significance of the correlation coefficient is discussed in more detail in the textbook (*ISP*, Chapter 10).

7.5   Spearman's rho

Step 1:

As for Pearson's correlation, select 'Analyze', 'Correlate', 'Bivariate' and the variables you want to correlate.

Select 'Spearman'.

If you don't want Pearson, deselect it.

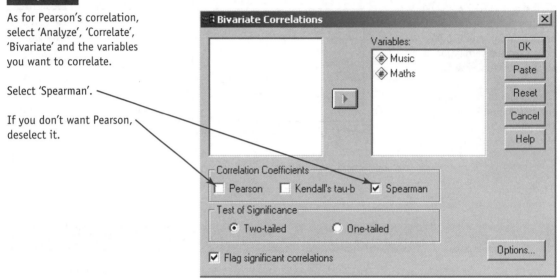

7.6   Interpreting the output

Spearman's rho between 'Maths' and 'Music' is –0.894.

The two-tailed significance level of this correlation is 0.001 or less, so the correlation is statistically significant.

The number of cases is 10. This information is also given in this cell.

Correlations

			Music	Maths
Spearman's rho	Music	Correlation Coefficient	1.000	–.894**
		Sig. (2-tailed)	.	.000
		N	10	10
	Maths	Correlation Coefficient	–.894**	1.000
		Sig. (2-tailed)	.000	.
		N	10	10

**. Correlation is significant at the 0.01 level (2-tailed).

7.7 Reporting the output

- The correlation reported to two decimal places is −0.89.
- The probability of achieving this correlation by chance is less than 0.001 (i.e. $p < 0.001$).
- We would report this in the following way: 'There is a statistically significant negative correlation between musical ability and mathematical ability (rho = −0.89, $DF = 8$, $p < 0.001$). Those with the highest musical ability tend to be those with the lowest mathematical ability and vice versa.'

7.8 Scatter diagram

Step 1:

Select 'Graphs' and 'Scatter/Dot…'.

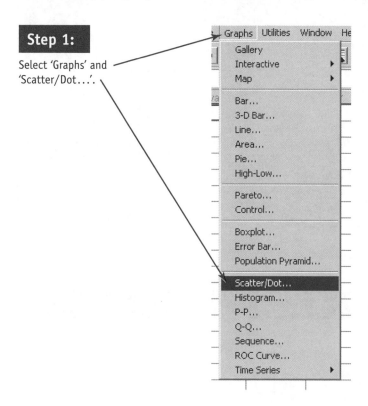

Step 2:

Select 'Define' as 'Simple' has already been selected. It is called the default.

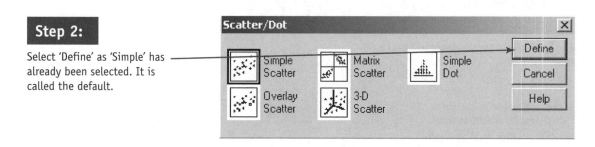

Step 3:

To have 'Music' as the vertical axis, select it and the ▶ button next to the 'Y Axis' box.

To have 'Maths' as the horizontal axis, select it and the ▶ button next to the 'X Axis' box.

Select 'OK'.

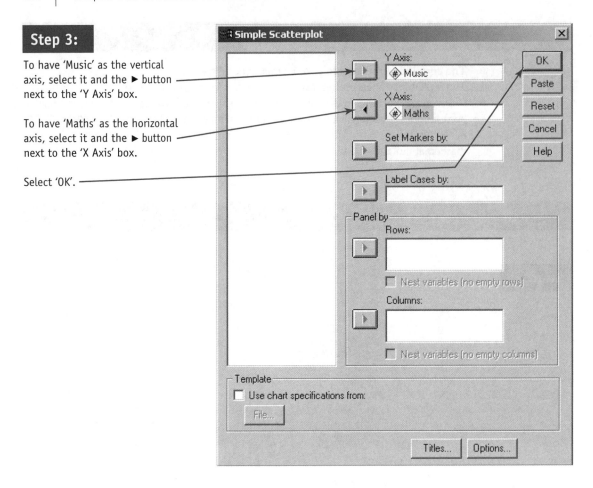

7.9 Interpreting the output

In this scattergram the scatter of points is relatively narrow, indicating that the correlation is high.

The slope of the scatter lies in a relatively straight line, indicating it is a linear rather than a curvilinear relationship.

The line moves from the upper left to the lower right, which signifies a negative correlation.

If the relationship is curvilinear, then Pearson's or Spearman's correlations may be misleading.

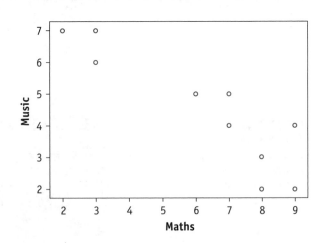

7.10 Reporting the output

■ You should never report a correlation coefficient without examining the scattergram for problems such as curved relationships or outliers (*ISP*, Chapter 7).

■ In a student project it should always be possible to include graphs of this sort. Unfortunately, journal articles and books tend to be restricted in the numbers they include because of the space they take and the impact on costs.

■ We could write of the scattergram: 'A scattergram of the relationship between mathematical ability and musical ability was examined. There was no evidence of a curvilinear relationship or the undue influence of outliers.'

8 Regression
Prediction with precision

Overview

- Where there is a relationship between two variables, it is possible to estimate or predict a person's score on one of the variables from their score on the other variable. The stronger the correlation, the better the prediction.

- Regression can be used on much the same data as the correlation coefficient. However, it is far less commonly used, partly because of the problem of comparability between values obtained from different sets of variables. (The beta weight can be used if such comparability is required.)

- The dependent variable in regression is the variable the value of which is to be predicted. It is also known as the criterion variable, the predicted variable or the Y-variable.

- The independent variable is the variable being used to make the prediction. It is also known as the predictor variable or the X-variable.

- Great care is needed not to get the independent variable and the dependent variable confused. This can easily happen with simple regression. The best way of avoiding problems is to examine the scatterplot or scattergram of the relationship between the two variables. Make sure that the horizontal x-axis is the independent variable and that the vertical y-axis is the dependent variable. One can then check what the cut point is approximately from the scattergram as well to get an idea of what the slope should be. The cut point is where the slope meets the vertical axis. These estimates may be compared with their calculated values to ensure that an error has not been made. If problems are found, the most likely reason is that the independent and dependent variables have been confused.

- The simple regression technique described in this chapter expresses relationships in terms of the original units of measurement of the variables involved. Thus, if two different studies use slightly different variables it is difficult to compare the outcomes of the studies using this form of regression.

- In regression, the relationship between two variables is described mathematically by the slope of the best fitting line through the points of the scattergram together with the point at which this regression line cuts the (vertical) axis of the scattergram. Therefore, the relationship between two variables requires the value of the slope (usually given the symbol B or b) and the intercept or cut point in the vertical axis (usually given the symbol a or described as the constant).

■ Regression becomes a much more important technique when one is using several variables to predict values on another variable. These techniques are known as multiple regression (see Chapters 28 and 29). When the dependent variable is a nominal category variable, then the appropriate statistical analysis will be a form of logistic regression (see Chapters 32 and 33).

We will illustrate the computation of simple regression and a regression plot with the data in Table 8.1 (*ISP*, Table 7.1), which gives a score for the musical ability and mathematical ability of 10 children. These data are identical to those used in the previous chapter on correlation. In this way, you may find it easier to appreciate the differences between regression and correlation.

Table 8.1   Scores on musical ability and mathematical ability for 10 children

Music score	Mathematics score
2	8
6	3
4	9
5	7
7	2
7	3
2	9
3	8
5	6
4	7

The music scores are the criterion or the dependent variable, while the mathematics scores are the predictor or independent variable. With regression, it is essential to make the criterion or dependent variable the vertical axis (*y*-axis) of a scatterplot and the predictor or independent variable the horizontal axis (*x*-axis).

8.1 Entering the data

If you have saved the data select the file. Otherwise enter the data again.

Step 1:

In 'Variable View' of the 'Data Editor' name the first column 'Music' and the second column 'Maths'.

Remove the two decimal places.

	Name	Type	Width	Decimals
1	Music	Numeric	8	0
2	Maths	Numeric	8	0

Step 2:

In 'Data View' of the 'Data Editor' enter the music data in the first column and the maths data in the second column.

	Music	Maths
1	2	8
2	6	3
3	4	9
4	5	7
5	7	2
6	7	3
7	2	9
8	3	8
9	5	6
10	4	7

8.2 Simple regression

Step 1:

Select 'Analyze', 'Regression' and 'Linear...'.

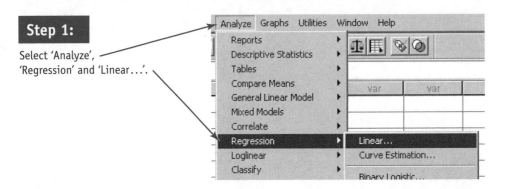

Step 2:

Select 'Music' and the ▶ button beside 'Dependent:' to put 'Music' in that box.

Select 'Maths' and the ▶ button beside 'Independent(s):' to put 'Maths' in that box.

Select 'Statistics...'.

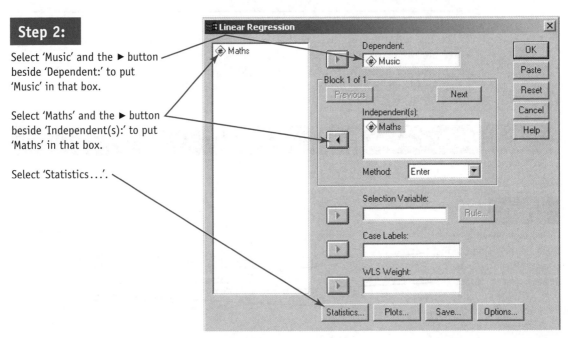

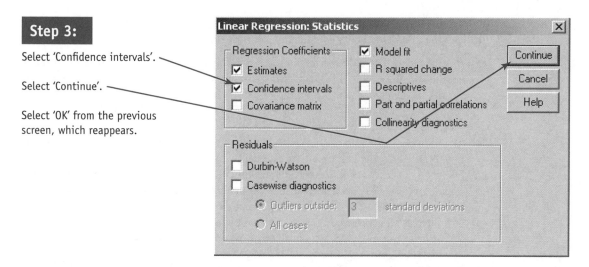

Step 3:

Select 'Confidence intervals'.

Select 'Continue'.

Select 'OK' from the previous screen, which reappears.

8.3 Interpreting the output

This last table of the output has the essential details of the regression analysis. It is very easy to reverse the independent variable and dependent variable accidentally. Check the table entitled 'Coefficients[a]'. Under the table the name of the dependent variable is given. In this case it is 'Music' which is our dependent variable. If it had read 'Maths' then we would have made a mistake and the analysis would need to be redone as the regression values would be incorrect.

The intercept or constant is 8.425. This is the point at which the regression line cuts the vertical axis.

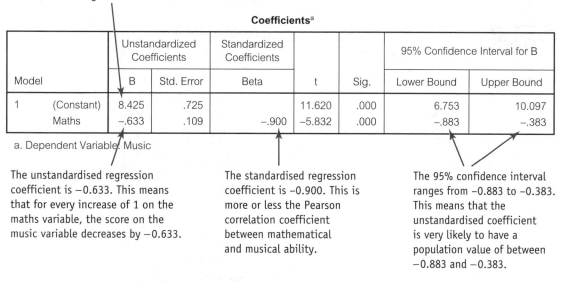

Coefficients[a]

Model		B	Std. Error	Beta	t	Sig.	Lower Bound	Upper Bound
		Unstandardized Coefficients		Standardized Coefficients			95% Confidence Interval for B	
1	(Constant)	8.425	.725		11.620	.000	6.753	10.097
	Maths	−.633	.109	−.900	−5.832	.000	−.883	−.383

a. Dependent Variable: Music

The unstandardised regression coefficient is −0.633. This means that for every increase of 1 on the maths variable, the score on the music variable decreases by −0.633.

The standardised regression coefficient is −0.900. This is more or less the Pearson correlation coefficient between mathematical and musical ability.

The 95% confidence interval ranges from −0.883 to −0.383. This means that the unstandardised coefficient is very likely to have a population value of between −0.883 and −0.383.

In simple regression involving two variables, it is conventional to report the regression equation as a slope (*b*) and an intercept (*a*) (see *ISP*, Chapter 8). SPSS does not quite follow this terminology. Unfortunately, at this stage the SPSS output is far more complex and detailed than the statistical sophistication of most students:

■ *B* is the slope. The slope of the regression line is called the unstandardised regression coefficient in SPSS. The unstandardised regression coefficient between 'music' and 'maths' is displayed under *B* and is −0.633, which rounded to two decimal places is −0.63. What this means is that for every increase of 1.00 on the horizontal axis, the score on the vertical axis changes by −0.633.

■ The 95% confidence interval for this coefficient ranges from −0.88 (−0.883) to −0.38 (−0.383). Since the regression is based on a sample and not the population, there is always a risk that the sample regression coefficient is not the same as that in the population. The 95% confidence interval gives the range of regression slopes within which you can be 95% sure that the population slope will lie.

■ The intercept *a* is referred to as the constant in SPSS. The intercept is presented as the '(Constant)' and is 8.425, which rounded to two decimal places is 8.43. It is the point at which the regression line cuts the vertical *y* axis.

■ The 95% confidence interval for the intercept is 6.753 to 10.097. This means that, based on the sample, the intercept of the population is 95% likely to lie in the range of 6.75 to 10.10.

■ The column headed 'Beta' gives a value of −0.900. This is actually the Pearson correlation between the two variables. In other words, if you turn your scores into standard scores (*z*-scores) the slope of the regression and the correlation coefficient are the same thing.

8.4 Regression scatterplot

It is generally advisable to inspect a scattergram of your two variables when doing regression. Follow the steps involved in plotting a scattergram as described in Chapter 7.

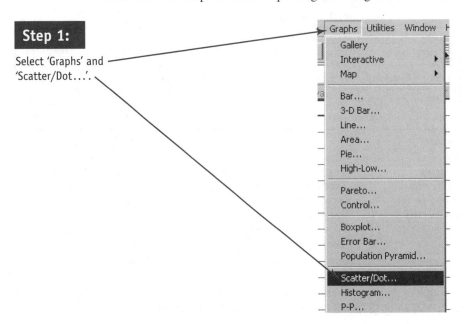

Step 1:

Select 'Graphs' and 'Scatter/Dot...'.

Step 2:

Select 'Define' as 'Simple' is
the pre-selected default.

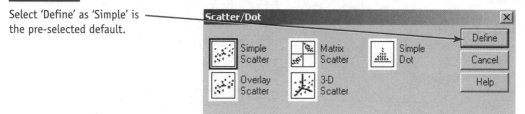

Step 3:

Select 'Music' and the ► button
beside 'Y Axis:' to put it in this
box as it is the criterion.

Select 'Maths' and the ► button
beside 'X Axis:' to put it in this
box as it is the predictor.

Select 'OK'.

The output is the same as that
for the correlation in section 7.9.

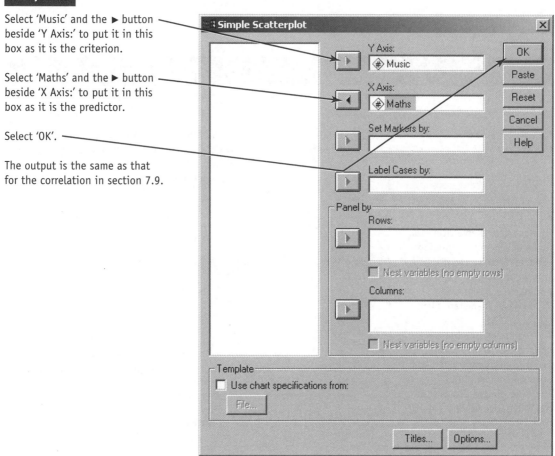

Step 4:

To fit a regression line to the scatterplot, double click anywhere in it which opens the 'Chart Editor'.

Select 'Elements' and 'Fit Line at Total'.

Select 'Close' in 'Properties' box.

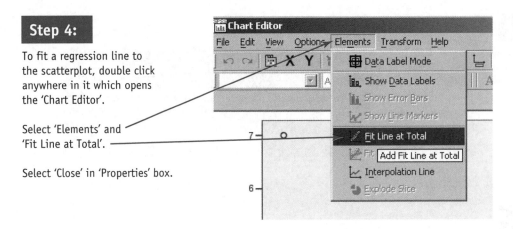

8.5 Interpreting the output

The points on the scatterplot are close to the regression line (i.e. the line is a good fit to the data). Furthermore, the points seem to form a straight line (i.e. the relationship is not curvilinear). Also, there is no sign of outliers – i.e. especially high or low points.

In *regression*, the vertical axis is the dependent or criterion variable. In this case it is 'Music'. It is a common error to mix up the axes in regression. If you have, then start again.

The regression line has a negative slope in this case; i.e. it slopes from top left down to bottom right. The *B*-weight therefore has a negative value.

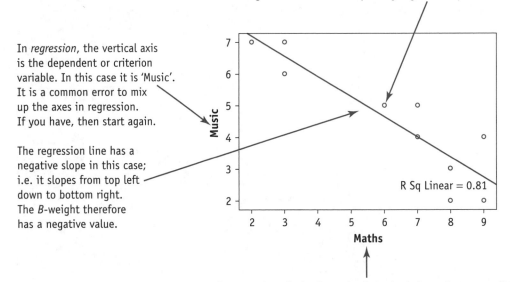

In *regression*, the horizontal axis is the independent or predictor variable. In this case it is 'Maths'. It is a common error to mix up the axes in regression. If you have, then re-do the analysis.

■ The regression line sloping from the top left down to bottom right indicates a negative relationship between the two variables. Remember that unless your axes intersect at zero on both the vertical and horizontal axes then your interpretation risks being mistaken.

■ The points seem relatively close to this line, which suggests that Beta (correlation) should be a large (negative) numerical value and that the confidence interval for the slope should be relatively small.

8.6 Reporting the scattergram

Although all of the output from SPSS is pertinent to a sophisticated user, many users might prefer to have the bare bones at this stage.

■ With this in mind, we could write about the analysis in this chapter as follows: 'The scatterplot of the relationship between mathematical and musical ability suggests a linear negative relationship between the two variables. It is possible to predict accurately a person's musical ability from their mathematical ability. The equation is $Y' = 8.43 + (-0.63X)$ where X is an individual's mathematics score and Y' is the best prediction of their musical ability score.'

■ An alternative would be to give the scatterplot and to write underneath $a = 8.43$ and $B = -0.63$.

■ One could add the confidence intervals as follows: 'The 95% confidence interval for the slope of the regression line is -0.88 to -0.38. Since this confidence interval does not include 0.00 the slope differs significantly from a horizontal straight line.' However, this would be a relatively sophisticated interpretation for novices in statistics.

9 Samples and populations
Generating a random sample

Overview

■ Random sampling is a key aspect of statistics. This chapter explains how random samples can be quickly generated. This is not a commonly used procedure in statistical analysis but can provide useful experience of the nature of random processes.

■ One can get a better feel for inferential statistics and sampling by obtaining random samples from your data to explore the variability in outcomes of further statistical analyses on these random samples. The variation in the characteristics of samples is known as sampling error and is the basis of inferential statistics.

■ Random sampling can also be used with huge sets of data to carry out preliminary analyses. In the past, when computer time was expensive and computer processing slow, this was of a great benefit.

■ Keep an eye on the dialogue boxes as you work through this chapter. You will notice options which allow you to select samples based on other criteria such as the date when the participants were interviewed.

In this chapter, the selection of random samples from a known set of scores is illustrated. The primary aim of this is to allow those learning statistics for the first time to try random sampling in order to get an understanding of sampling distributions. This should lead to a better appreciation of estimation in statistics and the frailty that may underlie seemingly hard nosed mathematical procedures. We will illustrate the generation of a random sample from a set of data consisting of the extraversion scores of the 50 airline pilots shown in Table 4.1.

Table 4.1 Extraversion scores of 50 airline pilots

3	5	5	4	4	5	5	3	5	2
1	2	5	3	2	1	2	3	3	3
4	2	5	5	4	2	4	5	1	5
5	3	3	4	1	4	2	5	1	2
3	2	5	4	2	1	2	3	4	1

9.1 Selecting a random sample

Step 1:

If you saved the data, select
the file. Otherwise enter
the data again.

Select 'Data' and 'Select Cases…'.

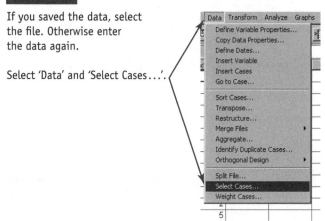

Step 2:

Select 'Random sample of cases'.

Select 'Sample'.

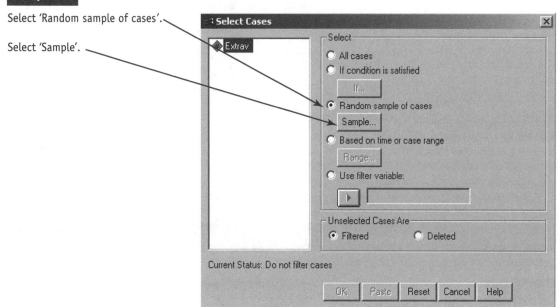

Step 3:

To select about 10% of all cases, enter '10' in the box beside 'Approximately'.

To select five cases exactly, select 'Exactly', enter '5' 'cases from the first' '50' 'cases'.

Select 'Continue'.

Select 'OK' from the previous screen, which reappears.

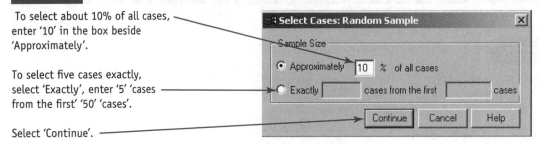

9.2 Interpreting the results

The cases which have been selected don't have a diagonal line across their case number and have a '1' in the new column created called 'filter_$'.

Cases which have not been selected have a diagonal across their case number and have a '0' in the new column called 'filter_$'.

	Extrav	filter_$
1	3	0
2	5	0
3	5	0
4	4	0
5	4	0
6	5	0
7	5	0
8	3	0
9	5	1
10	2	0
11	1	0
12	2	1
13	5	0
14	3	0

9.3 Statistical analysis on a random sample

Step 1:

To analyse this sample, select 'Analyze' and the analysis desired such as 'Descriptive Statistics' and 'Descriptives...'.

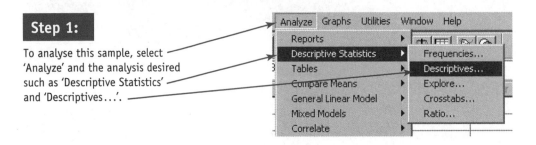

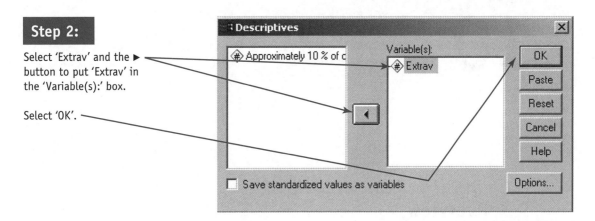

Step 2:

Select 'Extrav' and the ▶ button to put 'Extrav' in the 'Variable(s):' box.

Select 'OK'.

Descriptive Statistics

	N	Minimum	Maximum	Mean	Std. Deviation
Extrav	7	1	5	3.29	1.496
Valid N (listwise)	7				

Note that seven cases were selected. If exactly 10% is required, then 5 from 50 cases should be specified in Step 3 of Section 9.1.

10 Selecting cases

Overview

- This chapter explains how to select a particular subgroup from your sample. For example, you may wish to analyse the data only for young people or for women.
- It is possible to select subgroups based on multiple criteria.
- Sometimes the use of subgroups leads to a much clearer understanding of the trends in the data than would be possible if, for example, one used cross-tabulation by gender.

Sometimes we may wish to carry out computations on subgroups in our sample. For example we may want to correlate musical and mathematical ability (*a*) in girls and boys separately, (*b*) in older and younger children separately and (*c*) in older and younger girls and boys separately. To do this, we need a code for sex and age such as 1 for girls and 2 for boys. We also need to decide what age we will use as a cut-off point to determine which children fall into the younger age group and which children fall into the older age group. We will use age 10 as the cut-off point, with children aged 9 or less falling into the younger age group and children aged 10 or more falling into the older age group. Then we need to select each of the groups in turn and carry out the computation. We will illustrate the selection of cases with the data in Table 10.1, which shows the music and mathematics

Table 10.1 Scores on musical ability and mathematical ability for 10 children with their sex and age

Music score	Mathematics score	Sex	Age
2	8	1	10
6	3	1	9
4	9	2	12
5	7	1	8
7	2	2	11
7	3	2	13
2	9	2	7
3	8	1	10
5	6	2	9
4	7	1	11

scores of ten children together with their code for sex and their age in years. (The music and mathematics scores are the same as those previously presented in Table 7.1.)

Obviously the selection of cut-off points is important. You need to beware of inadvertently excluding some cases.

10.1 Entering the data

Step 1:

If you saved the data file for Chapter 7, select that file and define the new variables in 'Variable View' of the 'Data Editor'.

Otherwise, define the four variables.

Remove the two decimal places.

Save this file to use in Chapters 15 and 16.

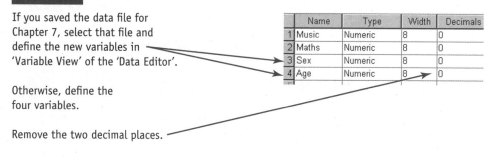

	Name	Type	Width	Decimals
1	Music	Numeric	8	0
2	Maths	Numeric	8	0
3	Sex	Numeric	8	0
4	Age	Numeric	8	0

Step 2:

Enter the data in 'Data View' of the 'Data Editor'.

	Music	Maths	Sex	Age
1	2	8	1	10
2	6	3	1	9
3	4	9	2	12
4	5	7	1	8
5	7	2	2	11
6	7	3	2	13
7	2	9	2	7
8	3	8	1	10
9	5	6	2	9
10	4	7	1	11

10.2 Selecting cases

Step 1:

Select 'Data' and 'Select Cases...'.

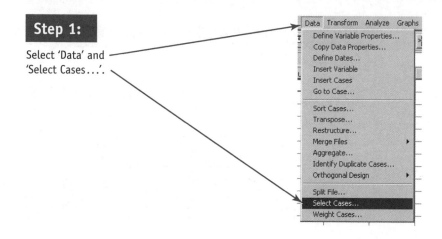

Data   Transform   Analyze   Graphs

Define Variable Properties...
Copy Data Properties...
Define Dates...
Insert Variable
Insert Cases
Go to Case...

Sort Cases...
Transpose...
Restructure...
Merge Files   ▶
Aggregate...
Identify Duplicate Cases...
Orthogonal Design   ▶

Split File...
Select Cases...
Weight Cases...

Step 2:

Select 'If condition is satisfied'.

Select 'If'.

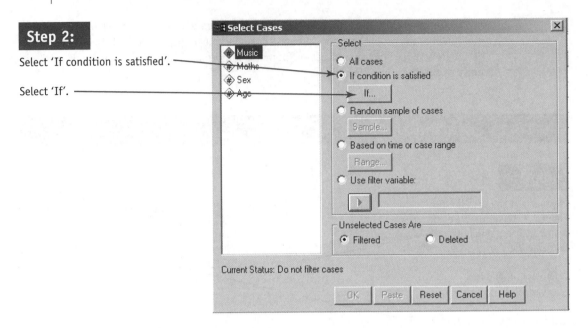

To select girls, select 'Sex' and the ▶ button.

Select '=' and '1'. Alternatively type in 'Sex = 1'.

Select 'Continue'.

Select 'OK' from the previous screen, which reappears.

Carry out the analysis you want (e.g. correlation).

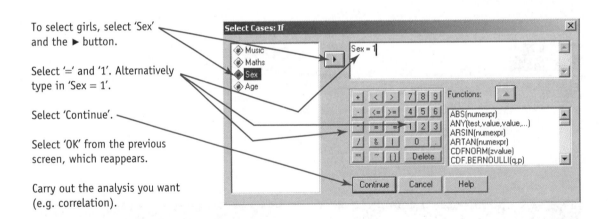

To select boys, select 'Data', 'Select Cases...' and 'If'.

Highlight '1' and replace it with '2'.

Select 'Continue' and then 'OK'.

Conduct your analysis (e.g. correlation).

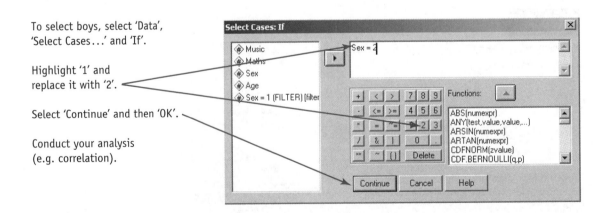

To select girls 9 years or younger, select 'Data', 'Select Cases...' and 'If'.

Highlight '2' and replace it with '1'.

Select '&' (the ampersand), 'Age', the ► button, '<=' (the less than or equal sign) and '9'. Or type this in.

Select 'Continue' and then 'OK'.

Conduct your analysis
(e.g. correlation).

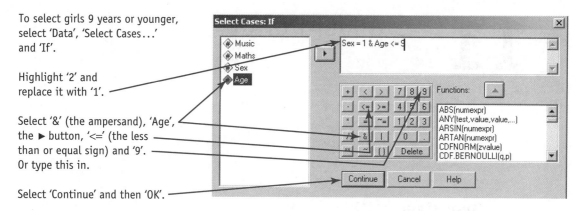

To select girls older than 9 years, select 'Data', 'Select Cases...' and 'If'.

Highlight '<=' and replace it with '>' (the greater than sign).

To see or remind you of what the signs mean, move the cursor to them and click on the right button of the mouse.

Select 'Continue' and then 'OK'.

Conduct your analysis
(e.g. correlation).

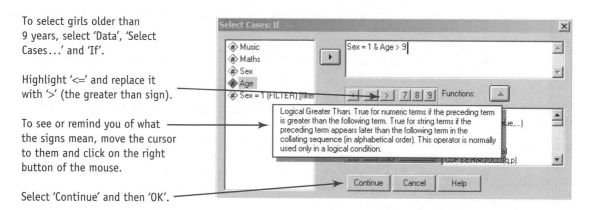

11 Standard error

Overview

- Standard error is an index of the variability of the means of many samples taken from the population. It is nothing other than the standard deviation, but applied to sample means rather than scores. In other words, standard error is the average amount by which the means of samples differ from the mean of the population from which they came.

- It is mostly used as an intermediate step in other statistical techniques such as the *t*-test. There is little need to calculate the standard error in its own right since it adds little or nothing that the standard deviation or variance cannot.

- Nevertheless, it can be used like variance or standard deviation as an index of the amount of variability in the scores on a variable. A knowledgeable researcher will find variance, standard deviation and standard error equally useful as indicators of the variability of scores.

- Standard error is an important concept in the calculation of confidence intervals. Indeed, it will occur in many contexts where the focus is on the characteristics of samples rather than scores.

- There are two versions of standard error. Standard error as applied to a set of scores and estimated standard error, which is used when trying to estimate the population standard error from the standard error of a sample. SPSS actually only calculates estimated standard error. Hence, for standard error in SPSS output read estimated standard error.

The computation of the estimated standard error of the mean is illustrated with the set of six scores of self-esteem presented in Table 11.1 (*ISP*, Table 11.3).

Table 11.1 Data for standard error example

Self-esteem scores	
5	6
7	4
3	5

11.1 Entering the data

Enter the data in the 'Data Editor'.

Label the variable 'Esteem'.

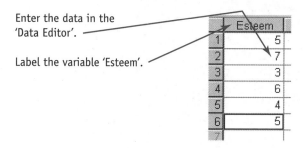

11.2 Estimated standard error of the mean

Step 1:

Select 'Analyze', 'Descriptive Statistics' and 'Descriptives...'.

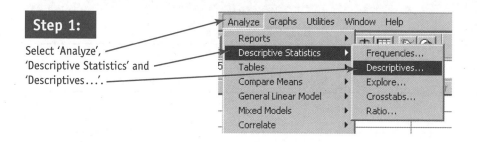

Step 2:

Select 'Esteem' and the ► button to put 'Esteem' in the 'Variable(s):' box.

Select 'Options...'.

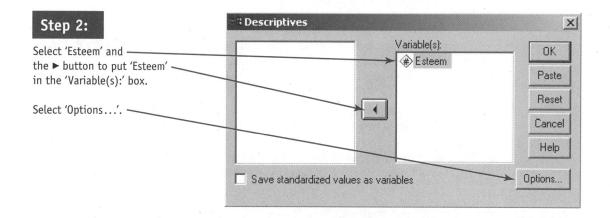

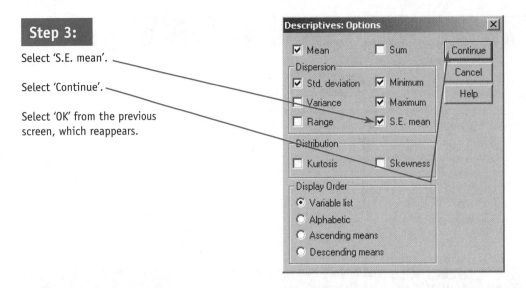

Step 3:

Select 'S.E. mean'.

Select 'Continue'.

Select 'OK' from the previous screen, which reappears.

11.3 Interpreting the output

Descriptive Statistics

	N	Minimum	Maximum	Mean		Std.
	Statistic	Statistic	Statistic	Statistic	Std. Error	Statistic
Esteem	6	3	7	5.00	.577	1.414
Valid N (listwise)	6					

The (estimated) standard error of the mean of this sample of six scores is 0.577. It is an indication of the average amount by which sample means differ from the mean of the population from which they came.

■ The table gives us the value of the standard error of sample means as 0.58, which is rounded to two decimal places. This is the average amount by which means of samples ($N = 6$) differ from the population mean.

■ It is an estimate based on a sample and should really be termed the estimated standard error.

■ The table includes other information such as the mean (5.00), the estimated population standard deviation based on this sample, and the minimum and maximum values in the data.

■ The final column gives the (estimated) standard deviation of the six scores, which is 1.41.

11.4 Reporting the output

Generally, in psychological statistics, one would not report the standard error of sample means on its own. It would be more usual to report it as part of certain tests of significance. However, in many circumstances it is just as informative as the variance or standard deviation of a sample as it bears a simple relationship to both of these.

12 The *t*-test

Comparing two samples of correlated/related scores

Overview

- The *t*-test is used to assess the statistical significance of the difference between the means of two sets of scores. That is, it helps to address the common research question of whether the average (i.e. mean) score for one set of scores differs from the average score for another set of scores.

- Statistical significance is assessed by using the variability in the available data to assess how likely various differences between the two means would be if there was no true difference between the two samples. The null hypothesis suggests that there is no difference between the sample means. Differences between sample means that would be very uncommon by chance if the null hypothesis were true are said to be statistically significant. They lead us to prefer the hypothesis that there is truly a difference between the two means that is unlikely to be a chance effect due to sampling.

- Because in research we invariably deal with samples of people drawn from the potential population, we need to estimate whether any difference we obtain between two sets of scores is statistically significant. That is, is the obtained difference between the two means so very different from a zero difference that it is unlikely that the samples come from the same population?

- There are two versions of the *t*-test. One is used when the two sets of scores to be compared come from a single set or sample of people or when the correlation coefficient between the two sets of scores is high. This is known as the related or correlated *t*-test. The other version of the *t*-test is used when the two different sets of scores come from different groups of participants. Refer to the next chapter if the two means you wish to compare come from distinct groups of participants.

- If you have used a matching procedure to make pairs of people similar on some other characteristics then you would also use the related *t*-test in this present chapter – especially if the two sets of scores correlate significantly.

- Data entry for related and unrelated variables is very different in SPSS so take care to plan your analysis before entering your data in order to avoid problems and unnecessary work.

- If you have more than two sets of scores to compare then refer to Chapter 21 on the related analysis of variance.

- The *t*-test described in this chapter is known as the related *t*-test. Basically this means that the two sets of scores are obtained from a single sample of participants.

There should be a correlation between the scores on the two measures since otherwise the two sets of scores are not related.

■ The related *t*-test works at its optimum if the distribution of the differences between the two sets of scores is approximately bell shaped (that is, if there is a normal distribution). If the distribution is very different from a bell shape, then one might consider using a related non-parametric statistics such as the Wilcoxon matched-pairs test (see Chapter 18).

The computation of a related *t*-test is illustrated with the data in Table 12.1, which shows the number of eye contacts made by the same babies with their mothers at 6 and 9 months (*ISP*, Table 12.6). The purpose of the analysis is to see whether the amount of eye contact changes between these ages.

Table 12.1   Number of one-minute segments with eye-contact at different ages

Baby	6 months	9 months
Clara	3	7
Martin	5	6
Sally	5	3
Angie	4	8
Trevor	3	5
Sam	7	9
Bobby	8	7
Sid	7	9

12.1 Entering the data

Step 1:

In 'Variable View' of the 'Data Editor' label the first row 'Six_mths' and the second row 'Nine_mths'.

Remove the two decimal places by changing the figure for the decimals to 0.

	Name	Type	Width	Decimals
1	Six_mths	Numeric	8	0
2	Nine_mths	Numeric	8	0

Step 2:

In 'Data View' of the 'Data Editor' enter the data in the first two columns.

(Save this data file to use in Chapter 18.)

	Six_mths	Nine_mths
1	3	7
2	5	6
3	5	3
4	4	8
5	3	5
6	7	9
7	8	7
8	7	9

12.2 The related *t*-test

Step 1:

Select 'Analyze', 'Compare Means' and 'Paired-Samples T Test...'.

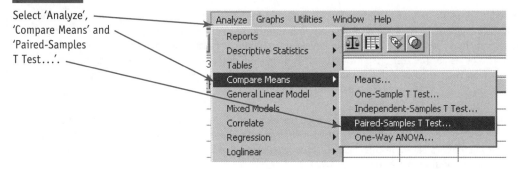

Step 2:

Select 'Six_mths' to put it besides 'Variable 1:' under 'Current Selections'.

Select 'Nine_mths' to put it besides 'Variable 2:' under 'Current Selections'.

Select the ▶ button to put these two variables in the 'Paired Variables:' box.

Select 'OK'.

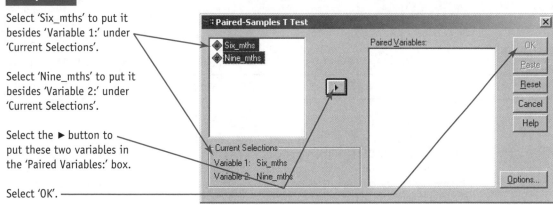

12.3 Interpreting the output

Paired Samples Statistics

		Mean	N	Std. Deviation	Std. Error Mean
Pair 1	Six_mths	5.25	8	1.909	.675
	Nine_mths	6.75	8	2.053	.726

The first table shows the mean, the number of cases and the standard deviation of the two groups. The mean for 'Six_mths' is 5.25 and its standard deviation is 1.909. The two standard deviations are very similar which is an advantage.

Paired Samples Correlations

	N	Correlation	Sig.
Pair 1 Six_mths & Nine_mths	8	.419	.301

The second table shows the degree to which the two sets of scores are correlated. The correlation between them is 0.419. This is a moderate correlation although it is not significant as the significance is greater than 0.05. Correlated tests such as the related *t*-test should have a substantial correlation between the two sets of scores. Be careful, this table is *not* the test of significance. It is a common mistake, among novices, to confuse this correlation between two variables with the significance of the difference between the two variables.

The first three columns containing figures are the basic components of the calculation of the related *t*-test. The mean of −1.500 is actually the difference between the 6 month and 9 month mean, so it is really the mean difference. The value of *t* is based on this mean difference (−1.500) divided by the standard error of the mean (0.756). This calculation gives the value of *t* (−1.984).

Paired Samples Test

		Paired Differences							
					95% Confidence Interval of the Difference				
		Mean	Std. Deviation	Std. Error Mean	Lower	Upper	t	df	Sig. (2-tailed)
Pair 1	Six_mths − Nine_mths	−1.500	2.138	.756	−3.287	.287	−1.984	7	.088

The third and last table shows the *t* value (−1.984), the degrees of freedom (7) and the two-tailed significance level (0.088). As the significance level is greater than 0.05 this difference is not significant. The one-tailed level is obtained by dividing it by 2 which is 0.044 and significant. However, unless the difference has been predicted in advance of data collection on the basis of strong theoretical and/or empirical reasons, only the two-tailed test is appropriate.

■ In the first table of the output, the mean number of eye contacts at 6 months ('Six_mths') and at 9 months ('Nine_mths') is displayed under 'Mean'. Thus the mean amount of eye contact is 5.25 at 6 months and 6.75 at 9 months.

■ The second table of the output gives the (Pearson) correlation coefficient between the two variables (eye contact at six months and eye contact at nine months). Ideally, the value of this should be sizeable (in fact it is 0.419) and statistically significant (which it is not with a two-tail significance level of 0.301). The related t-test assumes that the two variables are correlated, and you might consider an unrelated t-test (Chapter 13) to be more suitable in this case.

■ In the third table of the output, the difference between these two mean scores is presented under the 'Mean' of 'Paired Differences' and the standard error of this mean under 'Std. Error Mean'. The difference between the two means is −1.50 and the estimated standard error of means for this sample size is 0.76.

■ The t-value of the difference between the sample means, its degrees of freedom and its two-tailed significance level are also shown in this third table. The t-value is −1.984, which has an exact two-tailed significance level of 0.088 with 7 degrees of freedom.

12.4 Reporting the output

■ We could report these results as follows: 'The mean number of eye contacts at 6 months ($M = 5.25$, SD = 1.91) and at 9 months ($M = 6.75$, SD = 2.05) did not differ significantly ($t = -1.98$, $DF = 7$, two-tailed $p = 0.088$)'.

■ In this book, to be consistent, we will report the exact probability level for non-significant results as above. However, it is equally acceptable to report them as '$p > 0.05$' or NS (which is short for non-significant).

■ Notice that the findings would have been statistically significant with a one-tailed test. However, this would have to have been predicted with sound reasons prior to being aware of the data. In this case one would have written to the effect 'The two means differed significantly in the predicted direction ($t = 1.98$, $DF = 7$, one-tailed $p = 0.044$)'.

■ Once again, to be consistent throughout this book, we will report the exact probability level for significant findings where possible. Note that when SPSS displays the significance level as '.000', we need to present this as '$p < 0.001$' since the exact level is not given. It is equally acceptable to report significant probabilities as '$p < 0.05$', '$p < 0.01$' and '$p < 0.001$' as appropriate.

■ If you prefer to use confidence intervals, you could report your findings as: 'The mean number of eye contacts at 6 months was 5.25 (SD = 1.91) and at 9 months was 6.75 (SD = 2.05). The difference was 1.50. The 95% confidence interval for this difference is −3.29 to 0.29. Since the confidence interval passes through 0.00, the difference is not statistically significant at the two-tailed 5% level'.

■ Some statisticians advocate the reporting of confidence intervals rather than significance levels. However, it remains relatively uncommon to give confidence intervals.

13 The *t*-test
Comparing two groups of unrelated/uncorrelated scores

Overview

- The uncorrelated or unrelated *t*-test is used to calculate whether the means of two sets of scores are significantly different from each other. It is the most commonly used version of the *t*-test. Statistical signficance means that the two samples differ to an extent which is unlikely to be due to chance factors as a consequence of sampling. The variability inherent in the available data is used to estimate how likely it is that the difference between the two means would be if, in reality, there is no difference between the two samples.

- The unrelated *t*-test is used when the two sets of scores come from two different samples of people. (Refer to the previous chapter on the related *t*-test if your scores come from just one set of people or if you have employed a matching procedure.)

- Data entry for related and unrelated variables is very different in SPSS. So take care to plan your analysis before entering your data in order to avoid problems and unnecessary work. SPSS, however, is very flexible and errors of this sort are usually straightforward to correct using cut-and-paste and similar features.

- SPSS procedures for the unrelated *t*-test are very useful and go beyond usual textbook treatments of the topic. That is, they include an option for calculating the *t*-test when the variances of the two samples of scores are significantly different from each other. Most textbooks erroneously suggest that the *t*-test is too inaccurate when the variances of the two groups are unequal. This additional version of the unrelated *t*-test is rarely mentioned in statistics textbooks but is extremely valuable.

- If you have more than two sets of scores to compare, then refer to Chapter 20 on the unrelated analysis of variance.

The computation of an unrelated *t*-test is illustrated with the data in Table 13.1, which shows the emotionality scores of 12 children from two-parent families and 10 children from single-parent families (*ISP*, Table 13.8). In SPSS this sort of *t*-test is called an independent samples *t*-test. The purpose of the analysis is to assess whether emotionality scores are different in two-parent and lone-parent families.

Table 13.1   Emotionality scores in two-parent and lone-parent families

Two-parent family X_1	Lone-parent family X_2
12	6
18	9
14	4
10	13
19	14
8	9
15	8
11	12
10	11
13	9
15	
16	

13.1   Entering the data

Step 1:

In 'Variable View' of the 'Data Editor' label the first row 'Family'. This defines the two types of family.

Label the second row 'Emotion'. These are the emotionality scores.

Remove the two decimal places by changing the value here to 0 if necessary.

Step 2:

In 'Data View' of the 'Data Editor' enter the values of the two variables in the first two columns.

Save the data as a file to use in Chapter 18.

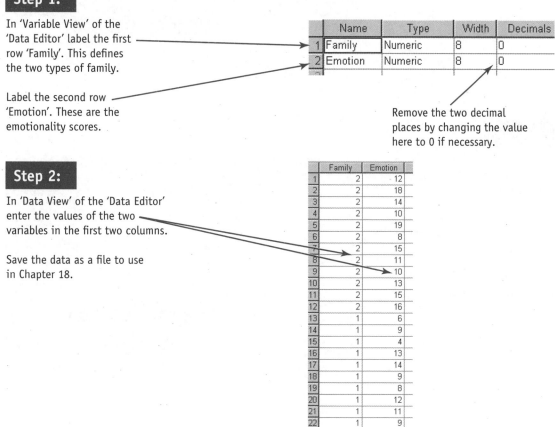

Take a good look at Step 2. Notice that there are two columns of data. The second column ('emotion') consists of the 22 emotionality scores from *both* groups of children. The data are not kept separate for the two groups; the 1s in the first column ('family') indicate, in our example, children from lone-parent families and the 2s indicate children from two-parent families. Thus a single column is used for the dependent variable (in this case, emotionality/'emotion') and another column for the independent variable (in this case, type of family/'family'). So each row is a particular child, and their independent variable and dependent variable scores are entered in two separate columns in the Data Editor.

13.2 Carrying out the unrelated *t*-test

Step 1:

Select 'Analyze', 'Compare Means' and 'Independent-Samples T Test...'.

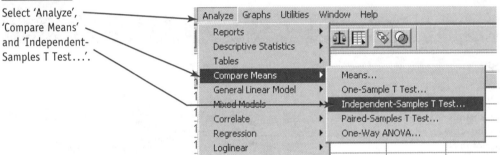

Step 2:

Select 'Emotion' and the ▶ button for the 'Test Variable(s):' box to put it there.

Select 'Family' and the ▶ button for the 'Grouping Variable:' box to put it there.

Select 'Define Groups...' to define the two groups.

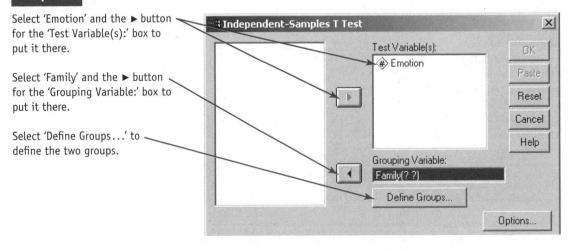

Step 3:

Enter '1' (code for one parent) besides 'Group 1:' and '2' (code for two parents) besides 'Group 2:'. Which group goes in which box is arbitrary.

Select 'Continue'. ———————

Select 'OK' from the previous screen, which reappears.

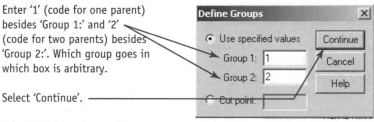

13.3 Interpreting the output

Group Statistics

	Family	N	Mean	Std. Deviation	Std. Error Mean
Emotion	1	10	9.50	3.100	.980
	2	12	13.42	3.370	.973

This first table shows for each group the number of cases, the mean and the standard deviation. The mean for the lone parents is 9.50. There is obviously a difference, therefore, between the two types of family. The question next is whether the two means differ significantly.

The value of t is simply the mean difference (-3.917) divided by the Standard Error of the Difference (1.382) which yields the value of -2.813.

Independent Samples Test

		Levene's Test for Equality of Variances		t-test for Equality of Means					95% Confidence Interval of the Difference	
		F	Sig.	t	df	Sig. (2-tailed)	Mean Difference	Std. Error Difference	Lower	Upper
Emotion	Equal variances assumed	.212	.650	−2.813	20	.011	−3.917	1.392	−6.821	−1.013
	Equal variances not assumed			−2.836	19.77	.010	−3.917	1.381	−6.800	−1.034

If the significance of Levene's test is greater than 0.05, which it is here at 0.650, use the information on this first row. If the significance of Levene's test is 0.05 or less, use the information on the second row. The second row gives the figures for when the variances are significantly different.

For equal variance, t is −2.813 which with 20 degrees of freedom is significant at 0.011 for the two-tailed level. To obtain the one-tailed level, divide this level by 2 which gives 0.006 rounded to three decimal places.

The output for the uncorrelated/unrelated *t*-test on SPSS is particularly confusing even to people with a good knowledge of statistics. The reason is that there are two versions of the uncorrelated/unrelated *t*-test. Which one to use depends on whether or not there is a significant difference between the (estimated) variances for the two groups of scores.

■ Examine the first table of the output. This contains the means and standard deviations of the scores on the dependent variable (emotionality) of the two groups. Notice that an additional figure has been added by the computer to the name of the column containing the dependent variable. This additional figure indicates which of the two groups the row refers to. If you had labelled your values, these value labels would be given in the table.

■ For children from two-parent families ('family 2') the mean emotionality score is 13.42 and the standard deviation of the emotionality scores is 3.37. For the children of lone-parent families ('family 1') the mean emotionality score is 9.50 and the standard deviation of emotionality is 3.10.

■ In the second table, read the line 'Levene's Test for Equality of Variances'. If the probability value is statistically significant then your variances are *unequal*. Otherwise they are regarded as equal.

■ Levene's test for equality of variances in this case tells us that the variances are equal because the *p* value of 0.650 is not statistically significant.

■ Consequently, you need the row for 'Equal variances assumed'. The *t*-value, its degrees of freedom and its probability are displayed. The *t*-value for equal variances is −2.813, which with 20 degrees of freedom has an exact two-tailed significance level of 0.011.

■ Had Levene's test for equality of variances been statistically significant (i.e. 0.05 or less), then you should have used the second row of the output which gives the *t*-test values for unequal variances.

13.4 Reporting the results

■ We could report the results of this analysis as follows: 'The mean emotionality scores of children from two-parent families ($M = 13.42$, SD $= 3.37$) is significantly higher ($t = -2.81$, DF $= 20$, two-tailed $p = 0.011$) than that of children in lone-parent families ($M = 9.50$, SD $= 3.10$).'

■ It is unusual to see the *t*-test for unequal variances in psychological reports. Many psychologists are unaware of its existence. So what happens if you have to use one? In order to clarify things, we would write: 'Because the variances for the two groups were significantly unequal ($F = 8.43$, $p < 0.05$), a *t*-test for unequal variances was used . . .'.

■ If you prefer to use the confidence intervals, you might write: 'The difference between the emotionality scores for the children from two-parent families ($M = 13.42$, SD $= 3.37$) and lone-parent families ($M = 9.50$, SD $= 3.10$) is −3.92. The 95% confidence interval for this difference is from −6.82 to −1.01. Since this interval does not include 0.00, the difference is statistically significant at the two-tailed 5% level.'

14 Chi-square
Differences between samples of frequency data

Overview

- Chi-square is generally used to assess whether two or more samples each consisting of frequency data (nominal data) differ significantly from each other. In other words, it is the usual statistical test to analyse cross-tabulation or contingency tables based on two nominal category variables.

- It can also be used to test whether a single sample differs significantly from a known population. The latter application is the least common because population characteristics are rarely known in research.

- It is essential to remember that chi-square analyses frequencies. These should *never* be converted to *percentages* for entry into SPSS as they will give misleading outcomes when calculating the value and significance of chi-square. This should be clearly distinguished from the use of percentages when one is trying to interpret what is happening in a contingency table.

- Also remember that a chi-square analysis needs to include the data from every individual only once. That is, the total frequencies should be the same as the number of people used in the analysis.

- The analysis and interpretation of 2×2 contingency tables are straightforward. However, interpretation of larger contingency tables is not quite so easy and may require the table to be broken down into a number of smaller tables. Partitioning chi-square, as this is known, usually requires adjustment to the significance levels to take into account the number of sub-analyses carried out. Consult a statistics textbook for more details.

- This chapter also includes the Fisher exact test, which can be useful in some circumstances when the assumptions of the chi-square are not met by your data (especially when the expected frequencies are too low).

- The McNemar test for significance of changes, which is closely related to chi-square, is also discussed.

- Versions of chi-square are used as measures of goodness-of-fit in some of the more advanced statistical techniques discussed later in this book such as logistic regression. A test of goodness-of-fit simply assesses the relationship between the available data and the predicted data based on a set of predictor variables. Consequently, it is essential to understand chi-square adequately, not simply because of its simple application but because of its role in more advanced statistical techniques.

Table 14.1   Relationship between favourite TV programme and sex

Respondents	Soap opera	Crime drama	Neither
Males	27	14	19
Females	17	33	9

The computation of chi-square with two or more samples is illustrated with the data in Table 14.1 (*ISP*, Table 14.8). This table shows which one of three types of television programme is favoured by a sample of 119 teenage boys and girls. To analyse a table of data like this one with SPSS, first we have to input the data into the Data Editor and weight the cells by the frequencies of cases in them.

- As we are working with a ready-made table, it is necessary to go through the 'Weighting Cases' procedure first (see Section 14.1). Otherwise, you would enter Table 14.1 case by case, indicating which category of the row and which category of the column each case belongs to (see Section 14.2). We need to identify each of the six cells in Table 14.1. The rows of the table represent the sex of the participants, while the columns represent the three types of television programme. We will then weight each of the six cells of the table by the number of cases in them.
- The first column, called 'Sex' in Step 1 of Section 14.1, contains the code for males (1) and females (2). (These values have also been labelled.)
- The second column, called 'Program', holds the code for the three types of television programme: soap opera (1), crime drama (2) and neither (3). (These values have also been labelled.)

14.1   Entering the data of Table 14.1 using the 'Weighting Cases' procedure

Step 1:

In 'Variable view' of the 'Data Editor' label the first three columns 'Sex', 'Program' and 'Freq', respectively.

Remove the two decimal places.

Label the values of 'Sex' and 'Program'.

	Name	Type	Width	Decimals	Label	Values
1	Sex	Numeric	8	0		{1, Males}...
2	Program	Numeric	8	0		{1, Soap}...
3	Freq	Numeric	8	0		None
4						

Step 2:

In 'Data View' of the 'Data Editor' enter the appropriate values. Each row represents one of the six cells in Table 14.1.

	Sex	Program	Freq
1	1	1	27
2	1	2	14
3	1	3	19
4	2	1	17
5	2	2	33
6	2	3	9
7			

Step 3:

To weight these cells, select 'Data' and 'Weight Cases...'.

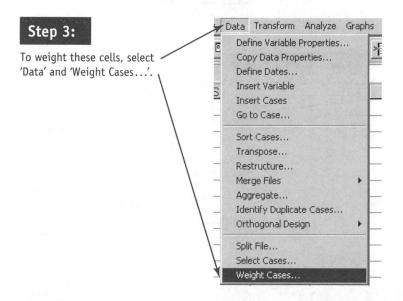

Data   Transform   Analyze   Graphs

- Define Variable Properties...
- Copy Data Properties...
- Define Dates...
- Insert Variable
- Insert Cases
- Go to Case...
- Sort Cases...
- Transpose...
- Restructure...
- Merge Files ▶
- Aggregate...
- Identify Duplicate Cases...
- Orthogonal Design ▶
- Split File...
- Select Cases...
- Weight Cases...

Step 4:

Select 'Freq', 'Weight cases by' and the ▶ button.

Select 'OK'.

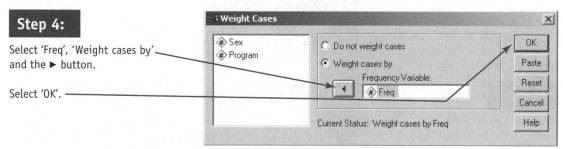

Weight Cases

- ⊛ Sex
- ⊛ Program

○ Do not weight cases

◉ Weight cases by

Frequency Variable:

◀   ⊛ Freq

Current Status: Weight cases by Freq

OK   Paste   Reset   Cancel   Help

14.2   Entering the data of Table 14.1 case by case

Enter the values for the two variables for each of the 119 cases.

	Sex	Program
1	1	1
2	1	1
3	1	1
4	1	1

14.3 Conducting a chi-square on Table 14.1

Step 1:

Select 'Analyze', 'Descriptive Statistics' and 'Crosstabs...'.

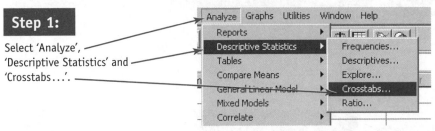

Step 2:

Select 'Sex' and the ▶ button for 'Row(s):' to put it there.

Select 'Program' and the ▶ button for 'Column(s):' to put it there.

Select 'Statistics...'.

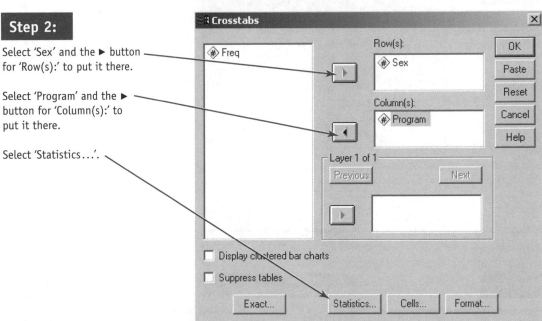

Step 3:

Select 'Chi-square'.

Select 'Continue'.

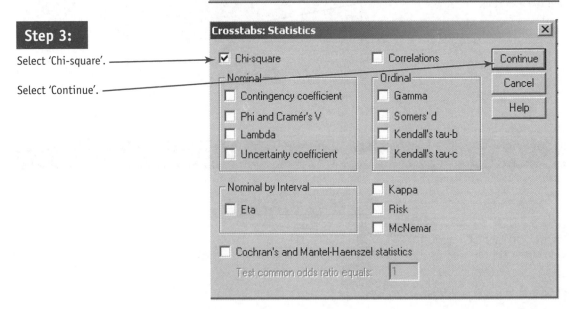

Step 4:

Select 'Cells'.

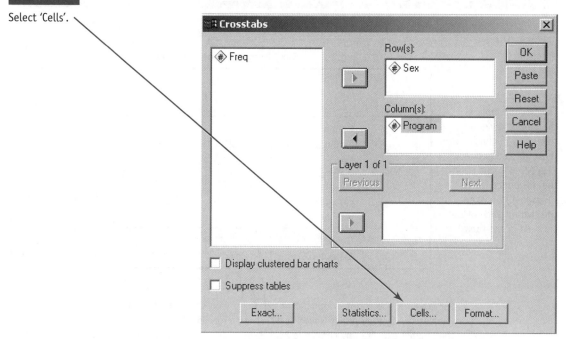

Step 5:

Select 'Expected' under 'Counts'.

Select 'Unstandardized' under 'Residuals'. (Residuals means differences.)

Select 'Continue'.

Select 'OK' from the previous screen, which reappears.

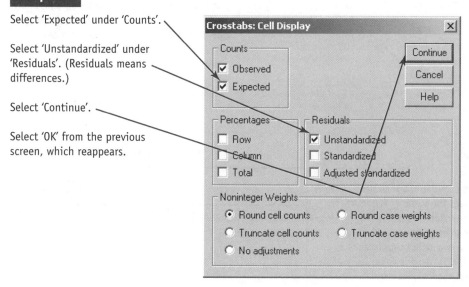

14.4 Interpreting the output for the chi-square

Sex * Program Crosstabulation

			Program			Total
			1	2	3	
Sex	1	Count	27	14	19	60
		Expected Count	22.2	23.7	14.1	60.0
		Residual	4.8	−9.7	4.9	
	2	Count	17	33	9	59
		Expected Count	21.8	23.3	13.9	59.0
		Residual	−4.8	9.7	−4.9	
Total		Count	44	47	28	119
		Expected Count	44.0	47.0	28.0	119.0

This second table of the output gives the frequency ('Count'), the expected frequency ('Expected Count') and the difference ('Residual') between the two for each of the six cells of the table.

For example, the count or number of females saying they prefer 'soaps' is 17, the number expected by chance is 21.8 and the difference between these is −4.8.

You should understand what the figures for 'Count' for the gender by programme cross-tabulation mean. They are equivalent to the original data table (Table 14.1). You could turn the figures into percentages (see the screenshot in Step 5 of section 14.3 which gives three different options – 'Row', 'Column' and 'Total' under percentages). Choosing column percentages would probably help you see that males tend to prefer soap operas and 'Neither' more than females. Females tend to prefer crime programmes more than males.

Chi-Square Tests

	Value	df	Asymp. Sig. (2-sided)
Pearson Chi-Square	13.518[a]	2	.001
Likelihood Ratio	13.841	2	.001
Linear-by-Linear Association	.000	1	.987
N of Valid Cases	119		

The third and last table gives the value of (Pearson's) chi-square (13.518), the degrees of freedom (2) and the two-tailed significance (0.001). As this value is less than 0.05, this chi-square is significant.

a. 0 cells (.0%) have expected count less than 5. The minimum expected count is 13.88.

■ The second table of the output shows the observed and expected frequencies of cases and the difference (residual) between them for each cell. The observed frequency (called 'Count') is presented first and the expected frequency (called 'Expected Count') second. The observed frequencies are always whole numbers, so they should be easy to spot. The expected frequencies are always expressed to one decimal place, so they are easily identified. Thus the first cell of the table (males liking soap opera) has an observed frequency of 27 and an expected frequency of 22.2.

■ The final column in this table (labelled 'Total') lists the number of cases in that row followed by the expected number of cases in the table. So the first row has 60 cases, which will always be the same as the expected number of cases (i.e. 60.0).

■ Similarly, the final row in this table (labelled 'Total') first presents the number of cases in that column followed by the expected number of cases in the table for that column. Thus the first column has 44 cases, which will always be equal to the expected number of cases (i.e. 44.0).

■ The chi-square value, its degrees of freedom and its significance level are displayed in the third table on the line starting with 'Pearson', the man who developed this test. The chi-square value is 13.518 which, rounded to two decimal places, is 13.52. Its degrees of freedom are 2 and its exact two-tailed probability is 0.001.

■ Also shown underneath this table is the 'minimum expected count' of any cell in the table, which is 13.88 for the last cell (females liking neither). If the minimum expected frequency is less than 5.0 then we should be wary of using chi-square. If you have a 2×2 chi-square and small expected frequencies occur, it would be better to use the Fisher exact test which SPSS includes in the output in these circumstances.

14.5 Reporting the output for the chi-square

There are two ways of describing these results. To the inexperienced eye they may seem very different but they amount to the same thing:

■ We could describe the results in the following way: 'There was a significant difference between the observed and expected frequency of teenage boys and girls in their preference for the three types of television programme ($\chi^2 = 13.51$, $DF = 2$, $p = 0.001$).'

■ Alternatively, and just as accurate: 'There was a significant association between sex and preference for different types of television programme ($\chi^2 = 13.51$, $DF = 2$, $p = 0.001$).'

■ In addition, we need to report the direction of the results. One way of doing this is to state that: 'Girls were more likely than boys to prefer crime programmes and less likely to prefer soap operas or both programmes.'

14.6 Fisher's exact test

The chi-square procedure computes Fisher's exact test for 2×2 tables when one or more of the four cells has an expected frequency of less than 5. Fisher's exact test would be computed for the data in Table 14.2 (*ISP*, Table 14.15).

Table 14.2   Photographic memory and sex

	Photographic memory	No photographic memory
Males	2	7
Females	4	1

14.7 Interpreting the output for Fisher's exact test

Sex * Memory Crosstabulation

			Memory		Total
			Photographic	Non-photographic	
Sex	Males	Count	2	7	9
		Expected Count	3.9	5.1	9.0
		Residual	−1.9	1.9	
	Females	Count	4	1	5
		Expected Count	2.1	2.9	5.0
		Residual	1.9	−1.9	
Total		Count	6	8	14
		Expected Count	6.0	8.0	14.0

This is the second of three tables in the output, showing the observed ('Count') and expected ('Expected Count') frequencies of the four cells.

Chi-Square Tests

	Value	df	Asymp. Sig. (2-sided)	Exact Sig. (2-sided)	Exact Sig. (1-sided)
Pearson Chi-Square	4.381[b]	1	.036		
Continuity Correction[a]	2.340	1	.126		
Likelihood Ratio	4.583	1	.032		
Fisher's Exact Test				0.91	.063
Linear-by-Linear Association	4.069	1	.044		
N of Valid Cases	14				

a. Computed only for a 2 × 2 table
b. 3 cells (75.0%) have expected count less than 5. The minimum expected count is 2.14.

The third and last table in the SPSS output. It shows the values of the statistics, their degrees of freedom and their significance levels. The significance of Fisher's exact test for this table is 0.091 at the two-tailed level and 0.063 at the one-tailed level.

14.8 Reporting the output for Fisher's exact test

■ We could write: 'There was no significant relationship between sex and the possession of a photographic memory (two-tailed Fisher exact $p = 0.091$)' or 'Males and females do not differ in the frequency of possession of a photographic memory (two-tailed Fisher exact $p = 0.091$).'

■ However, with such a small sample size, the finding might best be regarded as marginally significant and a strong recommendation made that further studies should be carried out in order to establish with more certainty whether girls actually do possess photographic memories more frequently.

14.9 One-sample chi-square

The computation of a one-sample chi-square is illustrated with the data in Table 14.3 (*ISP*, Table 14.18), which shows the observed and expected frequency of smiling in 80 babies. The expected frequencies were obtained from an earlier large-scale study.

Table 14.3   Data for a one-sample chi-square

	Clear smilers	Clear non-smilers	Impossible to classify
Observed frequency	35	40	5
Expected frequency	40	32	8

Step 1:

Enter the data in 'Data View' of the 'Data Editor' having named the variables and removed the two decimal places.

Label the three categories.

Weight the cells or cases with 'Freq'.

	Category	Freq
1	1	35
2	2	40
3	3	5

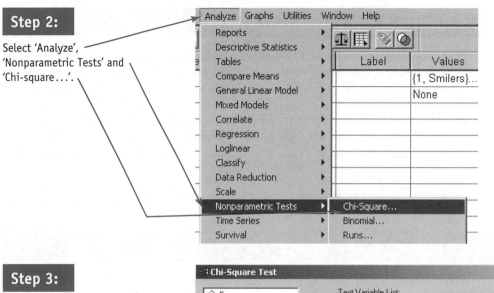

Step 2:

Select 'Analyze',
'Nonparametric Tests' and
'Chi-square...'.

Step 3:

Select 'Category' and the ▶
button to put it in the
'Test Variable List:' box.

Type in the expected frequencies
one at a time in the 'Values:'
box following each one with 'Add'.

Select 'OK'.

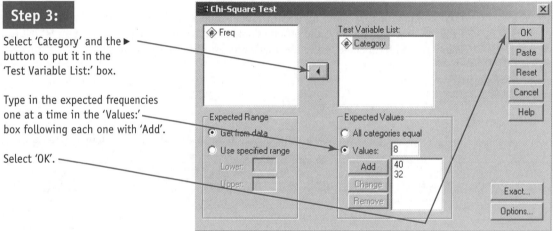

14.10 Interpreting the output for a one sample chi-square

Category

	Observed N	Expected N	Residual
Smilers	35	40.0	−5.0
Non-smilers	40	32.0	8.0
Unclassifiable	5	8.0	−3.0
Total	80		

The first of the two tables in the output shows the observed and the expected frequencies for
the three categories together with the difference or residual between them. The first column
shows the three categories, the second column the observed *N* or frequencies, the third column
the expected *N* or frequencies and the fourth column the residual or difference between the
observed and the expected frequencies. The observed frequency of smilers is 35 and the expected
frequency 40.0.

Test Statistics

	Category
Chi-Square[a]	3.750
df	2
Asymp. Sig.	.153

a. 0 cells (.0%) have expected frequencies less than 5. The minimum expected cell frequency is 8.0.

The second table shows the the value of chi-square (3.750), the degrees of freedom (2) and the significance level (0.153). As the significance level is less than 0.05, the observed frequencies do not differ significantly from those expected by chance.

14.11 Reporting the output for a one sample chi-square

We could describe the results of this analysis as follows: 'There was no statistical difference between the observed and expected frequency for the three categories of smiling in infants ($\chi^2 = 3.75$, $DF = 2$, $p = 0.153$).'

14.12 McNemar's test

The computation of McNemar's test is illustrated with the data in Table 14.4, which shows the number of teenage children who changed or did not change their minds about going to university after listening to a careers talk favouring university education (*ISP*, Table 14.19). The table gives the numbers who wanted to go to university before the talk and after it (30), those who wanted to go before the talk but not after it (10), those who wanted to go to university after the talk but not before it (50), and the numbers not wanting to go to university both before and after the talk (32).

Table 14.4   Students wanting to go to university before and after a careers talk

	1 Before talk 'yes'	2 Before talk 'no'
1 After talk 'yes'	30	50
2 After talk 'no'	10	32

Step 1:

Enter the data in 'Data View' of the 'Data Editor' having named the variables and removed the two decimal places.

Label value 1 as 'Yes' and value 2 as 'No'.

Weight the cells or cases with 'Freq'.

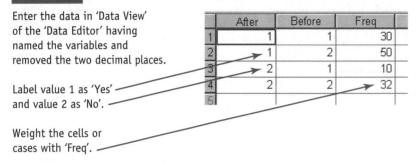

Step 2:

Select 'Analyze', 'Nonparametric Tests' and '2 Related Samples...'.

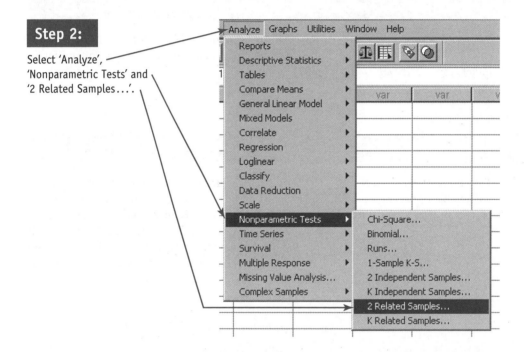

Step 3:

Select 'After', 'Before' and the ▶ button to put these two variables in the 'Test Pair(s) List:' box.

Select 'Wilcoxon' to de-select it.

Select 'McNemar'.

Select 'OK'.

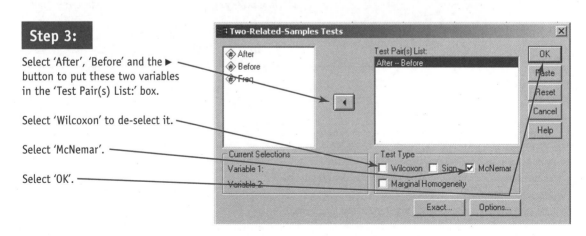

14.13 Interpreting the output for a McNemar test

The first of the two tables shows the frequencies of cases in the four cells as in Table 14.4. The two values, 1 and 2, have not been labelled.

After & Before

After	Before	
	1	2
1	30	50
2	10	32

The number who changed from wanting to go to university before hearing the talk to *not* wanting to go after hearing the talk (i.e. 10).

The number who changed from not wanting to go to university before hearing the talk to wanting to go after hearing the talk (i.e. 50).

The second table in the output shows the total number *N* of cases (122), the value of chi-square (25.350) and the significance level (0.000). Technically the significance level can never be zero. It is less than 0.001. As this is less than 0.05 it is significant. This means that there has been a significant change in the number of teenagers changing their minds about going to university after listening to a careers talk favouring university education.

Test Statistics[b]

	After & Before
N	122
Chi-Square[a]	25.350
Asymp. Sig.	.000

a. Continuity Corrected
b. McNemar Test

14.14 Reporting the output for a McNemar test

We can report the results of this analysis as follows: 'There was a significant increase in the number of teenagers who wanted to go to university after hearing the talk ($\chi^2 = 25.35$, $DF = 1$, $p < 0.001$).'

14.15 Chi-square without ready-made tables

In this chapter we have concentrated on how one can analyse data from pre-existing contingency tables. This is why we need the weighting procedure. However, you will not always be using ready-made tables. Any variables which consist of just a small number of nominal categories can be used for chi-square. For example, if one wished to examine the relationship between sex (coded 1 for male, 2 for female) and age (coded 1 for under 20 years, 2 for 20 to 39 years, and 3 for 40 years and over), the procedure is as follows.

■ Enter the sex codes for your, say, 60 cases in the first column of the Data Editor.
■ Enter the age categories for each of these cases in the equivalent row of the next column.
■ Carry out your chi-square. You do not go through the weighting procedure first. The frequencies in the cells are calculated for you by SPSS.

15 Missing values

Overview

■ Sometimes in research, you may not have a complete set of data from each participant. Missing values tells the computer how to deal with such situations.

■ Typically, when coding the variables for entry into the SPSS spreadsheet, the researcher chooses a distinctive value to denote a missing value on that variable. This value needs to be outside the possible range of actual values found in the data. Typically, numbers such as 9, 99 and 999 are used for missing values. It is possible to have more than one missing value for any variable. For example, the researcher may wish to distinguish between circumstances in which the participant refused to give an answer to a questionnaire and cases where the interviewer omitted the question for some reason.

■ Missing values can also be used to instruct the computer to ignore cases with a particular value(s) on particular variables.

■ One needs to be very careful when using missing values on SPSS. If a value has not been identified as a missing value for a particular variable, the computer will analyse what the researcher intended as a missing value as a real piece of data. This can seriously and misleadingly distort the analysis.

■ Missing values can be used in two main ways. In listwise deletion the case is deleted from the analysis if any missing values are detected for that case. This can rapidly deplete the number of participants in a study. The alternative is to simply delete the case from analyses which include the variables for which there is a missing value.

■ It is better to specify missing values as a value rather than type nothing under an entry. This is because typos made when typing in the data are too easily confused for an actual missing value.

When collecting data, information for some of the cases on some of the variables may be missing. Take, for example, the data in Table 15.1, which consists of the music and mathematics scores of 10 children with their code for gender and their age in years. There is no missing information for any of the four variables for any of the 10 cases. But suppose that

Table 15.1   Scores on musical ability and mathematical ability for 10 children with their sex and age

Music score	Mathematics score	Sex	Age
2	8	1	10
6	3	1	9
4	9	2	12
5	7	1	8
7	2	2	11
7	3	2	13
2	9	2	7
3	8	1	10
5	6	2	9
4	7	1	11

the first two cases were away for the music test so that we had no scores for them. It would be a pity to discard all the data for these two cases because we have information on them for the other three variables of mathematics, gender and age. Consequently we would enter the data for these other variables.

Although we could leave the music score cells empty for these two cases, what we usually do is to code missing data with a number which does not correspond to a possible value that the variable could take. Suppose the scores for the music test can vary from 0 to 10. We can use any number, other than 0 to 10, to signify a missing value for the music test. We will use the number 11 as the code for a missing music score so that the values in the first two rows of the first column are 11. We will also assume that the age for the third case is missing. We will use the number 0 as the code for age which is missing. Then we need to tell SPSS how we have coded missing data. If we do not do this, then SPSS will read these codes as real numbers.

Missing values can also be used to tell the computer to ignore certain values of a variable which you wish to exclude from your analysis. So, for example, you could use missing values in relation to chi-square to get certain categories ignored. Leaving a cell blank in the Data Editor spreadsheet results in a full stop (.) being entered in the cell if it is part of the active matrix of entries. On the output these are identified as missing values but they are best regarded as omitted values. We would recommend that you do not use blank cells as a way of identifying missing values since this does not distinguish between truly missing values and keyboard errors. Normally, substantial numbers such as 99 or 999 are the best way of identifying a missing value.

15.1 Defining missing values

Step 1:

Select the file from
Chapter 10 if you saved it.
Otherwise enter the data.

Change the 2 'Music' scores
of cases 1 and 2 to '11'.

Change the 'Age' of case 3 to '0'.

	Music	Maths	Sex	Age
1	11	8	1	10
2	11	3	1	9
3	4	9	2	0
4	5	7	1	8
5	7	2	2	11
6	7	3	2	13
7	2	9	2	7
8	3	8	1	10
9	5	6	2	9
10	4	7	1	11
11				

Step 2:

In 'Variable View' of the 'Data
Editor' select the right side of
the cell for 'Music' under 'Missing'.
An ellipsis of three dots appears.

Select 'Discrete missing values'
and type '11' in the box below.

Select 'OK'. '11' appears in
the 'Missing' cell for 'Music'.

Repeat this procedure for 'Age'
but type in '0' instead of '11'.

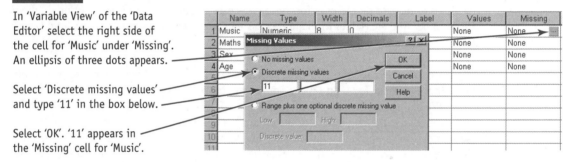

15.2 Pairwise and listwise options

Some of the options available when you have missing data are illustrated with the Correlate procedure, although similar kinds of options are available with some of the other statistical procedures.

Step 1:

Select 'Analyze',
'Correlate' and 'Bivariate...'.

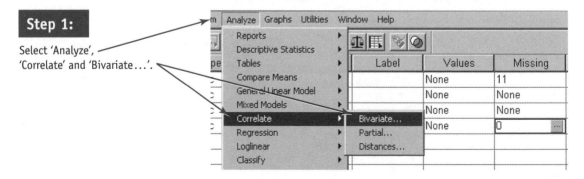

Step 2:

Select 'Music', 'Maths', 'Sex' and 'Age' and the ▶ button to put these four variables in the 'Variables:' box.

Select 'Options...'.

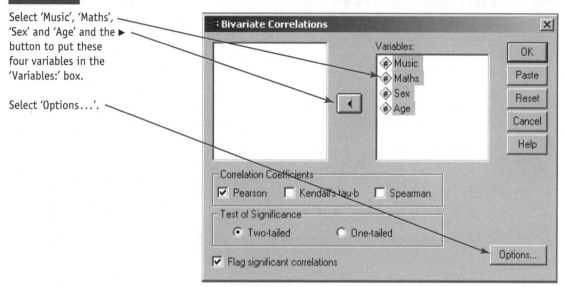

Step 3:

Note that the default 'Missing Values' option is pairwise. The output for pairwise is presented below first.

If you want listwise deletion, select 'Exclude cases listwise' and 'Continue'.

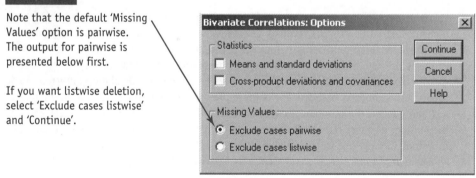

15.3 Sample output for pairwise deletion

8 cases   7 cases

Correlations

		Music	Maths	Sex	Age
Music	Pearson Correlation	1	−.923**	.293	.681
	Sig. (2-tailed)	.	.001	.482	.092
	N	8	8	8	7
Maths	Pearson Correlation	−.923**	1	−.161	−.550
	Sig. (2-tailed)	.001	.	.656	.125
	N	8	10	10	9
Sex	Pearson Correlation	.293	−.161	1	.118
	Sig. (2-tailed)	.482	.656	.	.762
	N	8	10	10	9
Age	Pearson Correlation	.681	−.550	.118	1
	Sig. (2-tailed)	.092	.125	.762	.
	N	7	9	9	9

9 cases

10 cases

**. Correlation is significant at the 0.01 level (2-tailed).

- Pairwise deletion means that a correlation will be computed for all cases which have non-missing values for any pair of variables. Since there are two missing values for the music test and no missing values for the mathematics test and gender, the number of cases on which these correlations will be based is 8. Since one value for age is missing for another case, the number of cases on which the correlation between music scores and gender is based is 7. As there are no missing values for the mathematics test and gender, the number of cases on which this correlation is based is 10. Finally, the number of cases on which the correlation between the mathematics score and age is 9 since there is one missing value for age and none for mathematics.
- *Notice that the number of cases varies for pairwise deletion of missing values.*

15.4 Sample output for listwise deletion

- In listwise deletion correlations are computed for all cases which have no missing values on the variables which have been selected for this procedure. In this example, the number of cases which have no missing values on any of the four variables selected is seven, which presents the output for this option.
- *Notice that the number of cases does not vary in listwise deletion of missing values.*

Correlations[a]

		Music	Maths	Sex	Age
Music	Pearson Correlation	1	−.956**	.354	.681
	Sig. (2-tailed)	.	.001	.437	.092
Maths	Pearson Correlation	−.956**	1	−.483	−.729
	Sig. (2-tailed)	.001	.	.272	.063
Sex	Pearson Correlation	.354	−.483	1	.088
	Sig. (2-tailed)	.437	.272	.	.852
Age	Pearson Correlation	.681	−.729	.088	1
	Sig. (2-tailed)	.092	.063	.852	.

**. Correlation is significant at the 0.01 level (2-tailed).
a. Listwise N=7

All cases are 7.

15.5 Interpreting the output

There is little in the output which has not been discussed in other chapters. The only thing to bear in mind is that the statistics are based on a reduced number of cases.

15.6 Reporting the output

Remember to report the actual sample sizes (or degrees of freedom) used in reporting each statistical analysis rather than the number of cases overall.

16 Recoding values

Overview

■ From time to time researchers need to alter how certain values of a variable are recorded by the computer; perhaps several different values need to be combined into one.

■ The recoding values procedure offers considerable flexibility by allowing quick and easy modifications to how any value has been coded numerically.

■ Because SPSS can quickly and easily recode values, it is good practice to enter as many data items as possible in their original form. This leaves the researcher with the greatest freedom to recode the data. If data have been recoded by the researcher prior to entry into the SPSS data spreadsheet, it is not possible to try an alternative coding of the original data. For example, if all of the scores are entered for a measure of extraversion for each participant, SPSS can be used to recode the entries (such as reversing the scoring of an item) or to compute a total based on all or some of the extraversion items. If the researcher calculates a score on extraversion manually before entering this into SPSS, it is not possible to rescore the questionnaire in a different way without adding the original scores anyway.

■ It is usually best to keep your original data intact. So always make sure that you create a brand new variable (new column) for the recoded variable. Do *not* change the original variables unless you are absolutely certain that you wish to change the original data forever.

Sometimes we need to recode values for a particular variable in our data. There can be many reasons for this, including:

■ To put together several categories of a nominal variable which otherwise would have very few cases. This is commonly employed in statistics such as chi-square.

■ To place score variables into ranges of scores.

■ To recode items needing to be scored in the reverse way (see Chapter 17).

We may wish to categorise our sample into two or more groups according to some variable such as age or intelligence. We will illustrate the recoding of cases with the data in Table 16.1, which shows the music and mathematics scores of 10 children together with

Table 16.1   Scores on musical ability and mathematical ability for 10 children with their sex and age

Music score	Mathematics score	Sex	Age
2	8	1	10
6	3	1	9
4	9	2	12
5	7	1	8
7	2	2	11
7	3	2	13
2	9	2	7
3	8	1	10
5	6	2	9
4	7	1	11

their code for gender and their age in years. The music and mathematics scores are the same as those previously presented in Table 7.1. Suppose that we wanted to compute the correlation between the music and mathematics scores for the younger and older children. To do this, we would first have to decide how many age groups we wanted. Since we have only 10 children we will settle for two groups. Next we decide what the cut-off point in age will be for the two groups. As we want two groups of similar size, we will select 10 as the cut-off point, with children younger than 10 falling into one group and children aged 10 or more into the other group. We will now use SPSS to recode age in this way.

16.1   Recoding values

Step 1:

Select the file from Chapter 10 if you saved it. Otherwise enter the data.

	Music	Maths	Sex	Age	
1	2	8	1	10	
2	6	3	1	9	
3	4	9	2	12	
4	5	7	1	8	
5	7	2	2	11	
6	7	3	2	13	
7	2	9	2	7	
8	3	8	1	10	
9	5	6	2	9	
10	4	7	1	11	
11					

Step 2:

Select 'Transform',
'Recode' and
'Into Different
Variables...'.

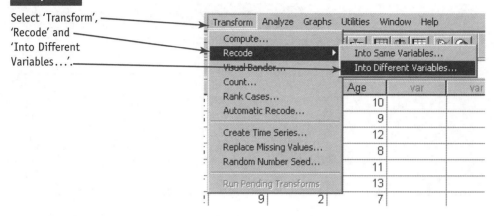

Step 3:

Select 'Age' and the ▶ button to
put 'Age' into the 'Numeric
Variable --> Output Variable:' box.

Type in the name of the new
variable (e.g. 'AgeRec') in
the 'Name:' box.

Select 'Change' to add this new
name to the 'Numeric Variable
--> Output Variable:' box.

Select 'Old and New Values...'.

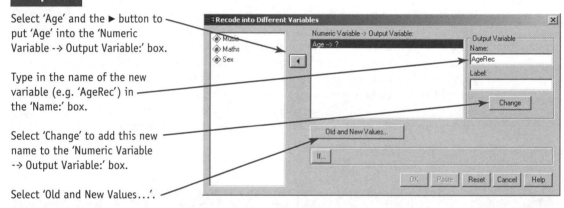

Step 4:

Select 'Range: Lowest through'
and type '9' in the box beside it.

Select 'Value:' under 'New Value'
and type '1' in the box beside it.

Select 'Add' to put 'Lowest thru 9
--> 1' into the 'Old --> New:' box.

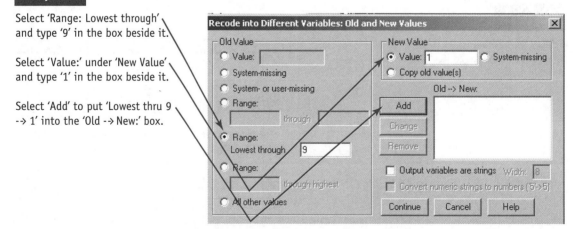

Step 5:

Select 'Range: through highest' and type '10' in the box beside it

Select 'Value:' under 'New Value' and type '2' in the box beside it.

Select 'Add' to put '10 thru Highest -> 2' into the 'Old -> New:' box.

Select 'Continue'.

Select 'OK' from the previous screen, which reappears.

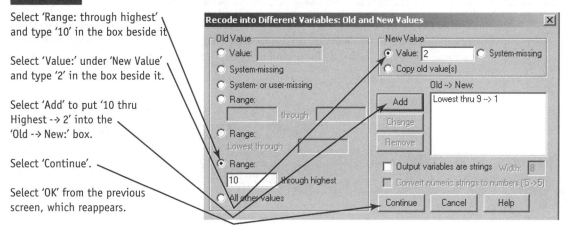

Step 6:

The new variable and its values are shown in 'Data View'. Check that these values are what you needed.

Age	AgeRec
10	2.00
9	1.00
12	2.00
8	1.00
11	2.00
13	2.00
7	1.00
10	2.00
9	1.00
11	2.00

With a complex set of data it is very easy to forget precisely what you have done to your data. Recoding can radically alter the output from a computer analysis. You need to carefully check the implications of any recodes before reporting them.

16.2 Recoding missing values

Note that if there are missing values (as for 'age' in Section 15.1, Step 1) it is necessary to code these by selecting 'System- or user-missing' in the 'Old Value' section of the 'Recode into Different Variables: Old and New Values' sub-dialogue box and selecting 'System-missing' in the 'New Value' section.

Always check that your recoding has worked as you intended by comparing the old and new values in the data editor for each new value for one or more cases.

16.3 Saving the recode procedure as a syntax file

You need to keep a note of how any new variables were created. The simplest way to do this is to write it down. Another way is to save what you have done as a syntax command by using the 'Paste' option in the main box of the procedure. The output for this procedure is shown below.

Select ▶ to run syntax commands. ─────────────

A syntax command. ─────────────────────▶

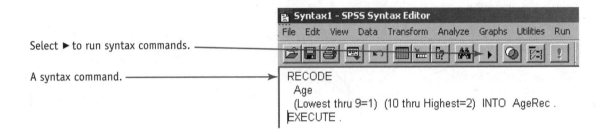

RECODE
  Age
  (Lowest thru 9=1) (10 thru Highest=2) INTO AgeRec .
EXECUTE .

Save this command as a file. You could use this file to carry out this procedure on another set of data if you wished. Before Windows was developed, SPSS commands were carried out with this kind of syntax command.

To check out this procedure select the column in 'Data View' containing recoded age and delete it. Select the Syntax window, select the whole of the command in it and run it with the button on the toolbar shown above.

17 Computing new variables

Overview

■ Computing new variables allows you to add, subtract, etc., scores on several variables to give you a new variable. For example, you might wish to add together several questions on a questionnaire to give an overall index of what the questionnaire is measuring.

■ One of the few disadvantages of SPSS for Windows is that no record is kept as to how the new variable was calculated in the first place. One can either keep a detailed written record of the formula used to compute the new variable or, if it is simple enough, then the variable label could be used to describe it.

■ When computing new variables, it is generally a wise precaution to do a few manual checks of cases. It is easy to inadvertently enter an incorrect formula which then gives a new variable that is not the one that you think you are creating.

When analysing data we may want to form a new variable out of one or more old ones. For example, when measuring psychological variables, several questions are often used to measure more or less the same thing. For instance, the following four statements might be used to assess satisfaction with life:

   a   I generally enjoy life.
   b   Some days things just seem to get me down.
   c   Life often seems pretty dull.
   d   The future looks hopeful.

Participants are asked to state how much they agree with each of these statements on the following four-point scale:

   1: Strongly agree   2: Agree   3: Disagree   4: Strongly disagree

We may use these four items to determine how satisfied people are with their lives by adding up their responses to all four of them.

   Notice a problem that frequently occurs when dealing with questionnaires: if you answer 'Strongly agree' to the first and fourth items you indicate that you enjoy life, whereas if you answer 'Strongly agree' to the second and third items you imply that

Table 17.1 Life satisfaction scores of three respondents

	a Enjoy life (recode)	b Get me down (no recode)	c Dull (no recode)	d Hopeful (recode)
Respondent 1	Agree (2 recoded as 3)	Agree (2)	Strongly disagree (4)	Agree (2 recoded as 3)
Respondent 2	Disagree (3 recoded as 2)	Disagree (3)	Agree (2)	Strongly disagree (4 recoded as 1)
Respondent 3	Strongly agree (1 recoded as 4)	Disagree (3)	Disagree (3)	Disagree (3 recoded as 2)

you are dissatisfied with life. We want higher scores to denote greater life satisfaction. Consequently, we will reverse the scoring for the *first* and *fourth* items as follows:

1: Strongly disagree   2: Disagree   3: Agree   4: Strongly agree

We can use the Recode procedure described in Chapter 16 to recode the values for the first and fourth items.

The data in Table 17.1 show the answers to the four statements by three individuals, and the way in which the answers to the first and fourth items have to be recoded. We will use these data to illustrate the SPSS procedure for adding together the answers to the four statements to form an index of life satisfaction.

17.1 Computing a new variable

Step 1:

Enter the (recoded) data, having named the variables as shown and removed the two decimal places.

	q1	q2	q3	q4
1	3	2	4	3
2	2	3	2	1
3	4	3	3	2

Step 2:

Select 'Transform' and 'Compute'.

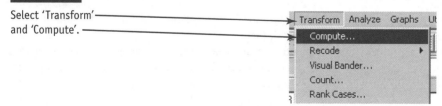

Transform   Analyze   Graphs   Ut

Compute...
Recode   ▶
Visual Bander...
Count...
Rank Cases...

Step 3:

Type a name for the new variable in the box under 'Target Variable:' (e.g. 'LifeSat').

Either type in or select the terms of the expression in the 'Numeric Expression:' box.

Select 'OK'.

Select 'Paste' to save this procedure as a syntax command.

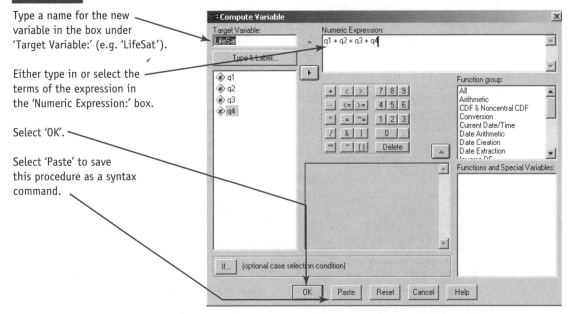

Step 4:

The new variable and its values are entered into the 'Data Editor'.

Check that the values are what they should be for a few cases.

Save the file if you want to use it again.

	q1	q2	q3	q4	LifSat
1	3	2	4	3	12.00
2	2	3	2	1	8.00
3	4	3	3	2	12.00
4					

17.2 Saving the compute procedure as a syntax file

To save this procedure as a syntax file, select 'Paste' in the main box. This syntax command appears in the Syntax window. (See Step 4.)

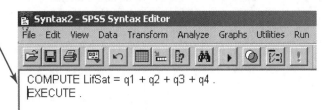

18 Ranking tests
Non-parametric statistics

Overview

■ Sometimes you may wish to know whether the means of two different sets of scores are significantly different from each other but feel that the requirement that the scores on each variable are roughly normally distributed (bell-shaped) is not fulfilled. Non-parametric tests can be used in these circumstances.

■ Non-parametric tests are ones which make fewer assumptions about the characteristics of the population from which the data came. This is unlike parametric tests (such as the *t*-test) which makes more assumptions about the nature of the population from which the data came. The assumption of normality (bell-shaped frequency curves) is an example of the sort of assumptions incorporated into parametric statistics.

■ Strictly speaking, non-parametric statistics do not test for differences in means. They cannot, since, for example, they use scores turned into ranks. Usually they test whether the ranks in one group are typically larger or smaller than the ranks in the other groups.

■ We have included the sign test and Wilcoxon's test for related data. In other words, they are the non-parametric equivalents to related *t*-test. The Wilcoxon test should be used in preference to the sign test when comparing score data.

■ The Mann–Whitney *U*-test is used for unrelated data. That is, it is the non-parametric equivalent to the unrelated *t*-test.

The computation of two non-parametric tests for related scores is illustrated with the data in Table 18.1, which was also used in Chapter 12 and which shows the number of eye contacts made by the same babies with their mothers at 6 and 9 months. Notice that the sign test (Section 18.1) and the Wilcoxon matched-pairs test (Section 18.4) produce different significance levels. The sign test seems rather less powerful at detecting differences than the Wilcoxon matched-pairs test.

Table 18.1   Number of one-minute segments with eye-contact at different ages

Baby	6 months	9 months
Clara	3	7
Martin	5	6
Sally	5	3
Angie	4	8
Trevor	3	5
Sam	7	9
Bobby	8	7
Sid	7	9

18.1   Related scores: sign test

Step 1:

Select the file of the data if you saved it. Otherwise enter the data.

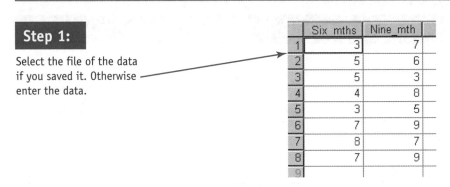

Step 2:

Select 'Analyze', 'Nonparametric Tests' and '2 Related Samples...'.

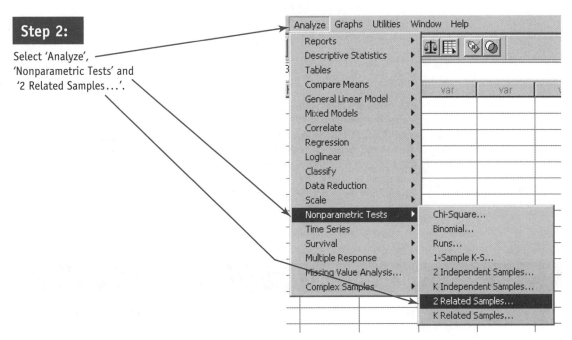

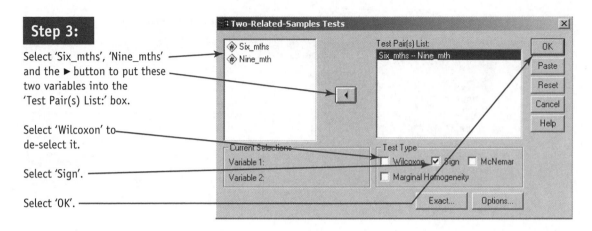

Select 'Six_mths', 'Nine_mths' and the ► button to put these two variables into the 'Test Pair(s) List:' box.

Select 'Wilcoxon' to de-select it.

Select 'Sign'.

Select 'OK'.

18.2 Interpreting the output for the sign test

The first of the two tables of output can be ignored. It shows the number of negative (2), positive (8) and no (0) differences in smiling between the two ages.

Frequencies

		N
Nine_mth - Six _mths	Negative Differences[a]	2
	Positive Differences[b]	6
	Ties[c]	0
	Total	8

a. Nine_mth < Six_mths
b. Nine_mth > Six_mths
c. Nine_mth = Six_mths

The second table shows the significance level of this test. The two-tailed probability is 0.289 or 29%, which is clearly not significant at the 5% level. The binomial distribution refers to the statistical technique by which probabilities can be found for samples consisting of just two different possible values, as is the case with the sign test (given that we ignore ties).

Test Statistics[b]

	Nine_mth - Six_mths
Exact Sig. (2-tailed)	.289[a]

a. Binomial distribution used.
b. Sign Test

18.3 Reporting the output for the sign test

We could report these results as follows: 'There was no significant change in the amount of eye contact between 6 and 9 months (sign test: $N = 8$, $p = 0.289$).'

18.4 Related scores: Wilcoxon test

The Wilcoxon test is the default option on the Two-Related-Samples Tests dialogue box. If you have previously de-selected it, reselect it. Then OK the analysis to obtain the Wilcoxon test output.

18.5 Interpreting the output for the Wilcoxon test

The first of the two tables of output can be ignored. It shows the number of negative (2), positive (6) and no (0) differences in the ranked data for the two ages as well as the mean and the sum of the negative and positive ranked data. The values of 'Nine_mths' are bigger than those for 'Six_mths'.

Ranks

		N	Mean Rank	Sum of Ranks
Nine_mth - Six_mths	Negative Ranks	2[a]	3.00	6.00
	Positive Ranks	6[b]	5.00	30.00
	Ties	0[c]		
	Total	8		

a. Nine_mth < Six_mths
b. Nine_mth > Six_mths
c. Nine_mth = Six_mths

The second table shows the significance level of this test. Instead of using tables of critical values, the computer uses a formula which relates to the *z*-distribution. The *z*-value is –1.706, which has a two-tailed probability of 0.088. This means that the difference between the two variables is not statistically significant at the 5% level.

Test Statistics[b]

	Nine_mth - Six_mths
Z	–1.706[a]
Asymp. Sig. (2-tailed)	.088

a. Based on negative ranks.
b. Wilcoxon Signed Ranks Test

18.6 Reporting the output for the Wilcoxon test

We could report these results as follows: 'There was no significant difference in the amount of eye contact by babies between 6 and 9 months (Wilcoxon: $N = 8$, $z = -1.71$, two-tailed $p = 0.088$).'

18.7 Unrelated scores: Mann–Whitney *U*-test

We will illustrate the computation of one non-parametric test for unrelated scores with the data in Table 18.2, which shows the emotionality scores of 12 children from two-parent families and 10 children from single-parent families.

Table 18.2   Emotionality scores in two-parent and lone-parent families

Two-parent family X_1	Lone-parent family X_2
12	6
18	9
14	4
10	13
19	14
8	9
15	8
11	12
10	11
13	9
15	
16	

Step 1:

Select the file of the data if you saved it. Otherwise enter the data.

Step 2:

Select 'Analyze', 'Nonparametric Tests' and '2 Independent Samples...'.

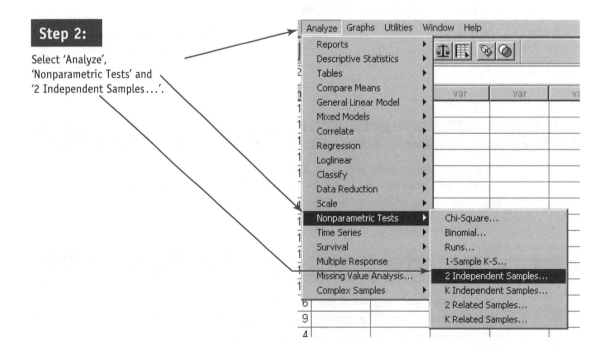

Step 3:

Select 'Emotion' and the ▶ button to put 'Emotion' in the 'Test Variable List:' box.

Select 'Family' and the ▶ button to put 'Family' in the 'Grouping Variable:' box.

Select 'Define Groups...'.

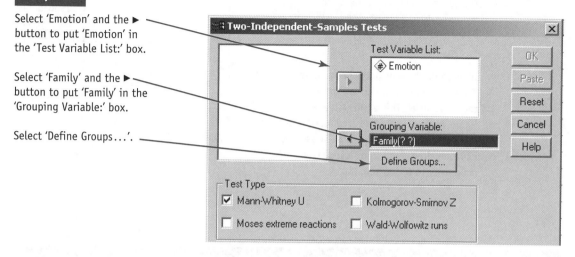

Step 4:

Type '1' (for one parent) in the box beside 'Group 1:'.

Type '2' (for two parent) in the box beside 'Group 2:'.

Select 'Continue'.

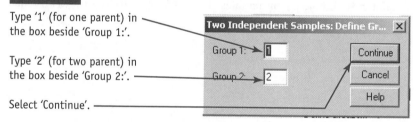

Select 'OK' from the previous screen, which reappears.

18.8 Interpreting the output for the Mann–Whitney *U*-test

The first of the two tables of the output can be ignored. It shows that the average rank given to 'Emotion' for the first group (i.e. value = 1) is 7.85, and the average rank given to the second group (i.e. value = 2) is 14.54. This means that the scores for Group 2 tend to be larger than those for Group 1.

Ranks

	Family	N	Mean Rank	Sum of Ranks
Emotion	1	10	7.85	78.50
	2	12	14.54	174.50
	Total	22		

Test Statistics[b]

	Emotion
Mann-Whitney U	23.500
Wilcoxon VV	78.500
Z	–2.414
Asymp. Sig. (2-tailed)	.016
Exact Sig. [2*(1-tailed Sig.)]	.014[a]

a. Not corrected for ties.

b. Grouping Variable: Family

The second table shows the basic Mann–Whitney statistic, the U-value, is 23.500, which is statistically significant at the 0.014 level.

In addition, the computer has printed out a Z-value of –2.414, which is significant at the 0.016 level. This is the value of the Mann–Whitney test when a correction for tied ranks has been applied. As can be seen, this has only altered the significance level marginally to 0.016 from 0.014.

18.9 Reporting the output for the Mann–Whitney *U*-test

We could report the results of this analysis as follows: 'The Mann–Whitney *U*-test found that the emotionality scores of children from two-parent families were significantly higher than those of children from lone-parent families ($U = 23.5$, $N_1 = 10$, $N_2 = 12$, two-tailed $p = 0.016$).'

19 The variance ratio test

Using the *F*-ratio to compare two variances

Overview

- The variance ratio test (*F*-test) indicates whether two unrelated sets of scores differ in the variability of the scores around the mean (i.e. are the variances significantly different?).
- This is clearly different from calculating whether two means are different, and one should remember that variances can be significantly different even though the means for the two sets of scores are the same. Consequently, examining the variances of the variables can be as important as comparing the means.
- Because few research questions are articulated in terms of differences in variance, researchers tend to overlook effects on variances and concentrate on differences between sample means. This should be avoided as far as possible.
- The *F*-test is probably more commonly found associated with the *t*-test and the analysis of variance.

To compute the variance ratio – or *F*-ratio – we divide the larger variance estimate by the smaller variance estimate. The variance estimate is produced by the Descriptives procedure first introduced in Chapter 5. The computation of the variance ratio is illustrated with the data in Table 19.1 (*ISP*, Table 19.2), which reports the emotional stability scores

Table 19.1 Emotional stability scores from a study of ECT to different hemispheres of the brain

Left hemisphere	Right hemisphere
20	36
14	28
18	4
22	18
13	2
15	22
9	1
Mean = 15.9	Mean = 15.9

of patients who have had an electric current passed through either the left or the right hemisphere of the brain. In this chapter, the method involves a little manual calculation. However, it provides extra experience with SPSS.

An alternative way of achieving the same end is to follow the *t*-test procedures in Chapter 13. You may recall that the Levene *F*-ratio test is part of the output for that *t*-test. Although Levene's test is slightly different, it is a useful alternative to the conventional *F*-ratio test.

19.1 Variance estimate

Step 1:

Enter the data. Code the left hemisphere as '1' and the right hemisphere as '2'. Label these two values. Call this variable 'Spheres' for short.

	Spheres	Emotion
1	1	20
2	1	14
3	1	18
4	1	22
5	1	13
6	1	15
7	1	9
8	2	36
9	2	28
10	2	4
11	2	18
12	2	2
13	2	22
14	2	1

Step 2:

Select 'Analyze', 'Compare Means' and 'Means...'.

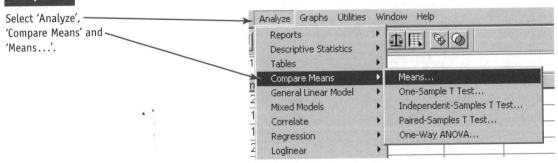

Step 3:

Select 'Emotion' and the ▶ button beside the 'Dependent List:' box to put it there.

Select 'Spheres' and the ▶ button beside the 'Independent List:' box to put it there.

Select 'Options...'.

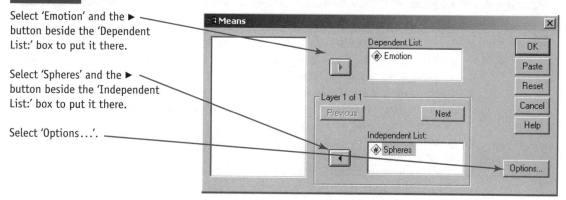

Step 4:

Select 'Variance' and the ▶ button to put it in the 'Cell Statistics:' box.

Select 'Continue'.

Select 'OK' from the previous screen, which reappears.

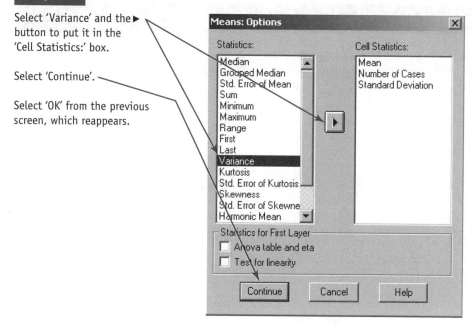

Report

Emotion

Spheres	Mean	N	Std. Deviation	Variance
Left	15.86	7	4.451	19.810
Right	15.86	7	13.837	191.476
Total	15.86	14	9.875	97.516

The variances for the two groups are in the last column of this table. It is 19.810 for the left-hemisphere group.

19.2 Calculating the variance ratio from the output

- Divide the larger variance estimate in the output by the smaller variance estimate. The larger variance estimate is 191.476 (for 'Right'), which divided by the smaller one of 19.810 (for 'Left') gives a variance or F-ratio of 9.6656. This ratio is 9.66 when rounded *down* to two decimal places.
- Look up the statistical significance of this ratio in a table of critical values of F-ratios where the degrees of freedom for the numerator (191.48) and the denominator (19.81) of the ratio are both 6.
- The 0.05 critical value of the F-ratio with 6 degrees of freedom in the numerator and denominator is 4.28.
- The F-ratio we obtained is 9.66, which is larger than the 0.05 critical value of 4.28 (see *ISP*, Significance Table 19.1 where the nearest critical value is 4.4 with 5 degrees of freedom in the numerator).

19.3 Reporting the variance ratio

We could report these findings as: 'The variance of emotionality scores of patients in the right-hemisphere condition was significantly larger than those of patients in the left-hemisphere condition ($F_{6,6} = 9.66$, $p < 0.05$).'

20 Analysis of variance (ANOVA)
Introduction to the one-way unrelated or uncorrelated ANOVA

Overview

- The unrelated/uncorrelated analysis of variance indicates whether several (two or more) groups of scores have very different means. It assumes that each of the sets of scores comes from different individuals. It is not essential to have equal numbers of scores for each set of scores.

- The different groups correspond to the independent variable. The scores correspond to the dependent variable.

- Basically the analysis of variance calculates the variation between scores and the variation between the sample means. Both of these can be used to estimate the variation in the population. If the two estimates are very different, it means that the variation due to the independent variable is greater than could be expected on the basis of the variation between scores. If this disparity is big enough, the difference in variability is statistically significant. This means that the independent variable is having an effect on the scores.

- The interpretation of the analysis of variance can be difficult when more than two groups are used. The overall analysis of variance may be statistically significant, but it is difficult to know which of the three or more groups is significantly different from the other groups.

- The solution is to break the analysis into several separate comparisons to assess which sets of scores are significantly different from other sets of scores. That is, which of the groups are significantly different from other groups.

- Ideally an adjustment should be made for the number of comparisons being made (see Chapter 23 on multiple comparisons for information on better methods for doing this than those described in this chapter). This adjustment is necessary because the more statistical comparisons that are made, the more likely it is that some of the comparisons will be statistically significant.

The computation of a one-way unrelated analysis of variance is illustrated with the data in Table 20.1 (*ISP*, Table 20.2), which shows the scores of different participants in three conditions. It is a study of the effect of different hormone and placebo treatments on depression. So drug is the independent variable and depression the dependent variable.

Table 20.1   Data for a study of the effects of hormones

Group 1 Hormone 1	Group 2 Hormone 2	Group 3 Placebo control
9	4	3
12	2	6
8	5	3

20.1 One-way unrelated ANOVA

Step 1:

Enter the data. Code the 3
conditions '1', '2' and '3',
respectively. Label them
'Hormone 1', 'Hormone 2'
and 'Placebo control'.

Save this file to use in
Chapters 23 and 24.

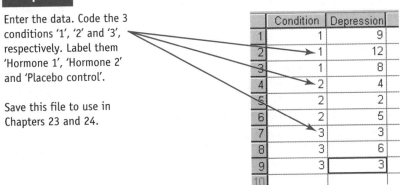

Step 2:

Select 'Analyze',
'Compare Means' and
'One-Way ANOVA...'.

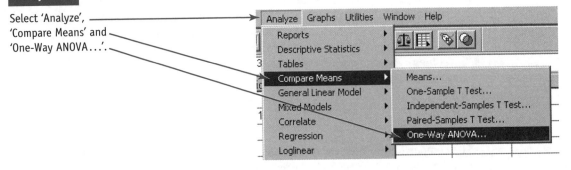

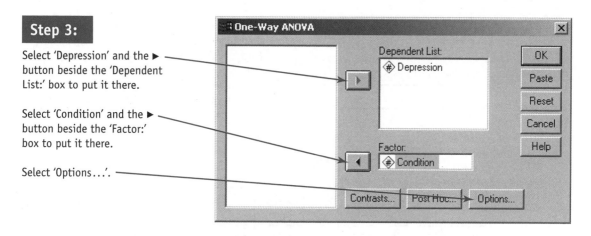

Step 3:

Select 'Depression' and the ► button beside the 'Dependent List:' box to put it there.

Select 'Condition' and the ► button beside the 'Factor:' box to put it there.

Select 'Options…'.

Step 4:

Select 'Descriptive' and 'Homogeneity of variance test'.

Select 'Continue'.

Select 'OK' from the previous screen, which reappears.

20.2 Interpreting the output

Descriptives

Depression

	N	Mean	Std. Deviation	Std. Error	95% Confidence Interval for Mean		Minimum	Maximum
					Lower Bound	Upper Bound		
Hormone 1	3	9.67	2.082	1.202	4.50	14.84	8	12
Hormone 2	3	3.67	1.528	.882	−.13	7.46	2	5
Placebo control	3	4.00	1.732	1.000	−.30	8.30	3	6
Total	9	5.78	3.308	1.103	3.23	8.32	2	12

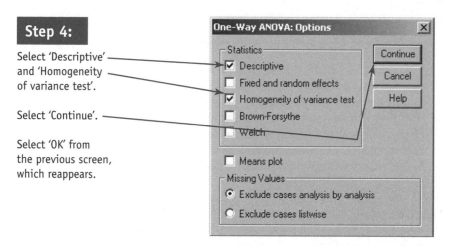

The first table provides various descriptive statistics such as the number *N* of cases, the mean and the standard deviation for the three conditions and the total sample.

Test of Homogeneity of Variances

Depression

Levene Statistic	df1	df2	Sig.
.293	2	6	.756

The second table gives Levene's test of how similar the variances are. As this test is not significant (with a significance of 0.756), the variances are similar or homogeneous. If the variances were not similar, we should try to transform the scores to make them so. Otherwise there may be problems in interpreting the analysis of variance.

ANOVA

Depression

	Sum of Squares	df	Mean Square	F	Sig.
Between Groups	68.222	2	34.111	10.586	.011
Within Groups	19.333	6	3.222		
Total	87.556	8			

The third table shows the results of the analysis of variance. The F-ratio is significant at 0.011 as it is less than 0.05.

- The F-ratio is the between groups mean square divided by the within groups mean square, which gives an F-ratio of 10.586 (34.111/3.222 = 10.5869).
- This indicates that there is a significant difference between the three groups. *However it does not necessarily imply that all the means are significantly different from each other. In this case, one suspects that the means 3.67 and 4.00 are not significantly different.*
- Which of the means differ from the others can be further determined by the use of multiple-comparison tests such as the unrelated t-test. To do this, follow the procedure for the unrelated t-test described in Chapter 13. You do not have to re-enter your data. However, do an unrelated t-test defining the groups as 1 and 2, then redefine the groups as 1 and 3, and finally redefine the groups as 2 and 3. In our example, group 1 is significantly different from groups 2 and 3, which do not differ significantly from each other. (See *ISP*, Chapter 13 for more details.)
- Because we are doing three comparisons, the exact significance level of each t-test should be multiplied by 3 to obtain the Bonferroni significance level.

20.3 Reporting the output

We could report the results of the output as follows: 'The effect of the drug treatment was significant overall ($F_{2,6}$ = 10.58, p = 0.011). When a Bonferroni adjustment was made for the number of comparisons, the only significant difference was between the means of hormone treatment 1 and hormone treatment 2 (t = 4.02, DF = 4, two-tailed $p < 0.05$). The mean of hormone treatment 1 (M = 9.67, SD = 2.08) was significantly greater than that for hormone treatment 2 (M = 3.67, SD = 1.53). There was no significant difference between the mean of the placebo control and the mean of either hormone treatment 1 or hormone treatment 2.'

21 Analysis of variance for correlated scores or repeated measures

Overview

■ The correlated/related analysis of variance indicates whether several (two or more) sets of scores have very different means. However, it assumes that a single sample of individuals has contributed scores to each of the different sets of scores and that the correlation coefficients between sets of scores are large.

■ If your data do not meet these requirements then turn back to Chapter 20 on the unrelated analysis of variance.

■ Changes in scores on a variable over time is a typical example of the sort of study which is appropriate for the correlated/related analysis of variance.

■ If properly used, correlated/related designs can be extremely effective in that fewer participants are required to run the study. The reason is that once participants are measured more than once, it becomes possible to estimate the individual differences component of the variation in the data. In a study of memory, for example, some participants will tend to do well whatever the condition and others will tend to do poorly. These individual differences can be identified and adjusted for in the analysis. What would be classified as error variation in an unrelated analysis of variance, is separated into two components – the individual differences component (within subjects error) and residual error. Effectively this means that the error term is reduced because the individual difference component has been removed. Since the error term is smaller, it is possible to get significant results with smaller numbers of participants than would be possible with an unrelated design.

The computation of a one-way correlated analysis of variance is illustrated with the data in Table 21.1, which shows the scores of the same participants in three different conditions (*ISP*, Table 21.10).

Table 21.1   Pain relief scores from a drugs experiment

	Aspirin	'Product X'	Placebo
Bob Robertson	7	8	6
Mavis Fletcher	5	10	3
Bob Polansky	6	6	4
Ann Harrison	9	9	2
Bert Entwistle	3	7	5

21.1   One-way correlated ANOVA

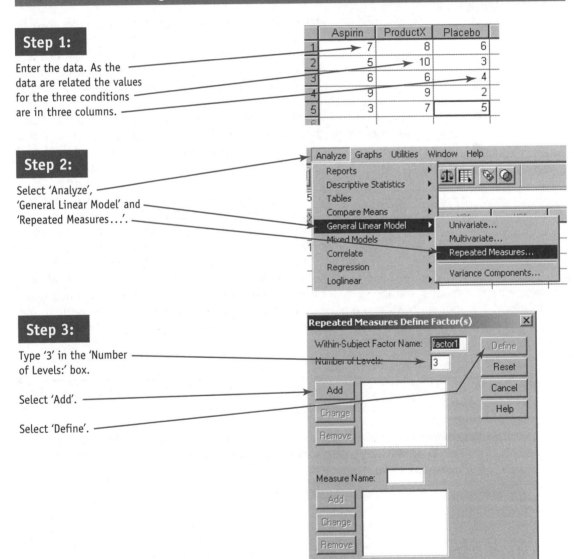

Step 1:

Enter the data. As the data are related the values for the three conditions are in three columns.

Step 2:

Select 'Analyze', 'General Linear Model' and 'Repeated Measures...'.

Step 3:

Type '3' in the 'Number of Levels:' box.

Select 'Add'.

Select 'Define'.

Step 4:

Select each variable individually or all three together and the ▶ button beside the 'Within-Subjects Variables:' box to put them there.

Select 'Options...'.

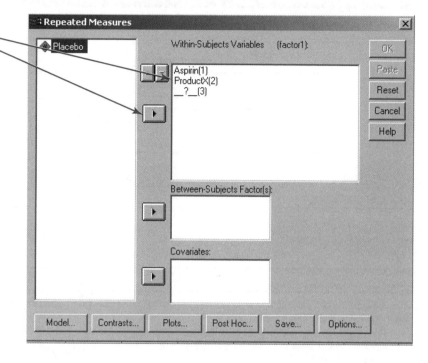

Step 5:

Select 'Descriptive statistics'.

Select 'Continue'.

Select 'OK' from the previous screen, which reappears.

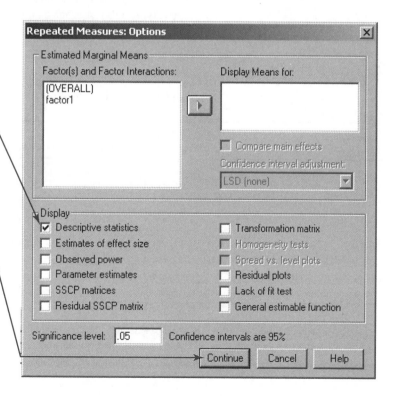

21.2 Interpreting the output

The output gives seven tables. Only the more important ones are shown in this section.

Descriptive Statistics

	Mean	Std. Deviation	N
Aspirin	6.00	2.236	5
ProductX	8.00	1.581	5
Placebo	4.00	1.581	5

The second table gives the mean and standard deviation for the three groups.

Mauchly's Test of Sphericity[b]

Measure: MEASURE_1

					Epsilon[a]		
Within Subjects Effect	Mauchly's W	Approx. Chi-Square	df	Sig.	Greenhouse-Geisser	Huynh-Feldt	Lower-bound
factor1	.862	.444	2	.801	.879	1.000	.500

Tests the null hypothesis that the error covariance matrix of the orthonormalized transformed dependent variables is proportional to an identity matrix.

a. May be used to adjust the degrees of freedom for the averaged tests of significance. Corrected tests are displayed in the Tests of Within-Subjects Effects table.

b Design: Intercept
   Within Subjects Design: factor1

The fourth table gives the results for Mauchly's test of sphericity. As this test is not significant, sphericity is assumed and we do not have to adjust the significance levels for the analysis. If it is significant, then one of the alternative tests in the next output box should be used.

Tests of Within-Subjects Effects

Measure: MEASURE_1

Source		Type III Sum of Squares	df	Mean Square	F	Sig.
factor1	Sphericity Assumed	40.000	2	20.000	5.106	.037
	Greenhouse-Geisser	40.000	1.758	22.752	5.106	.045
	Huynh-Feldt	40.000	2.000	20.000	5.106	.037
	Lower-bound	40.000	1.000	40.000	5.106	.087
Error(factor1)	Sphericity Assumed	31.333	8	3.917		
	Greenhouse-Geisser	31.333	7.032	4.456		
	Huynh-Feldt	31.333	8.000	3.917		
	Lower-bound	31.333	4.000	7.833		

Very little of the output is needed. Mostly it consists of similar analyses using slightly different tests. These are used when Mauchly's test is significant in the previous output table.

The fifth table gives the significance of the F ratio. It is 0.037 when sphericity is assumed.

■ The F-ratio is the mean square (MS) for factor1 (20.000) divided by the Error(factor1) mean square (3.917). It is 5.106 (20.000/3.917 = 5.1059).

■ The exact significance level of this F-ratio is 0.037. Since this value is smaller than 0.05, we would conclude that there is a significant difference in the mean scores of the three conditions overall.

■ In order to interpret the meaning of the ANOVA as it applies to your data, you need to consider the means of each of the three groups of scores which are displayed in the second table. They are 6.00, 8.00 and 4.00. Which of these means are significantly different from the other means?

■ You also need to remember that if you have three or more groups, you need to check where the significant differences lie between the pairs of groups. The related t-test procedure in Chapter 12 explains this. For the present example, only the difference between the means for product X and the placebo was significant. Because you are doing several t-tests, each exact probability for the t-tests should be multiplied by the number of t-tests being carried out. In our example, there are three comparisons, so each exact probability should be multiplied by three. This is known as the Bonferroni adjustment or correction (see *ISP*, Chapter 23).

21.3 Reporting the output

■ We could describe the results of this analysis in the following way. 'A one-way correlated analysis of variance showed a significant treatment effect for the three conditions ($F_{2,8}$ = 5.10, p = 0.037). The aspirin mean was 6.00, the product X mean 8.00, and the placebo mean was 4.00. None of the three treatments differed from one another with related t-tests when a Bonferroni adjustment was made for the number of comparisons.'

■ This could be supplemented by an analysis of variance summary table such as Table 21.2. Drugs is 'factor1' in the output, and residual error is 'Error(factor1)' from the fifth table in the output.

Table 21.2 Analysis of variance summary table

Source of variation	Sum of squares	Degrees of freedom	Mean square	F-ratio
Drugs	40.00	2	20.00	5.11*
Residual error	31.33	8	3.92	

* Significant at 5% level.

22 Two-way analysis of variance for unrelated/uncorrelated scores

Overview

■ Two-way analysis of variance allows you to compare the means of a dependent variable when there are *two* independent variables.

■ If you have more than one *dependent* variable then you simply repeat the analysis for each dependent variable separately. On the other hand, if the several dependent variables are measuring much the same thing then they could be combined into a single overall measure using the summing procedures described in Chapter 17.

■ With SPSS, you do *not* need equal numbers of scores in each condition of the independent variable. If it is possible to have equal numbers in each condition, however, the analysis is optimal statistically.

■ Although the two-way ANOVA can be regarded as an efficient design in so far as it allows two different independent variables to be incorporated into the study, its ability to identify interactions may be more important. An interaction is simply a situation in which the combined effect of two variables is greater than the sum of the effects of each of the two variables acting separately.

■ The two-way ANOVA can be tricky to interpret. It is important to concentrate on the means in each condition and not simply on the the complexities of the statistical output. It is important to note that ANOVAs proceed according to certain rules. The main effects are identified prior to the interactions. Sometimes, unless care is taken, the interaction is mistaken for the main effects – simply because variation is claimed for the main effects before it is claimed for the interaction. As with most statistical analyses, it is important to concentrate as much on the patterns of means in the data as the statistical probabilities.

The computation of a two-way unrelated analysis of variance is illustrated with the data in Table 22.1. The table shows the scores of different participants in six conditions, reflecting the two factors of sleep deprivation and alcohol (*ISP*, Table 22.11). The purpose of the analysis is to evaluate whether the different combinations of alcohol and sleep deprivation differentially affect the mean number of mistakes made.

Table 22.1   Data for sleep deprivation experiment: number of mistakes on video test

	Sleep deprivation		
	4 hours	**12 hours**	**24 hours**
Alcohol	16	18	22
	12	16	24
	17	25	32
No alcohol	11	13	12
	9	8	14
	12	11	12

22.1 Two-way unrelated ANOVA

Step 1:

Enter the data. The two codes for 'Alcohol' (1 = Alcohol and 2 = No alcohol) are in the first column.

The three codes for 'SleepDep' are in the second column (1 = 4 hrs, 2 = 12 hrs and 3 = 24 hrs).

The errors are in the third column. Label these codes in this way. Remove the decimal places in 'Variable View'.

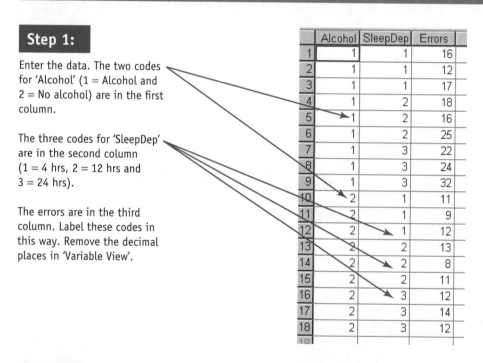

Step 2:

Select 'Analyze', 'General Linear Model' and 'Univariate...'.

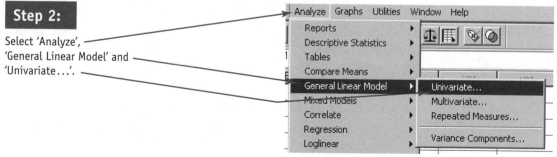

Step 3:

Select 'Errors' and the ▶ button beside the 'Dependent Variable:' box to put it there. Select 'Alcohol' and 'SleepDep' either singly or together and the ▶ button beside 'Fixed Factor(s):' to put them there.

Select 'Options...'.

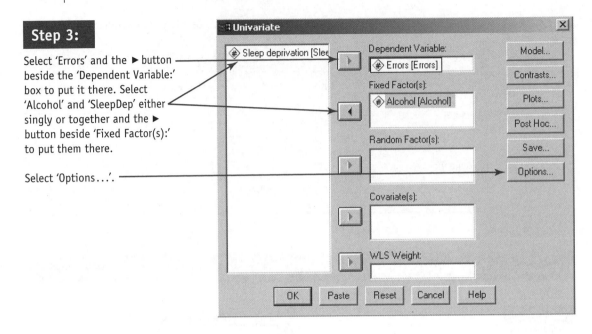

Step 4:

Select 'Descriptive statistics' and 'Homogeneity tests'.

Select 'Continue'.

In previous screen which reappears, select 'Plots...'

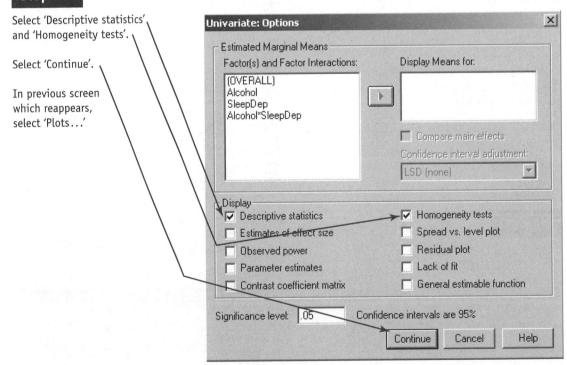

Step 5:

Select 'Alcohol' and the ▶ button beside the 'Horizontal Axis:' box to put it there.

Select 'SleepDep' and the ▶ button beside the 'Separate Lines:' box to put it there.

Select 'Add'.

Select 'Continue'.

Select 'OK' from the previous screen, which reappears.

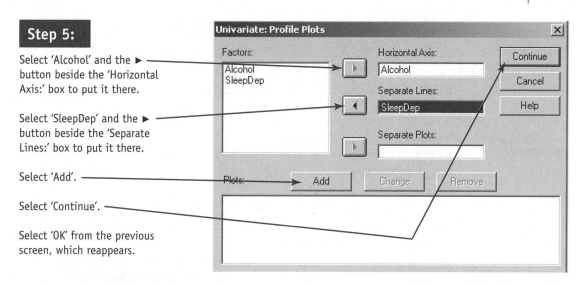

22.2 Interpreting the output

Descriptive Statistics

Dependent Variable: Errors

The second table provides the means, standard deviations and number (*N*) of cases for the two variables of 'Alcohol' and 'Sleep deprivation' separately and together. So the mean for the 'Alcohol' condition is given against the 'Total' for 'Sleep deprivation' (i.e. 20.22). The mean for the '4 hrs' 'Sleep deprivation' is given against the 'Total' for 'Alcohol' (i.e. 12.83).

Alcohol	Sleep deprivation	Mean	Std. Deviation	N
Alcohol	4 hrs	15.00	2.646	3
	12 hrs	19.67	4.726	3
	24 hrs	26.00	5.292	3
	Total	20.22	6.099	9
No alcohol	4 hrs	10.67	1.528	3
	12 hrs	10.67	2.517	3
	24 hrs	12.67	1.155	3
	Total	11.33	1.871	9
Total	4 hrs	12.83	3.061	6
	12 hrs	15.17	5.981	6
	24 hrs	19.33	8.066	6
	Total	15.78	6.330	18

Levene's Test of Equality of Error Variances[a]

Dependent Variable: Errors

F	df1	df2	Sig.
2.786	5	12	.068

Tests the null hypothesis that the error variance of the dependent variable is equal across groups.

a. Design: Intercept+Alcohol+SleepDep+Alcohol * SleepDep

The third table gives Levene's test to see if the variances are similar. As the significance of this test is 0.068 (which is above 0.05), the variances are similar. If this test was significant, the scores should be transformed, say, by using a logarthimic scale to make the variances similar. This is a matter of trial and error – try different transformations until the variances become the same.

Tests of Between-Subjects Effects

Dependent Variable: Errors

Source	Type III Sum of Squares	df	Mean Square	F	Sig.
Corrected Model	546.444[a]	5	109.289	9.739	.001
Intercept	4480.889	1	4480.889	399.287	.000
Alcohol	355.556	1	355.556	31.683	.000
SleepDep	130.111	2	65.056	5.797	.017
Alcohol * SleepDep	60.778	2	30.389	2.708	.107
Error	134.667	12	11.222		
Total	5162.000	18			
Corrected Total	681.111	17			

a. R Squared = .802 (Adjusted R Squared = .720)

The fourth table gives the significance levels for the two variables of 'Alcohol' and 'SleepDep' and their interaction.

- In the analysis of variance table the F-ratio for the two main effects ('Alcohol' and 'SleepDep') is presented first.
- For the first variable of alcohol the F-ratio is 31.683, which is significant at less than the 0.0005 level. Since there are only two conditions for this effect we can conclude that the mean score for one condition is significantly higher than that for the other condition.
- For the second variable of sleep deprivation it is 5.797, which has an exact significance level of 0.017. In other words, this F-ratio is statistically significant at the 0.05 level, which shows that the means of the three sleep conditions are dissimilar.
- Which of the means differ from the others can be further determined by the use of multiple-comparison tests such as the unrelated t-test.
- The F-ratio for the two-way interaction between the two variables ('Alcohol * SleepDep') is 2.708. As the exact significance level of this ratio is 0.107 we conclude that there was no significant interaction.

This plot is shown for the means of the six conditions. It has been edited with the 'Chart Editor'. The style of the different coloured lines has been changed so that they can be more readily distinguished.

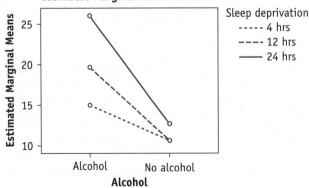

Step 1:

To change the style of line, double click on the plot to select the 'Chart Editor'.

Select the line in the legend to be changed.

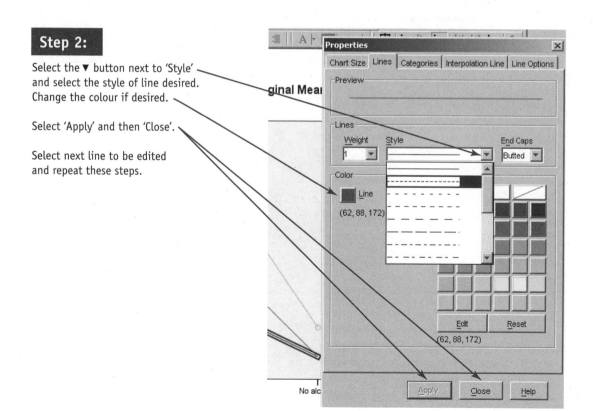

Step 2:

Select the ▼ button next to 'Style' and select the style of line desired. Change the colour if desired.

Select 'Apply' and then 'Close'.

Select next line to be edited and repeat these steps.

22.3 Reporting the output

■ We could report the results of the output as follows: 'A two-way unrelated ANOVA showed that significant effects were obtained for alcohol ($F_{2,12} = 31.68$, $p < 0.001$) and sleep deprivation ($F_{2,12} = 5.80$, $p = 0.017$) but not for their interaction ($F_{2,12} = 2.70$, $p = 0.107$).'

■ It is usual to give an analysis of variance summary table. A simple one, like that shown in Table 22.2, would leave out some of the unnecessary information in the third table in the output.

■ Because the 'SleepDep' factor has more than two conditions, we need to use an appropriate multiple-comparison test to determine the means of which groups differ significantly (see Chapters 21 and 23).

■ We also need to report the means and standard deviations of the groups which differ significantly. These descriptive statistics are given in the second table of the output.

Table 22.2   Analysis of variance summary table

Source of variation	Sums of squares	Degrees of freedom	Mean square	F-ratio	Probability
Alcohol	355.56	1	355.56	31.68	< 0.001
Sleep deprivation	130.11	2	65.06	5.80	< 0.05
Alcohol with sleep deprivation	60.78	2	30.39	2.71	not significant
Error	134.67	12	11.22		

23 Multiple comparisons in ANOVA

Overview

- This chapter extends the coverage of multiple t-tests from Chapters 20 and 21. It explains how to decide which particular pairs of means are significantly different from each other in the analysis of variance.
- The technique is used when you have more than two means. It adds no further information if there are only two means.
- ANOVAs with more than two pairs of means are almost certain to benefit from employing multiple-comparison methods.
- It is not possible to give definitive advice as to which multiple-comparison test to use in different situations as there is no clear consensus in the literature.

Knowing precisely where significant differences lie between different conditions of your study is important. The overall trend in the ANOVA may only tell you part of the story. SPSS has a number of post hoc procedures which are, of course, applied after the data are collected and not planned initially. They all do slightly different things. There is a thorough discussion of them in Howell (2002). We will illustrate the use of these multiple-comparison procedures (using the data in Table 23.1, which were previously discussed in Chapter 20).

Table 23.1   Data for a study of the effects of hormones

Group 1 Hormone 1	Group 2 Hormone 2	Group 3 Placebo control
9	4	3
12	2	6
8	5	3

23.1 Multiple-comparison tests

Step 1:

Select the data file if you saved it. Otherwise enter the data.

	Condition	Depression
1	1	9
2	1	12
3	1	8
4	2	4
5	2	2
6	2	5
7	3	3
8	3	6
9	3	3

Step 2:

Select 'Analyze', 'Compare Means' and 'One-Way ANOVA...'.

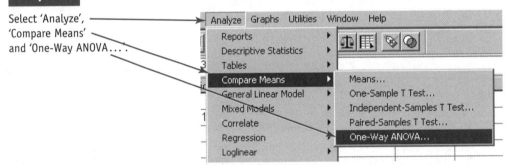

Analyze	Graphs	Utilities	Window	Help
Reports	▶			
Descriptive Statistics	▶			
Tables	▶			
Compare Means	▶	Means...		
General Linear Model	▶	One-Sample T Test...		
Mixed Models	▶	Independent-Samples T Test...		
Correlate	▶	Paired-Samples T Test...		
Regression	▶	One-Way ANOVA...		
Loglinear	▶			

Step 3:

Select 'Depression' and the ▶ button beside the 'Dependent List:' box to put it there.

Select 'Condition' and the ▶ button beside the 'Factor:' box to put it there.

Select 'Post Hoc...'.

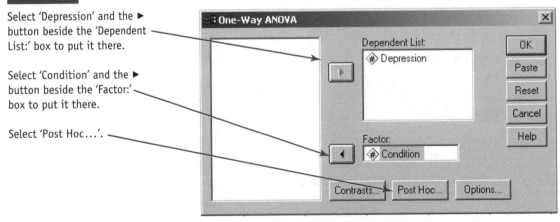

Step 4:

Select 'Tukey', 'Duncan' and 'Scheffe'.

Select 'Continue'.

Select 'OK' from the previous screen, which reappears.

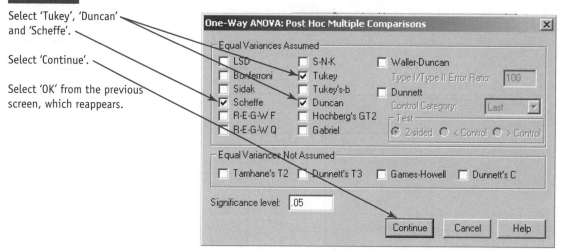

23.2 Interpreting the output

ANOVA

Depression

	Sum of Squares	df	Mean Square	F	Sig.
Between Groups	68.222	2	34.111	10.586	.011
Within Groups	19.333	6	3.222		
Total	87.556	8			

The first table shows the results for the analysis of variance. The F-ratio for the between groups effect (i.e. the effects of hormones) is 10.586, which has an exact significance level of 0.011. In other words, the between groups effect is significant. Overall the means for the three groups differ.

The second and last tables give the results for the three multiple comparison tests.

Multiple Comparisons

Dependent Variable: Depression

	(I) Condition	(J) Condition	Mean Difference (I-J)	Std. Error	Sig.	95% Confidence Interval Lower Bound	95% Confidence Interval Upper Bound
Tukey HSD	Hormone 1	Hormone 2	6.000*	1.466	.015	1.50	10.50
		Placebo control	5.667*	1.466	.019	1.17	10.16
	Hormone 2	Hormone 1	−6.000*	1.466	.015	−10.50	−1.50
		Placebo control	−.333	1.466	.972	−4.83	4.16
	Placebo control	Hormone 1	−5.667*	1.466	.019	−10.16	−1.17
		Hormone 2	.333	1.466	.972	−4.16	4.83
Scheffe	Hormone 1	Hormone 2	6.000*	1.466	.018	1.30	10.70
		Placebo control	5.667*	1.466	.023	.97	10.37
	Hormone 2	Hormone 1	−6.000*	1.466	.018	−10.70	−1.30
		Placebo control	−.333	1.466	.975	−5.03	4.37
	Placebo control	Hormone 1	−5.667*	1.466	.023	−10.37	−.97
		Hormone 2	.333	1.466	.975	−4.37	5.03

*. The mean difference is significant at the .05 level.

For example, using Tukey HSD test, the Hormone 1 mean is significantly different from the Hormone 2 mean (sig. = 0.015) and the Placebo control mean (sig. = 0.019)

Homogeneous Subsets

Depression

	Condition	N	Subset for alpha = .05 — 1	Subset for alpha = .05 — 2
Tukey HSD[a]	Hormone 2	3	3.67	
	Placebo control	3	4.00	
	Hormone 1	3		9.67
	Sig.		.972	1.000
Duncan[a]	Hormone 2	3	3.67	
	Placebo control	3	4.00	
	Hormone 1	3		9.67
	Sig.		.828	1.000
Scheffe[a]	Hormone 2	3	3.67	
	Placebo control	3	4.00	
	Hormone 1	3		9.67
	Sig.		.975	1.000

Hormone 2 and Placebo control are in same subset – i.e. not significantly different.

Hormone 1 is the only group in this second subset. Consequently it is significantly different from the other two group means.

Means for groups in homogeneous subsets are displayed.
a. Uses Harmonic Mean Sample Size = 3.000.

■ The final table, entitled 'Homogeneous Subsets', lists the sets of means which do not *differ* significantly from each other. So taking the rows for Tukey HSD, there are two subsets of means. Subset 1 indicates that the Hormone 2 and Placebo control means of 3.67 and 4.00 do not differ significantly. Subset 2 contains just the Hormone 1 mean of 9.67. Thus the mean of Hormone 1 differs significantly from the means of both Hormone 2 and the Placebo control. However, the means of Hormone 2 and the Placebo control do not differ significantly. The pattern is identical for the Duncan and Scheffé tests in this case – it is not always so.

■ Therefore the three multiple-comparison tests all suggest the same thing: that there are significant differences between Hormone 1 and Hormone 2, and between Hormone 1 and the Placebo control. There are no other differences. So, for example, it is not possible to say that Hormone 1 and Hormone 2 are significantly different.

■ The choice between the three tests is not a simple matter. Howell (2002) makes some recommendations.

23.3 Reporting the output

We could report the results of the output as follows: 'A one-way unrelated analysis of variance showed an overall significant effect for the type of drug treatment ($F_{226} = 10.59$, $p = 0.011$). Scheffé's range test found that the Hormone 1 group differed from the Hormone 2 group ($p = 0.018$) and the Placebo control ($p = 0.023$) but no other significant differences were found.'

Reference

Howell, D. (2002), *Statistical Methods for Psychology* (5th edn, Duxbury Press: Boston).

24 Analysis of covariance (ANCOVA) and two-way mixed analysis of variance (ANOVA) designs

Overview

■ The analysis of covariance allows the researcher to control or adjust for variables which correlate with your dependent variable before comparing the means on the dependent variable. These variables are known as covariates of the dependent variable.

■ To the extent that the levels of the covariates are different for your different research conditions, unless you adjust your dependent variable for the covariates you will confuse the effects of your independent variables with the influence of the pre-existing differences between the conditions caused by different levels of the covariates.

■ By controlling for the covariates, essentially you are taking their effect away from your scores on the dependent variable. Thus having adjusted for the covariates, the remaining variation between conditions cannot be due to the covariates.

■ One common use of ANCOVA is in pre-test/post-test designs. Assume that the pre-test suggests that the different conditions of the experiment have different means prior to testing (e.g. the experimental and control groups are different), ANCOVA may be used to adjust for these pre-test differences.

■ A mixed analysis of variance design is merely a two-way (or three-way, etc.) research design which contains *both* unrelated and related independent variables.

■ Mixed designs generate rather more complex measures of error estimates compared to other forms of the ANOVA. This means that special care needs to be taken when producing appropriate summary tables.

The analysis of covariance is much the same as the analysis of variance dealt with elsewhere but with one major difference. This is that the effects of additional variables (covariates) are taken away as part of the analysis. It is a bit like using partial correlation to get rid of the effects of a third variable on a correlation. We will illustrate the computation of an analysis of covariance (ANCOVA) with the data shown in Table 24.1, which are the same as those presented in Table 20.1 except that depression scores taken immediately prior to the three treatments have been included.

Table 24.1   Data for a study of the effects of hormones (analysis of covariance)

Group 1 Hormone 1		Group 2 Hormone 2		Group 3 Placebo control	
Pre	Post	Pre	Post	Pre	Post
5	9	3	4	2	3
4	12	2	2	3	6
6	8	1	5	2	3

It could be that differences in depression prior to the treatment affect the outcome of the analysis. Essentially by adjusting the scores on the dependent variable to get rid of these pre-existing differences, it is possible to disregard the possibility that these pre-existing differences are affecting the analysis. So, if (*a*) the pre-treatment or test scores are correlated with the post-treatment or test scores, and (*b*) the pre-test scores differ between the three treatments, then these pre-test differences can be statistically controlled by covarying them out of the analysis.

24.1 One-way ANCOVA

Step 1:

Enter the data. The first two columns are the same as the data in Chapters 20 and 23. The data for the third column are new.

	Condition	Posttest	Pretest
1	1	9	5
2	1	12	4
3	1	8	6
4	2	4	3
5	2	2	2
6	2	5	1
7	3	3	2
8	3	6	3
9	3	3	2

Step 2:

Select 'Analyze', 'General Linear Model' and 'Univariate...'.

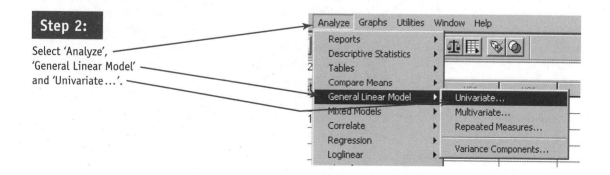

Analyze   Graphs   Utilities   Window   Help

Reports
Descriptive Statistics
Tables
Compare Means
General Linear Model   ▶   Univariate...
Mixed Models   Multivariate...
Correlate   Repeated Measures...
Regression
Loglinear   Variance Components...

Step 3:

Select 'Posttest' and the ▶ button beside the 'Dependent Variable:' box to put it there.

Select 'Condition' and the ▶ button beside the 'Fxed Factor(s):' box to put it there.

Select 'Pretest' and the ▶ button beside the 'Covariate(s):' box to put it there.

Select 'Options...'.

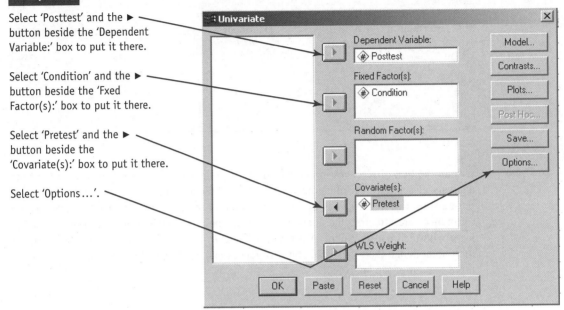

Step 4:

Select 'Condition' and the ▶ button to put it in the 'Display Means for:' box.

Select 'Descriptive statistics'.

Select 'Continue'.

Select 'OK' from the previous screen, which reappears.

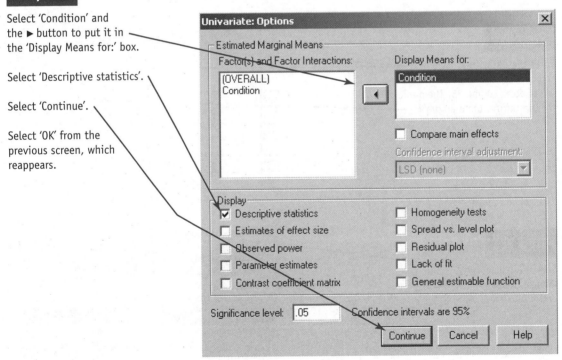

24.2 Interpreting the output

The second table shows the unadjusted means for the three conditions.

Descriptive Statistics

Dependent Variable: Posttest

This table simply gives the means for the three conditions at the post-test. Total is the average post-test score in the original data.

Condition	Mean	Std. Deviation	N
Hormone 1	9.67	2.082	3
Hormone 2	3.67	1.528	3
Placebo control	4.00	1.732	3
Total	5.78	3.308	9

The fourth and last table shows the adjusted means for these three conditions. The adjusted means of the three treatments are what the means are when all groups are adjusted to be identical on the covariate (in this case pre-treatment depression scores).

Condition

Dependent Variable: Posttest

The means for the post-test given in this output table have been adjusted for the effect of the covariate on the three conditions. The effect of the covariate has effectively been removed from the data.

Condition	Mean	Std. Error	95% Confidence Interval	
			Lower Bound	Upper Bound
Hormone 1	10.881[a]	1.955	5.856	15.906
Hormone 2	2.952[a]	1.443	−.756	6.661
Placebo control	3.500[a]	1.269	.237	6.763

a. Covariates appearing in the model are evaluated at the following values: Pretest = 3.11.

■ The adjusted mean is 10.881 for the first treatment, 2.952 for the second treatment and 3.500 for the third treatment.

■ We can see that these adjusted means seem to differ from the unadjusted means shown in the second table of the output. For the first treatment the adjusted mean is 10.88 and the unadjusted mean is 9.67. For the second treatment the adjusted mean is 2.95 and the unadjusted mean is 3.67, while for the third treatment the adjusted mean is 3.50 and the unadjusted mean is 4.00.

The third table shows the F-ratio for the analysis of covariance.

Tests of Between-Subjects Effects

Dependent Variable: Posttest

Source	Type III Sum of Squares	df	Mean Square	F	Sig.
Corrected Model	70.151[a]	3	23.384	6.718	.033
Intercept	27.684	1	27.684	7.953	.037
Pretest	1.929	1	1.929	.554	.490
Condition	26.425	2	13.213	3.796	.099
Error	17.405	5	3.481		
Total	388.000	9			
Corrected Total	87.556	8			

a. R Squared = .801 (Adjusted R Squared = .682)

Following removal of the effects of the covariate, there is not a significant difference between the means of the three conditions as the significance is 0.099 which is not statistically significant.

- The F-ratio for the main effect is 3.796 (13.213/3.481 = 3.796).
- The probability of this F-ratio is 0.099. In other words, it is greater than the 0.05 critical value and so is not statistically significant.

24.3 Reporting the output

- We could report the results of the output as follows: 'A one-way ANCOVA showed that when pre-test depression was covaried out, the main effect of treatment on post-test depression was not significant ($F_{225} = 3.79$, $p = 0.099$). The covariate, pre-treatment depression-scores had a significant effect on post-treatment depression scores.' You would normally also report the changes to the means once the covariate has been removed.
- In addition, we would normally give an ANCOVA summary table as in Table 24.2.

Table 24.2   ANCOVA summary table for effects of treatments on depression controlling for pre-treatment depression

Source of variance	Sums of squares	Degrees of freedom	Mean square	F-ratio
Covariate (pre-treatment depression scores)	43.73	1	43.73	12.56*
Main effect (treatment)	26.43	2	13.21	3.80
Residual error	17.41	5	3.48	

* Significant at 5% level.

24.4 Two-way mixed ANOVA design

A two-way mixed analysis of variance has one unrelated factor and one related factor. Factors are independent variables. This analysis is illustrated with the data in Table 24.3 (*ISP*, Table 24.6), which consists of the self-esteem scores of children measured before and after an experimental manipulation in which half the children (chosen at random) were praised for good behaviour (experimental condition) while the other half were given no feedback (control condition).

Table 24.3   Pre- and post-test self-esteem scores in two conditions

Conditions	Children	Pre-test	Post-test
Control	1	6	5
	2	4	6
	3	5	7
Experimental	4	7	10
	5	5	11
	6	5	12

Step 1:

Enter the data. The codes for the two conditions (1 = Control and 2 = Experimental) are in the 1st column. Label these values as such. The pre-test and post-test scores are in the second and third columns.

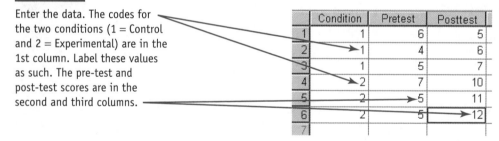

Step 2:

Select 'Analyze', 'General Linear Model' and 'Repeated Measures...'.

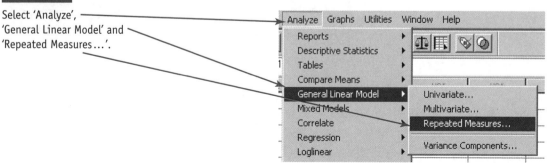

Step 3:

Type '2' in the 'Number of Levels:' box.

Select 'Add'.

Select 'Define'.

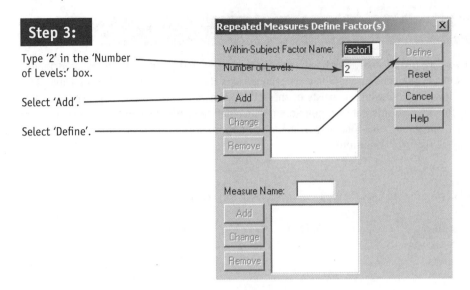

Step 4:

Select 'Pretest' and 'Posttest' either alone or together and the ► button beside the 'Within-Subjects Variables:' box to put them there.

Select 'Condition' and the ► button beside the 'Between-Subjects Factor(s):' box to put it there.

Select 'Options...'.

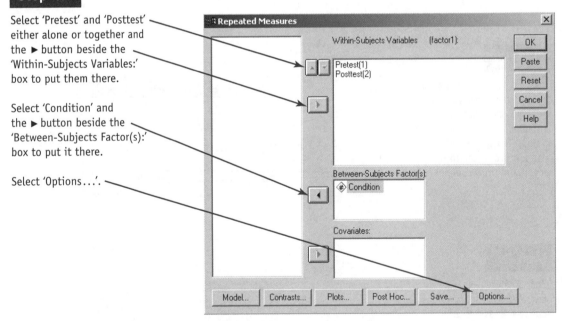

Step 5:

Select 'Descriptive statistics' and 'Homogeneity tests'.

Select 'Continue'.

In previous box which reappears, select 'Plots...'.

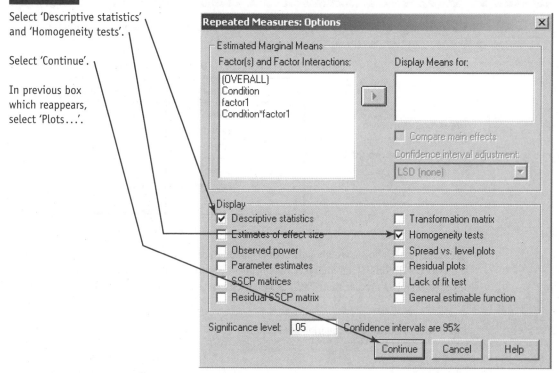

Step 6:

Select 'factor1' ('Pretest' 'Posttest') and the ► button beside the 'Horizontal Axis:' box to put it there.

Select 'Condition' and the ► button beside the 'Separate Lines:' box to put it there.

Select 'Add'.

Select 'Continue'.

Select 'OK' from the previous screen, which reappears.

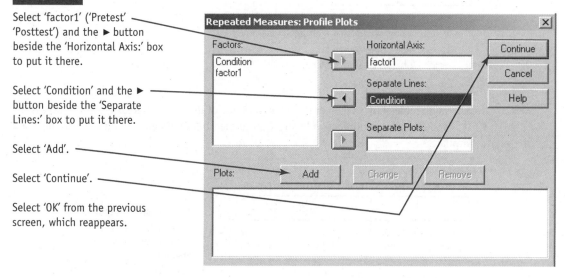

24.5 Interpreting the output

The output gives 10 tables and a plot. Only the more important tables are shown here.

Descriptive Statistics

The second table gives the mean and standard deviation for the two groups.

	Condition	Mean	Std. Deviation	N
Pretest	Control	5.00	1.000	3
	Experimental	5.67	1.155	3
	Total	5.33	1.033	6
Posttest	Control	6.00	1.000	3
	Experimental	11.00	1.000	3
	Total	8.50	2.881	6

The third table shows whether the covariances matrices of the post-test are equal across the two conditions. This analysis of variance assumes that they are. As the significance level of 0.951 is greater than 0.05, the matrices are similar and this assumption is met.

Box's Test of Equality of Covariance Matrices[a]

Box's M	.757
F	.115
df1	3
df2	2880.000
Sig.	.951

Check that this value is *not* less than 0.05. If it is not significant (as it is here), the covariances of the post-test groups are equal.

Tests the null hypothesis that the observed covariance matrices of the dependent variables are equal across groups.
a. Design: Intercept+Condition
   Within Subjects Design: factor1

The ninth table shows whether the error variance of the two variables is similar across the two conditions. A significance level of more than 0.05 indicates that these variances are similar.

Levene's Test of Equality of Error Variances[a]

	F	df1	df2	Sig.
Pretest	.308	1	4	.609
Posttest	.000	1	4	1.000

Check these for significance. Significance means that the error variances are significantly different for the two or more conditions – either for the pre-test or the post-test.

Tests the null hypothesis that the error variance of the dependent variable is equal across groups.
a. Design: Intercept+Condition
   Within Subjects Design: factor1

The eighth table contains information for the F-test. The F-test that is of particular interest to us is that for the interaction between the within-subjects and between-subjects factor (factor1 * Condition). This F-ratio is 7.682 and has a probability value of 0.05. In other words, this interaction is just significant. If we look at the means for the four groups we can see that while the mean for the control condition increases little from pre-test (5.00) to post-test (6.00), the mean for the experimental condition shows a larger increase from pre-test (5.67) to post-test (11.00).

Tests of Within-Subjects Contrasts

Measure: MEASURE_1

Source	factor1	Type III Sum of Squares	df	Mean Square	F	Sig.
factor1	Linear	30.083	1	30.083	16.409	.015
factor1 * Condition	Linear	14.083	1	14.083	7.682	.050
Error(factor1)	Linear	7.333	4	1.833		

This indicates a just significant interaction between pre-test/post-test and experimental condition. In other words, there are differences between the cells which cannot be explained by the pre-existing differences between the groups of participants or simply by changes in all conditions between the pre-test and the post-test. Take a look at Table 24.5 which will help clarify the trends in the means.

- ■ To determine whether these increases were statistically significant we could run a related t-test between the pre- and post-test scores for the two conditions separately (with Bonferroni adjustment for the number of comparisons carried out).
- ■ We could also see whether the two conditions differed at pre-test and at post-test with an unrelated t-test for the two test periods separately.

The plot or graph below shows the means of the four cells which may help you to grasp more quickly the relationships between them. This has been edited to change the style of lines, as described in Chapter 22.

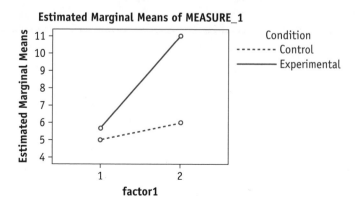

24.6 Reporting the output

- We could report the results of the output as follows: 'The interaction between the two conditions and the change over time was statistically significant ($F_{1,4} = 7.68$, $p = 0.05$). While the pre-test means did not differ significantly ($t = 0.76$, $DF = 4$, two-tailed $p = 0.492$), the post-test mean for the experimental condition ($M = 11.00$, SD = 1.00) was significantly higher ($t = 6.12$, $DF = 4$, two-tailed $p = 0.004$) than that for the control condition ($M = 6.00$, SD = 1.00). The increase from pre-test ($M = 5.67$, SD = 1.15) to post-test ($M = 11.00$, SD = 1.00) was significant for the experimental condition ($t = 4.44$, $DF = 2$, two-tailed $p = 0.047$) but not for the control condition ($t = 1.00$, $DF = 2$, two-tailed $p = 0.423$).'
- An analysis of variance table for this analysis is presented in Table 24.4.
- It is also useful to include a table of means (M) and standard deviations (SD) as shown in Table 24.5.

Table 24.4 ANCOVA summary table for a two-way mixed design

Source of variance	Sums of squares	Degrees of freedom	Mean square	F-ratio
Between-subjects factor	24.08	1	24.08	72.25*
Between-subjects error	1.33	1	1.33	
Within-subjects factor	30.08	1	30.08	16.41*
Within-subjects error	7.33	4	1.83	
Interaction	14.08	1	14.08	7.68*

* Significant at 0.05 level.

Table 24.5 Means and standard deviations of the pre- and post-tests for the control and experimental conditions

Conditions	Pre-test		Post-test	
	M	SD	*M*	SD
Control	5.00	1.00	6.00	1.00
Experimental	5.67	1.15	11.00	1.00

25 Reading ASCII or text files into the Data Editor

Overview

- Sometimes you have a computer file of data which you wish to use on SPSS. This chapter tells you how to use data not specifically entered into the SPSS Data Editor spreadsheet.
- Although student work will rarely require the use of ASCII files, there are a number of databases of archived data which researchers may wish to analyse.
- It is worth noting that sometimes data from other spreadsheets can be entered into SPSS. For example, data from Excel spreadsheets can simply be cut and pasted into SPSS though not the spreadsheet in its entirety. SPSS data can be saved as an Excel file.

25.1 Introduction

SPSS for Windows is one of many different computer programs for analysing data. There are circumstances in which researchers might wish to take data sets which have been prepared for another computer and run those data through SPSS for Windows. It can be expensive in time and/or money to re-enter data, say, from a big survey into the Data Editor spreadsheet. Sometimes, the only form in which the data are available is as an archive electronic data file; the original questionnaires may have been thrown away. No matter the reason for using an imported data file, SPSS for Windows can accept files in other forms. In particular, data files are sometimes written as simple text or ASCII files, as these can be readily transferred from one type of computer to another. ASCII stands for American Standard Code for Information Interchange. To analyse an ASCII data file you first need to read it into the Data Editor.

Suppose, for example, that you had an ASCII data file called 'data.txt' which consisted of the following numbers:

1118
2119
3218

Obviously you cannot sensibly use an ASCII file until you know exactly where the information for each variable is. However, we do know where and what the information is for the small file above. The figures in the first column simply number the three different participants for whom we have data. The values in the second column contain the code for gender, with '1' representing females and '2' males. While the values in the third and fourth column indicate the age of the three people. We would carry out the following procedure to enter this ASCII data file into the Data Editor.

25.2 Reading an ASCII or text data file

Step 1:

Select 'File' and
'Read Text Data...'.

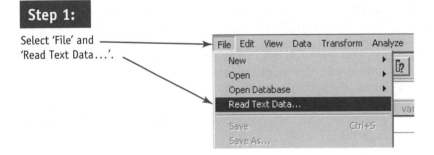

Step 2:

Select the ▼ button of
the 'Look in:' box to find
the data file (e.g. data).

Select the file.

Select 'Open'.

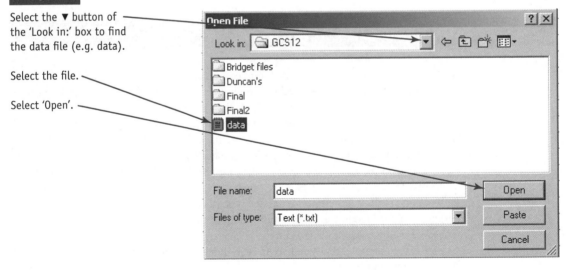

Step 3:

Select 'Next >'.

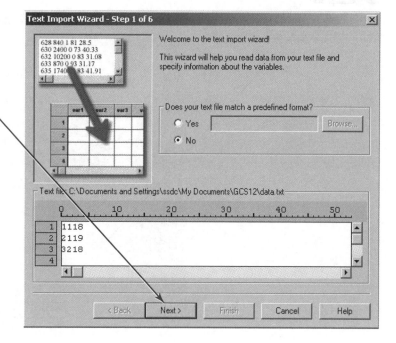

Step 4:

Select 'Next >'.

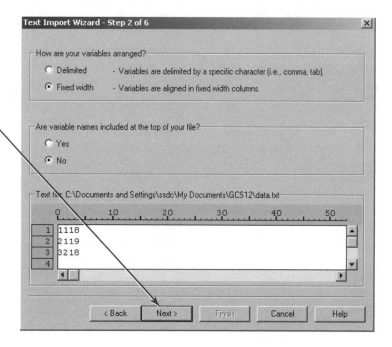

Step 5:

Select 'Next >'.

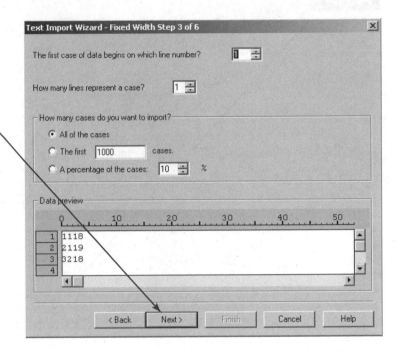

Step 6:

Click immediately after the first column as this column contains the number of the participant.

Click after the second column which holds the code for gender.

The last two columns contain age.

Select 'Next >'.

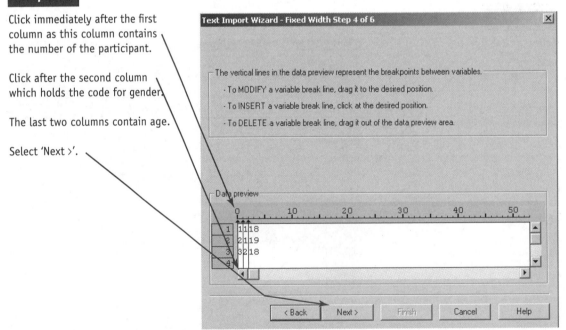

Step 7:

Select 'Next >'.

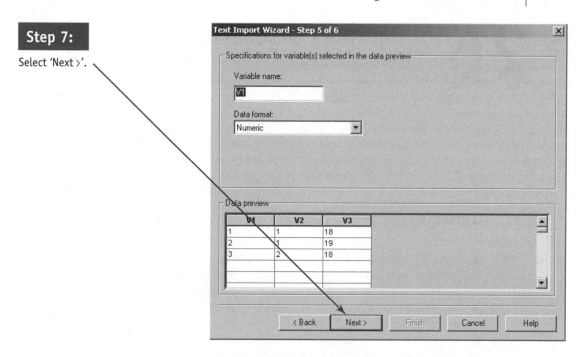

Step 8:

Select 'Finish'.

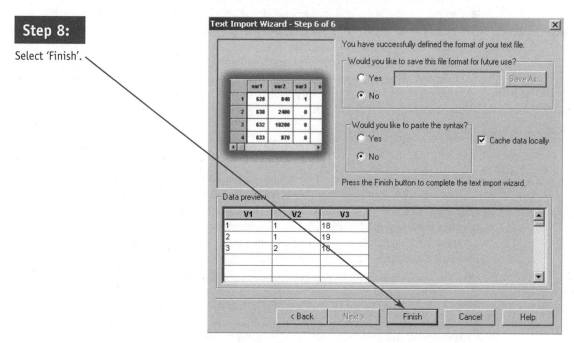

The text data has now been
entered into the 'Data Editor'
and can be saved as an SPSS file.

	V1	V2	V3
1	1	1	18.0
2	2	1	19.0
3	3	2	18.0

26 Partial correlation

Overview

■ If you suspect that a correlation between two variables is affected by their correlations with yet another variable, it is possible to adjust for the effects of this additional variable by using the partial correlation procedure.

■ The correlation between two variables (before partialling) is known as the zero-order correlation.

■ Using SPSS, it is also possible to simultaneously control for several variables which may be affecting the correlation coefficient.

■ If the variable to be controlled for consists of a small number of nominal categories, it is useful to explore the correlations for separate sets of cases based on the control variable. For example, if gender is to be controlled, then separate your sample into a male subsample and then a female subsample. Explore what the correlations between your main variables are for these two groups. Often this clarifies the effect of partialling in unanticipated ways.

SPSS for Windows cannot easily compute partial correlations from a matrix of zero-order correlations (i.e. entering the values of the correlations between the variables under analysis directly). Consequently, we will illustrate the computation of partial correlations with the raw scores in Table 26.1, which represent a numerical intelligence test score, a verbal intelligence test score and age in years. We will correlate the two test scores partialling out age.

Table 26.1 Numerical and verbal intelligence test scores and age

Numerical scores	Verbal scores	Age
90	90	13
100	95	15
95	95	15
105	105	16
100	100	17

26.1 Partial correlation

Step 1:

In 'Variable View' of the 'Data Editor' name the three columns 'Num_IQ', 'Verb_IQ' and 'Age'.

Remove the two decimal places by setting the number to 0.

	Name	Type	Width	Decimals
1	Num_IQ	Numeric	8	0
2	Verb_IQ	Numeric	8	0
3	Age	Numeric	8	0

Step 2:

In 'Data View' of the 'Data Editor' enter the numerical IQ scores in the first column, the verbal IQ scores in the second column and age in the third column.

	Num_IQ	Verb_IQ	Age
1	90	90	13
2	100	95	15
3	95	95	15
4	105	105	16
5	100	100	17

Step 3:

Select 'Analyze', 'Correlate' and 'Partial...'.

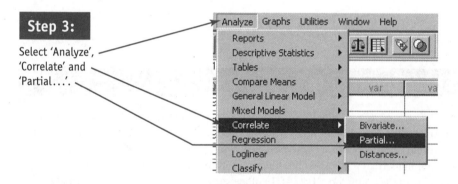

Analyze	Graphs	Utilities	Window	Help

- Reports ▶
- Descriptive Statistics ▶
- Tables ▶
- Compare Means ▶
- General Linear Model ▶
- Mixed Models ▶
- Correlate ▶ → Bivariate...
- Regression ▶ → Partial...
- Loglinear ▶ → Distances...
- Classify ▶

Step 4:

Select 'Num_IQ' and 'Verb_IQ' and the ▶ button to put these two variables into the 'Variables:' box.

Select 'Age' and the ▶ button to put it into the 'Controlling for:' box.

Select 'OK'.

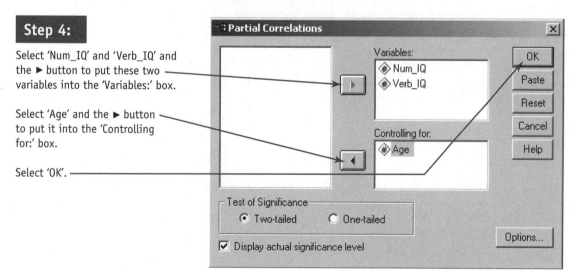

Partial Correlations

Variables:
- Num_IQ
- Verb_IQ

Controlling for:
- Age

OK | Paste | Reset | Cancel | Help

Test of Significance
- ● Two-tailed ○ One-tailed

☑ Display actual significance level

Options...

26.2 Interpreting the output

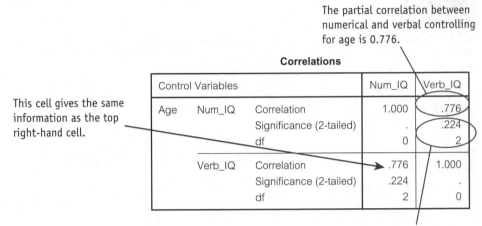

The partial correlation between numerical and verbal controlling for age is 0.776.

This cell gives the same information as the top right-hand cell.

Correlations

Control Variables			Num_IQ	Verb_IQ
Age	Num_IQ	Correlation	1.000	.776
		Significance (2-tailed)	.	.224
		df	0	2
	Verb_IQ	Correlation	.776	1.000
		Significance (2-tailed)	.224	.
		df	2	0

The two-tailed significance is 0.224 which is not significant. There are two degrees of freedom.

26.3 Reporting the results

We should mention the original correlation between numerical and verbal intelligence which is 0.92. So we could report the results as follows: 'The correlation between numerical and verbal intelligence is 0.92 ($DF = 3$, two-tailed $p = 0.025$). However, the correlation between numerical and verbal intelligence controlling for age declines to 0.78, which is not significant (two-tailed $p = 0.224$). In other words, there is no significant relationship between numerical and verbal intelligence when age is controlled.'

27 Factor analysis

Overview

- There are two types of factor analysis: exploratory and confirmatory factor analysis. SPSS does not compute confirmatory factor analysis directly. Exploratory factor analysis is probably the more important and SPSS has a very complete package of options for this.

- (Exploratory) factor analysis allows one to make sense of a complex set of variables by reducing them to a smaller number of factors (or supervariables) which account for many of the original variables. Although it is possible to obtain valuable insights from a matrix of correlations between several variables, the sheer size of the matrix may make this difficult even with a relatively small number of variables.

- Factor analysis is commonly used when trying to understand the pattern of responses of people completing closed-ended questionnaires. The items measuring similar things can be identified through factor analysis and, consequently, the structure of replies to the questionnaire.

- Factor analysis, however, includes a variety of techniques and approaches which you may find bewildering. We provide a 'standard' approach which will serve the purposes of most researchers well.

- Factor analysis requires a degree of judgement, especially on the matter of the number of factors to extract. The speed of computer factor analyses means that more than one approach may be tried even within quite a short analysis session. It is a useful exercise to explore the effects of varying the method of analysis in order to assess the effect of this on one's conclusions.

The computation of a principal components factor analysis is illustrated with the data in Table 27.1, which consist of scores on six variables for nine individuals. This is only for illustrative purposes; it would be considered a ludicrously small number of cases to do a factor analysis on. Normally, you should think of having at least two or three times as many cases as you have variables. The following is a standard factor analysis which is adequate for most situations. However, SPSS has many options for factor analysis.

Table 27.1   Scores of nine individuals on six variables

Individual	Batting	Crosswords	Darts	Scrabble	Juggling	Spelling
1	10	15	8	26	15	8
2	6	16	5	25	12	9
3	2	11	1	22	7	6
4	5	16	3	28	11	9
5	7	15	4	24	12	7
6	8	13	4	23	14	6
7	6	17	3	29	10	9
8	2	18	1	28	8	8
9	5	14	2	25	10	6

27.1 Principal components analysis with orthogonal rotation

Step 1:

Enter the data.

Step 2:

Select 'Analyze', 'Data Reduction' and 'Factor...'.

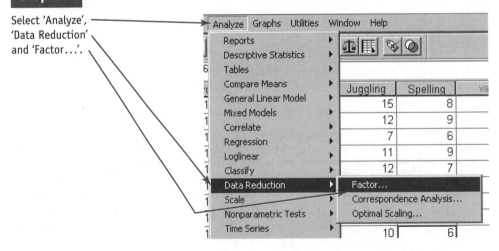

Step 3:

Select the six variables either individually or together and the ▶ button to put them in the 'Variables:' box.

Select 'Descriptives...'.

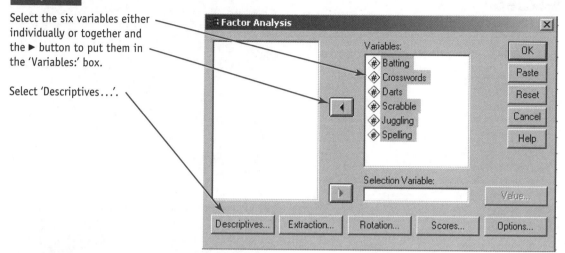

Step 4:

Select 'Coefficients'.

Select 'Continue'.

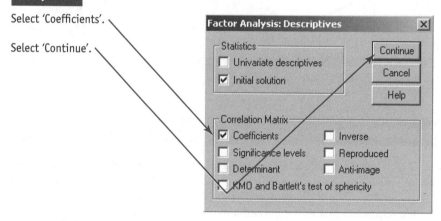

Step 5:

Select 'Scree plot'.

Select 'Continue'.

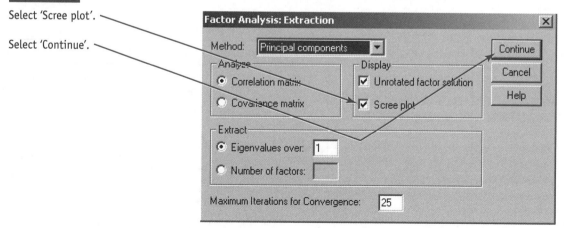

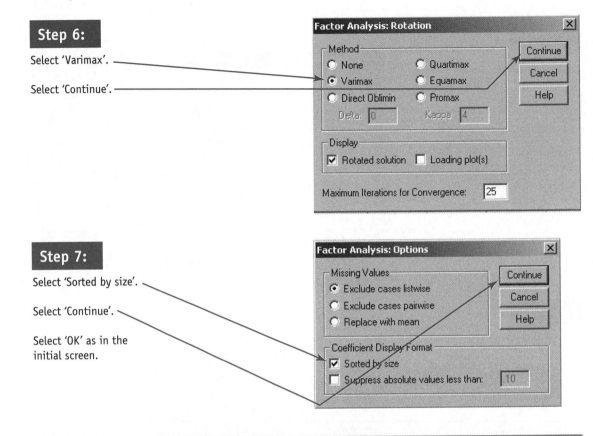

Step 6:

Select 'Varimax'.

Select 'Continue'.

Step 7:

Select 'Sorted by size'.

Select 'Continue'.

Select 'OK' as in the initial screen.

27.2 Interpreting the output

■ The first table presents the correlation matrix. From this it appears that there are two groups of variables that are strongly intercorrelated. One consists of batting, juggling and darts, and the other of crosswords, Scrabble and spelling. These have been indicated – but remember that as a correlation matrix is symmetrical that only the lower half below the diagonal has been marked. Normally in factor analysis the correlation matrix is much more difficult to decipher than this. Our data are highly stylised.

Correlation Matrix

		Batting	Crosswords	Darts	Scrabble	Juggling	Spelling
Correlation	Batting	1.000	.000	.910	−.047	.963	.096
	Crosswords	.000	1.000	.081	.883	.023	.795
	Darts	.910	.081	1.000	−.005	.902	.291
	Scrabble	−.047	.883	−.005	1.000	−.080	.789
	Juggling	.963	.023	.902	−.080	1.000	.108
	Spelling	.096	.795	.291	.789	.108	1.000

Because factor analysis usually involves a lot of variables and there is a limit to what can be got onto a computer screen, normally the correlation matrix is difficult to see in its entirety.

■ The third table shows that two principal components factors were initially extracted in this case. The computer ignores factors with an eigenvalue of less than 1.00. This is because such factors consists of uninterpretable error variation. Of course, your analysis may have even more (or less) factors.

Total Variance Explained

Component	Initial Eigenvalues			Extraction Sums of Squared Loadings			Rotation Sums of Squared Loadings		
	Total	% of Variance	Cumulative %	Total	% of Variance	Cumulative %	Total	% of Variance	Cumulative %
1	2.951	49.186	49.186	2.951	49.186	49.186	2.876	47.931	47.931
2	2.579	42.981	92.167	2.579	42.981	92.167	2.654	44.236	92.167
3	.264	4.401	96.567						
4	.124	2.062	98.630						
5	.058	.974	99.604						
6	.024	.396	100.000						

Extraction Method: Principal Component Analysis.

The first two factors (components) will be analysed further by the computer as their eigenvalues are larger that 1.00.

■ The scree plot also shows that a break in the size of eigenvalues for the factors occurs after the second factor: the curve is fairly flat after the second factor. Since it is important in factor analysis to ensure that you do not have too many factors, you may wish to do your factor analysis and rotation stipulating the number of factors once you have the results of the scree test. (This can be done by inserting the number in the 'Number of factors:' in the 'Factor Analysis: Extraction' sub-dialogue box.) In the case of our data this does not need to be done since the computer has used the first two factors and ignored the others because of the minimum eigenvalue requirement of 1.00. It is not unusual for a component analysis to be recomputed in the light of the pattern which emerges.

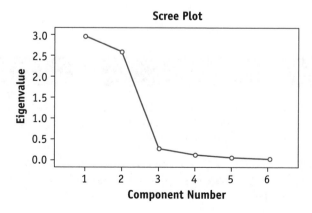

Scree Plot

■ These two components are then orthogonally rotated and the loadings of the six variables on these two factors are shown in the fifth table entitled 'Rotated Component Matrix'.

Rotated Component Matrix[a]

	Component	
	1	2
Batting	.980	−.012
Juggling	.979	−.011
Darts	.962	.104
Crosswords	.006	.951
Scrabble	−.078	.951
Spelling	.153	.914

Extraction Method: Principal Component Analysis.
Rotation Method: Varimax with Kaiser Normalization.
a. Rotation converged in 3 iterations.

■ The variables are ordered or sorted according to their loading on the first factor from those with the highest loadings to those with the lowest loadings. This helps interpretation of the factor since the high loading items are the ones which primarily help you decide what the factor is.

■ On the first factor, batting has the highest loading (0.980) followed by juggling (0.979) and darts (0.962).

■ On the second factor, crosswords has the highest loading (0.951) followed by Scrabble (0.951) and spelling (0.914). The apparent lack of difference in size of loading of crosswords and Scrabble is due to rounding. This can be seen if you double click on the rotated-component matrix table and then double click on these two loadings in turn.

■ We would interpret the meaning of these factors in terms of the content of the variables that loaded most highly on them.

■ The percentage of variance that each of the orthogonally rotated factors accounts for is given in the third table under '% of variance' in the 'Rotation Sums of Squared Loadings' section. It is 47.931 for the first factor and 44.236 for the second factor.

27.3 Reporting the output

It would be usual to tabulate the factors and variables, space permitting. Since the data in our example are on various tests of skill, the factor analysis table might be as in Table 27.2. The figures have been given to two decimal places.

■ The exact way of reporting the results of a factor analysis will depend on the purpose of the analysis. One way of describing the results would be as follows. 'A principal components factor analysis was conducted on the correlations of the six variables.

Two factors were initially extracted with eigenvalues equal to or greater than 1.00. Orthogonal rotation of the factors yielded the factor structure given in Table 27.2. The first factor accounted for 48% of the variance and the second factor 44%. The first factor seems to be hand–eye coordination and the second factor seems to be verbal flexibility.' With factor analysis, since the factors have to be interpreted, differences in interpretation may occur.

Table 27.2   Orthogonal factor loading matrix for six skills

Variable	Factor 1	Factor 2
Skill at batting	0.98	−0.01
Skill at crosswords	0.01	0.95
Skill at darts	0.96	0.10
Skill at Scrabble	−0.08	0.95
Skill at juggling	0.98	−0.01
Skill at spelling	0.15	0.91

28 Stepwise multiple regression

Overview

- Stepwise multiple regression is a way of choosing predictors of a particular dependent variable on the basis of statistical criteria.
- Essentially the statistical procedure decides which independent variable is the best predictor, the second best predictor, etc.
- The emphasis is on finding the best predictors at each stage. When predictors are highly correlated with each other and with the dependent variable, often one variable becomes listed as a predictor and the other variable is not listed. This does not mean that the latter variable is *not* a predictor, merely that it adds nothing to the prediction that the first predictor has not already done. Sometimes the best predictor is only marginally better than the second predictor and minor variations in the procedures may affect which of the two is chosen as the predictor.
- There are a number of multiple regression variants. Stepwise is usually a good choice though one can enter all variables simultaneously as an alternative. Similarly, one can enter all of the variables simultaneously and gradually eliminate predictors one by one if eliminating does little to change the overall prediction.
- It is possible to enter variables as different groups for analysis. This is called hierarchical multiple regression and can, for example, be selected alongside stepwise procedures. The use of blocks is discussed in the next chapter.

The computation of a stepwise multiple regression analysis is illustrated with the data shown in Table 28.1, which consist of scores for six individuals on the four variables of educational achievement, intellectual ability, school motivation and parental interest, respectively.

Because this is for illustrative purposes and to save space, we are going to enter these data 20 times to give us a respectable amount of data to work with. Obviously you would *not* do this if your data were real. It is important to use quite a lot of research participants or cases for multiple regression. Ten or 15 times your number of variables would be reasonably generous. Of course, you can use less for data-exploration purposes.

Table 28.1   Data for stepwise multiple regression

Educational achievement	Intellectual ability	School motivation	Parental interest
1	2	1	2
2	2	3	1
2	2	3	3
3	4	3	2
3	3	4	3
4	3	2	2

28.1   Stepwise multiple regression analysis

Step 1:

Enter the data.
The 'Freq' variable is for weighting these six cases 20 times using the 'Weight Cases...' procedure.

Save this data file to use in Chapter 29.

	Achievement	Ability	Motivation	Interest	Freq
1	1	2	1	2	20
2	2	2	3	1	20
3	2	2	3	3	20
4	3	4	3	2	20
5	3	3	4	3	20
6	4	3	2	2	20
7					

Step 2:

Select 'Analyze', 'Regression' and 'Linear...'.

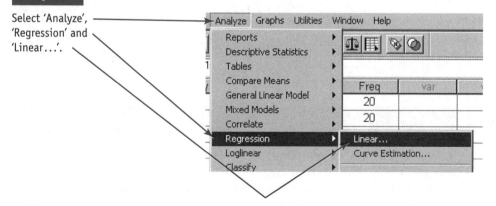

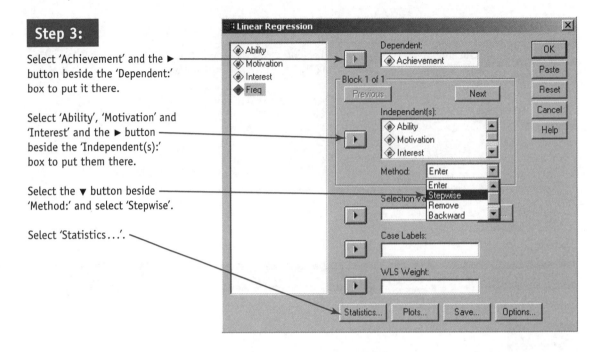

Step 3:

Select 'Achievement' and the ▶ button beside the 'Dependent:' box to put it there.

Select 'Ability', 'Motivation' and 'Interest' and the ▶ button beside the 'Independent(s):' box to put them there.

Select the ▼ button beside 'Method:' and select 'Stepwise'.

Select 'Statistics…'.

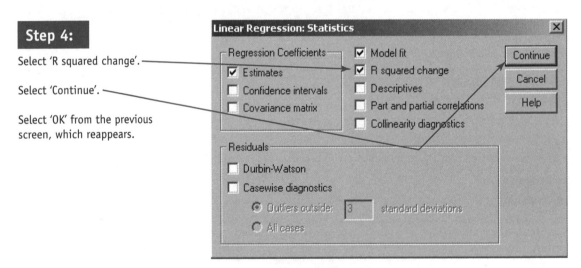

Step 4:

Select 'R squared change'.

Select 'Continue'.

Select 'OK' from the previous screen, which reappears.

28.2 Interpreting the output

■ There is a great deal of information in the output. Multiple regression is a complex area and needs further study in order to understand all of its ramifications. In interpreting the results of this analysis we shall restrict ourselves to commenting on the following statistics: multiple R, R-square, adjusted R-square, B, beta and R-square change. (Most of these are dealt with in a simple fashion in the accompanying statistics text (see *ISP*, Chapter 28).)

■ In stepwise multiple regression, each new step is discussed as a 'Model'. In this example, two significant steps were involved. The first step (Model 1) uses the predictor 'Ability'. The second step (Model 2) is built on this predictor with the addition of a second predictor 'Motivation'. Generally, it is reasonable to concentrate on the model with the higher or highest number.

■ Notice how badly the first table in particular is laid out. If you double click on a table it will be enclosed in a rectangle. To move any but the first line, move the cursor to that line. When it changes to a double-arrow ($\leftrightarrow$), click the left button of the mouse and, holding the left button down, move the line to the position you want before releasing the button. By dragging the column dividers in this way you should be able to obtain a better and more easily read table.

Variables Entered/Removed[a]

Model	Variables Entered	Variables Removed	Method
1	Ability	.	Stepwise (Criteria: Probability -of- F-to-enter <= .050, Probability -of- F-to-remove >= .100).
2	Motivation	.	Stepwise (Criteria: Probability -of- F-to-enter <= .050, Probability -of- F-to-remove >= .100).

a. Dependent Variable: Achievement

■ The second table of the output 'Model Summary' gives the values of multiple R, R-square and adjusted R-square for the two steps (Models). This is really a table of the multiple correlation coefficients between the models and the criterion. It also includes statistics indicating the improvement of fit of the models with the data. Each model in this example gives an improvement in fit. This can be seen from the final figures where the change in fit is significant for both Model 1 and Model 2. (The regression weights (B and beta) are to be found in the fourth table of the output entitled 'Coefficients'.)

Model Summary

Model	R	R Square	Adjusted R Square	Std. Error of the Estimate	Change Statistics				
					R Square Change	F Change	df1	df2	Sig. F Change
1	.701[a]	.491	.487	.689	.491	113.786	1	118	.000
2	.718[b]	.515	.507	.675	.024	5.850	1	117	.017

a. Predictors: (Constant), Ability
b. Predictors: (Constant), Ability, Motivation

The most important thing is that the 'Sig. F Change' indicates the improvement in fit for the two models is significant.

- The predictor that is entered on the first step of the stepwise analysis (Model 1) is the predictor which has the highest correlation with the criterion. In this example this predictor is 'Ability'. (Note 'a' immediately underneath the 'Model Summary' table indicates this.)
- As there is only predictor in the regression equation on the first step, multiple R is the same as the correlation between 'Ability' and 'Achievement' (the dependent or criterion variable). In this case it is 0.701, or 0.70 to two decimal places.
- R-square is simply the multiple correlation coefficient squared, which in this instance is 0.491, or 0.49 to two decimal places. This indicates that 49% of the variance in the criterion is shared with or 'explained by' the first predictor.
- Adjusted R-square is R-square which has been adjusted for the size of the sample and the number of predictors in the equation. The effect of this adjustment is to reduce the size of R-square, so adjusted R-square is 0.487, or 0.49 to two decimal places.
- The variable which is entered second in the regression equation is the predictor which generally explains the second greatest significant proportion of the variance in the criterion. In this example, this variable is 'Motivation'.
- The multiple R, R-square and adjusted R-square for Model 2 are 0.718, 0.515 and 0.507, respectively which, rounded to two decimal places, are 0.72, 0.52 and 0.51. As might be expected, these values are bigger than for the corresponding figures for Model 1. This is to be expected because there is an additional predictor contributing to a better prediction.
- In Model 2, then, two variables ('Ability' and 'Motivation') explain or account for 51% of the variance in the criterion.
- R-square change presented under 'Change Statistics' in the second table shows the increase in the proportion of the variance in the criterion variable ('Achievement') by predictors that have been entered after the first predictor ('Ability'). In this case there is only one other predictor ('Motivation'). This predictor explains a further 2.4% of the variance in the criterion.
- Examine the table headed 'Coefficients'. Find the column headed 'Beta' in the table. The first entry is 0.701 for Model 1. This is exactly the same as the value of the multiple correlation above for Model 1. That is because beta is the standardised regression coefficient which is the same as the correlation when there is only one predictor. It is as if all your scores had been transformed to z-scores before the analysis began.

Coefficients[a]

Model		Unstandardized Coefficients		Standardized Coefficients		
		B	Std. Error	Beta	t	Sig.
1	(Constant)	.100	.234		.428	.669
	Ability	.900	.084	.701	10.667	.000
2	(Constant)	−.167	.254		−.656	.513
	Ability	.833	.087	.649	9.561	.000
	Motivation	.167	.069	.164	2.419	.017

a. Dependent Variable: Achievement

The quickest way to access the output from multiple regression is to concentrate on the final model's output in the table labelled 'Coefficients'. Ignore the row for constants, then concentrate on the remaining rows. These give the important predictors of the dependent variable. These are clearly 'Ability' and 'Motivation', both of which contribute significantly.

B-weights are hard to interpret since they are dependent on the scale of measurement involved. Beta weights are analogous to correlation coefficients. Both beta weights are positive so there is a positive relation between each predictor and the dependent variable. Ability has a correlation of 0.649 with 'Achievement', and 'Motivation' contributes an additional independent correlation of 0.164 with 'Achievement'.

The *t*-values plus their corresponding 'Sig.' values indicates that the two independent variables contribute significantly to the prediction.

- Beta is 0.649 for the first predictor ('Ability') and 0.164 for the second predictor ('Motivation').
- The analysis stops at this point, as the third predictor ('Interest') does not explain a further significant proportion of the criterion variance. Notice that in the final table of the output entitled 'Excluded Variables', 'Interest' has a *t*-value of 0.000 and a significance level of 1.0000. This tells us that 'Interest' is a non-significant predictor of the criterion ('Achievement').

28.3 Reporting the output

- There are various ways of reporting the results of a stepwise multiple regression analysis. In such a report we should include the following kind of statement. 'In the stepwise multiple regression, intellectual ability was entered first and explained 49% of the variance in educational achievement ($F_{1,118} = 113.76$, $p < 0.001$). School motivation was entered second and explained a further 2% ($F_{1,117} = 5.85$, $p = 0.017$).

Greater educational attainment was associated with greater intellectual ability and school motivation.'

■ A table is sometimes presented. There is no standard way of doing this, but Table 28.2 is probably as clear as most.

Table 28.2   Stepwise multiple regression of predictors of educational achievement (only significant predictors are included)

Variable	Multiple R	B	Standard error b	Beta	t	Significance of t
Intellectual ability	0.70	0.83	0.09	0.65	9.56	0.001
School motivation	0.72	0.17	0.07	0.16	2.42	0.05

29 Hierarchical multiple regression

Overview

- Hierarchical multiple regression allows the researcher to decide which order to use for a list of predictors.

- This is achieved by putting the predictors or groups of predictors into blocks of variables. The computer will carry out the regression taking each block in the order that it was entered into SPSS. So it provides a way of forcing the variables to be considered in the sequence chosen by the researcher. Rather than let the computer decide on statistical criteria as in the previous chapter, the researcher decides which should be the first predictor, the second predictor, and so forth.

- A block may be a single predictor or it may be a group of predictors. The order in which variables are put in a block does not matter as they are treated altogether as a group.

- This order of the blocks is likely to be chosen on theoretical grounds. One common procedure is to put variables which need to be statistically controlled in the first block. The consequence of this is that the control variables are partialled out before the rest of the blocks are analysed.

- Since the researcher is trying to produce models of the data, the multiple regression may be varied to example the effects of, say, entering the blocks in a different order.

- Hierarchical multiple regression is used to calculate the path coefficients in a simple path analysis.

The computation of a hierarchical multiple-regression analysis is illustrated with the data shown in Table 29.1, which consist of scores for six individuals on the four variables of educational achievement, intellectual ability, school motivation and parental interest.

We have added a further variable, social class, which is on a scale of 1 to 5, with 5 being the highest social class. Hierarchical analysis is used when variables are entered in an order predetermined by the researcher on a 'theoretical' basis rather than in terms of statistical criteria. This is done by ordering the independent variables in terms of blocks of the independent variables, called 'Block 1', 'Block 2', etc. A block may consist of just

Table 29.1   Data for hierarchical multiple regression

Educational achievement	Intellectual ability	School motivation	Parental interest	Social class
1	2	1	2	2
2	2	3	1	1
2	2	3	3	5
3	4	3	2	4
3	3	4	3	3
4	3	2	2	2

one independent variable or several. In this particular analysis, we will make Block 1 social class ('Class'), which is essentially a demographic variable which we would like to control for. Block 2 will be intellectual ability ('Ability'). Block 3 will be school motivation ('Motivation') and parental interest ('Interest'). The dependent variable or criterion to be explained is educational achievement ('Achievement').

In our example, the model essentially is that educational achievement is affected by intellectual ability, which is partly determined by motivational factors such as school motivation and parental interest. Social class is being controlled for in this model since we are not regarding it as a psychological factor.

When doing a path analysis, it is often necessary to do several hierarchical multiple regressions. One re-does the hierarchical multiple regression using different blocks and in different orders so that various models of the interrelationships can be explored.

29.1 Hierarchical multiple-regression analysis

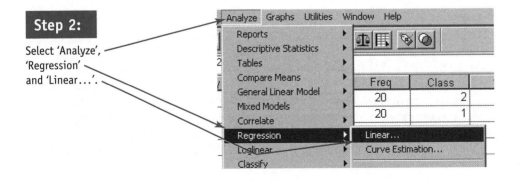

Step 1:

Select the data file if you saved it. Otherwise enter the data. A fifth variable, 'Class', has been put in the sixth column.

	Achievement	Ability	Motivation	Interest	Freq	Class
1	1	2	1	2	20	2
2	2	2	3	1	20	1
3	2	2	3	3	20	5
4	3	4	3	2	20	4
5	3	3	4	3	20	3
6	4	3	2	2	20	2
7						

Step 2:

Select 'Analyze', 'Regression' and 'Linear...'.

Analyze   Graphs   Utilities   Window   Help

Reports
Descriptive Statistics
Tables
Compare Means
General Linear Model
Mixed Models
Correlate
Regression   ▶   Linear...
Loglinear   Curve Estimation...
Classify

Freq	Class
20	2
20	1

Step 3:

Select 'Achievement' and the ▶ button beside the 'Dependent:' box to put it there.

Select 'Class' and the ▶ button beside the 'Independent(s):' box to put it there.

Select 'Next'.

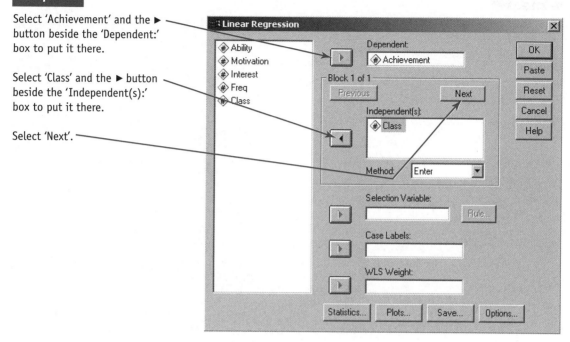

Step 4:

Select 'Ability' and the ▶ button beside the 'Independent(s):' box to put it there.

Note this is 'Block 2 of 2'.

Select 'Next'.

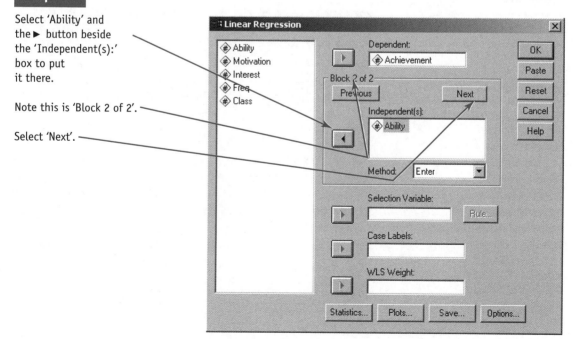

Step 5:

Select 'Motivation' and 'Interest' and the ▶ button beside the 'Independent(s):' box to put them there.

Select 'Statistics'.

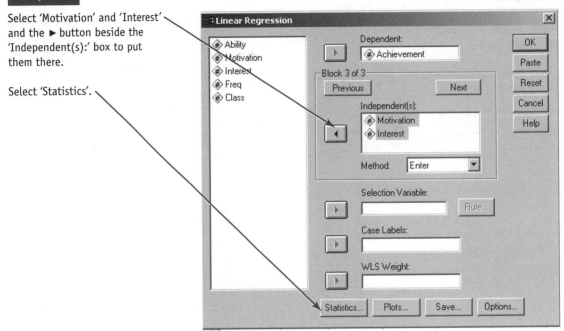

Step 6:

Select 'R squared change'.

Select 'Continue'.

Select 'OK' from the previous screen, which reappears.

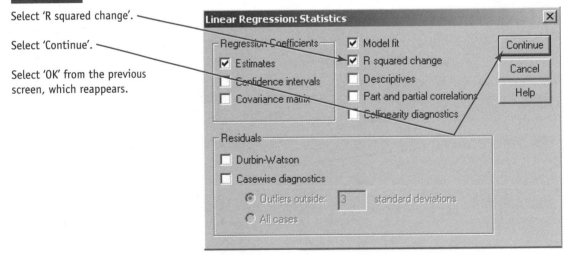

29.2   Interpreting the output

■ As summarised in the second table of the output entitled 'Model Summary', the variable entered on the first block is 'Class' (social class). The R-square for this block is effectively 0.0 (0.004), which means that social class explains 0% of the variance of educational achievement.

Model Summary

Model	R	R Square	Adjusted R Square	Std. Error of the Estimate	Change Statistics				
					R Square Change	F Change	df1	df2	Sig. F Change
1	.065[a]	.004	−.004	.963	.004	.497	1	118	.482
2	.714[b]	.509	.501	.679	.505	120.333	1	117	.000
3	.769[c]	.591	.577	.626	.082	11.500	2	115	.000

a. Predictors: (Constant), Class
b. Predictors: (Constant), Class, Ability
c. Predictors: (Constant), Class, Ability, Motivation, Interest

■ The statistical significance of the F-ratio of 0.497 for this block or model is 0.482. As this value is above the critical value of 0.05, this means that the regression equation at this first stage does not explain a significant proportion of the variance in educational achievement.

■ The variable entered on the second block is 'Ability' (intellectual ability). The adjusted R-square for this block or model is 0.501, which means that intellectual ability together with social class explain 50.1% of the variance of educational achievement.

■ The statistical significance of the F-ratio for this block is 0.000 which means that it is less than 0.001. As this value is much lower than the critical value of 0.05, the first two steps of the regression equation explain a significant proportion of the variance in educational achievement.

■ The variables entered on the third and final block are 'Motivation' (school motivation) and 'Interest' (parental interest). The adjusted R-square for this block is 0.557, which means that all four variables explain 55.7% of the variance of educational achievement.

■ The F-ratio for this block is 0.000. As this value is much lower than the critical value of 0.05, the first three steps in the regression equation explain a significant proportion of the variance in educational achievement.

■ The simplest interpretation of the output comes from examining the fourth table entitled 'Coefficients' of the output. Especially useful are the 'Beta' column and the 'Sig.' (of t) column. These tell us that the correlation (beta) between 'Class' (social class) and 'Achievement' (educational achievement) is −0.439 when the other predictors are taken into account. This correlation is significant at the 0.000 level which means that it is less than 0.001. This coefficient is now significant because the two variables of 'Ability' and 'Interest' suppress the zero-order coefficient between 'Class' and 'Achievement'. Having controlled for social class in Block 1, the correlation between 'Ability' (intellectual ability) and 'Achievement' (educational achievement) is 0.730. This is also significant at the 0.000 level. Finally, having controlled for

'Class' (social class) and 'Ability' (intellectual ability), the correlations for each of the variables in Block 3 (school motivation and parental interest) with educational achievement ('Achievement') are given separately.

Coefficients[a]

Model		Unstandardized Coefficients		Standardized Coefficients		
		B	Std. Error	Beta	t	Sig.
1	(Constant)	2.369	.205		11.543	.000
	Class	.046	.065	.065	.705	.482
2	(Constant)	.250	.241		1.036	.302
	Class	−.100	.048	−.140	−2.082	.040
	Ability	.950	.087	.740	10.970	.000
3	(Constant)	−.562	.284		−1.984	.050
	Class	−.313	.068	−.439	−4.615	.000
	Ability	.938	.084	.730	11.180	.000
	Motivation	.187	.068	.185	2.769	.007
	Interest	.438	.130	.314	3.374	.001

a. Dependent Variable : Achievement

The quickest way to access the output is to concentrate on the third model in the above data. The output indicates that when 'Class', 'Ability', 'Motivation' and 'Interest' are all entered that each has a significant association with the dependent variable 'Achievement'. Class has a negative relationship whereas the others have a positive one.

29.3 Reporting the output

■ There are various ways of reporting the results of a hierarchical multiple-regression analysis. In such a report we would normally describe the percentage of variance explained by each set or block of predictors (from the value of the R-square).

■ One way of reporting these results is to state that: 'In a hierarchical multiple regression, potential predictors of achievement were entered in blocks. Social class was entered first, then intellectual ability was added in the second block, and school motivation and parental interest were added in the final block. The final model indicated that social class was a negative predictor ($B = -0.31$), intellectual ability was a positive predictor $B = 0.94$), and school motivation and parental interest were also positive predictors ($B = 0.19$ and 0.44). All predictors were significant at the 1% level.'

■ One would also need to summarise the regression equation as in Table 29.2.

Table 29.2   Hierarchical multiple regression of predictors of educational achievement

Blocks	B	Standard error B	Beta
Block 1			
Social class	−0.31	0.07	−0.44*
Block 2			
Intellectual ability	0.94	0.08	0.73*
Block 3			
School motivation	0.19	0.07	0.19*
Parental interest	0.44	0.13	0.31*

* Significant at 0.01.

30 Item reliability and inter-rater agreement

Overview

- Reliability is a complex matter, as the term refers to a range of very different concepts and measures. It is easy to confuse them.

- Item alpha reliability and split-half reliability assess the internal consistency of the items in a questionnaire – that is, do the items tend to be measuring much the same thing?

- Split-half reliability on SPSS refers to the correlation between scores based on the first half of items you list for inclusion and the second half of the items. This correlation can be adjusted statistically to maintain the original questionnaire length.

- Coefficient alpha is merely the average of all possible split-half reliabilities for the questionnaire and so may be preferred, as it is not dependent on how the items are ordered. Coefficient alpha can be used as a means of shortening a questionnaire while maintaining or improving its internal reliability.

- Inter-rater reliability (here assessed by kappa) is essentially a measure of agreement between the ratings of two different raters. Thus it is particularly useful for assessing codings or ratings by 'experts' of aspects of open-ended data; in other words, the quantification of qualitative data. It involves the extent of exact agreement between raters on their ratings compared to what agreement would be expected by chance. Note then that it is different from the correlation between raters, which does not require *exact* agreement to achieve high correlations but merely that the ratings increase relatively for both raters.

- Other forms of reliability, such as the consistency of a measure taken at two different points in time (test–retest reliability), could be assessed simply using the correlation coefficient (Chapter 7).

30.1 Item alpha reliability

The answers of 10 people to the four items of a questionnaire are shown in Table 30.1. These data will be used to illustrate two measures of item reliability known as alpha reliability and split-half reliability.

Table 30.1 Data for 10 cases from a four-item questionnaire

Cases	Item 1	Item 2	Item 3	Item 4
1	1	3	5	6
2	2	1	1	2
3	1	1	1	1
4	5	2	4	2
5	6	4	3	2
6	5	4	5	6
7	4	5	3	2
8	2	1	2	1
9	1	2	1	1
10	1	1	2	2

Step 1:

Enter the data.

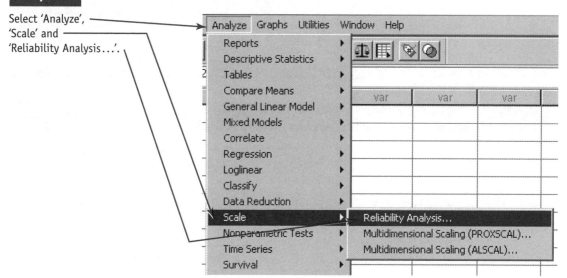

Step 2:

Select 'Analyze',
'Scale' and
'Reliability Analysis...'.

Step 3:

Select the four items singly or together and the ► button to put them in the 'Items:' box.

Select 'Statistics...'.

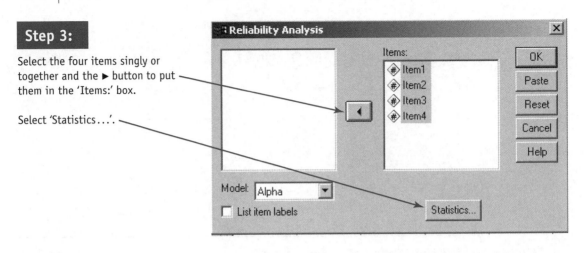

Step 4:

Select 'Scale if item deleted'.

Select 'Continue'.

Select 'OK' from the previous screen, which reappears.

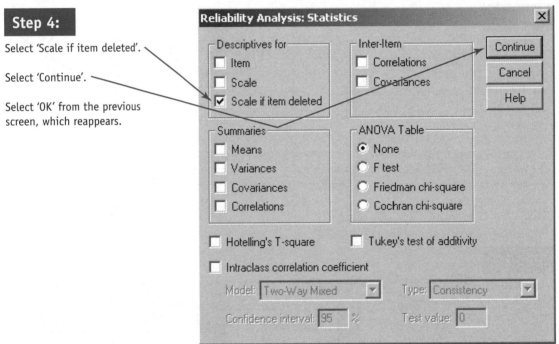

30.2 Interpreting the output

Case Processing Summary

		N	%
Cases	Valid	10	100.0
	Excluded[a]	0	.0
	Total	10	100.0

The first table shows the number of cases on which the analysis is based, that is 10.

a. Listwise deletion based on all variables in the procedure.

The second table shows the alpha reliability of the four items and is 0.811, which rounded to two decimal places is 0.81.

Reliability Statistics

Cronbach's Alpha	N of Items
.811	4

Item-Total Statistics

	Scale Mean if Item Deleted	Scale Variance if Item Deleted	Corrected Item-Total Correlation	Cronbach's Alpha if Item Deleted
Item 1	7.60	18.933	.490	.840
Item 2	8.00	19.556	.718	.731
Item 3	7.70	17.789	.842	.671
Item 4	7.90	18.767	.547	.806

This is the alpha reliability of scale with one of the items dropped. From this column we can see that if we remove the first item ('Item 1'), the alpha reliability of the remaining three items of the scale increases slightly to 0.840 from 0.811. Since this is a very small change, Item 1 is probably best retained.

30.3 Reporting the output

One way of reporting the results of this analysis is as follows: 'The alpha reliability of the four item scale was 0.81, indicating that the scale had good reliability.' An alpha of 0.80 or above is considered satisfactory.

30.4 Split-half reliability

The previous data are reused for this analysis.

Select the ▼ button in the 'Model:' window and 'Split-half'.

Select 'OK'.

(De-select 'Scale if item deleted' in 'Statistics...' if you wish.)

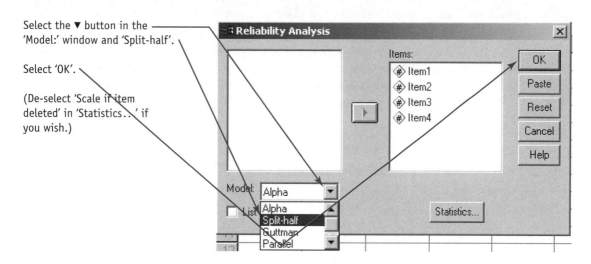

30.5 Interpreting the output

The last line of the second table shows the (Guttman) split reliability of the four items as 0.646, which rounded to two decimal places is 0.65.

Reliability Statistics

Cronbach's Alpha	Part 1	Value	.777
		N of Items	2[a]
	Part 2	Value	.904
		N of Items	2[b]
	Total N of Items		4
Correlation Between Forms			.477
Spearman-Brown	Equal Length		.646
Coefficient	Unequal Length		.646
Guttman Split-Half Coefficient			.646

a. The items are: Item 1, Item 2.
b. The items are: Item 3, Item 4.

30.6 Reporting the output

One way of reporting the results of this analysis is as follows: 'The split-half reliability of the four-item scale was 0.65, indicating that the scale had only moderate reliability.'

30.7 Inter-rater agreement (kappa)

Kappa is used to measure the agreement between two raters, taking into account the amount of agreement that would be expected by chance. We will illustrate its computation for the data in Table 30.2, which shows the ratings by a forensic psychologist and a psychiatrist of 12 sex offenders in terms of the offenders being no risk (1), a moderate risk (2) or a high risk (3) to the public.

Table 30.2   Ratings of risk by two professionals of 12 offenders

Sex offenders	Forensic psychologist	Psychiatrist
1	3	3
2	3	3
3	3	3
4	1	1
5	1	2
6	3	3
7	2	3
8	3	3
9	2	3
10	3	3
11	3	3
12	3	3

Step 1:

Enter the data.

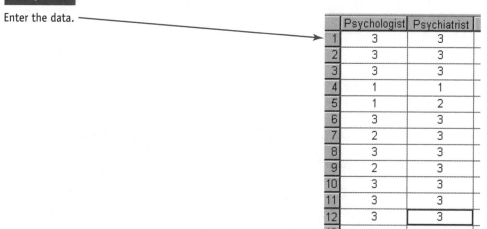

Step 2:

Select 'Analyze', 'Descriptive Statistics' and 'Crosstabs…'.

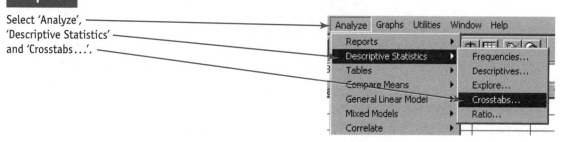

Step 3:

Select 'Psychologist' and the ▶
button beside 'Row(s):'
to put it there.

Select 'Psychiatrist' and the ▶
button beside 'Column(s):'
to put it there.

Select 'Statistics...'.

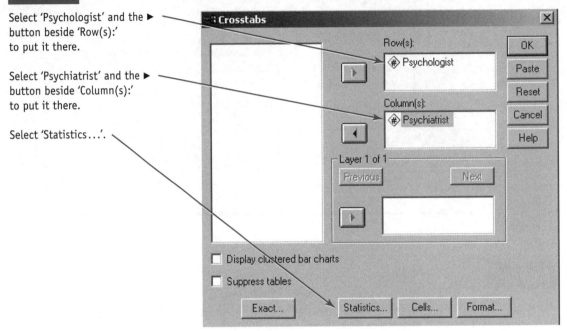

Step 4:

Select 'Kappa'.

Select 'Continue'.

Select 'OK' from the
previous screen, which
reappears.

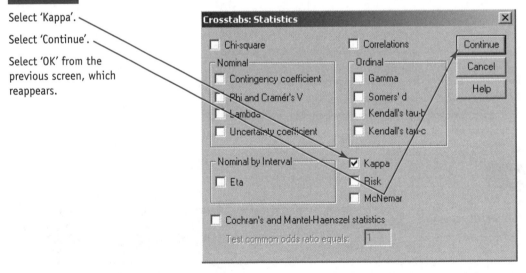

30.8   Interpreting the output

In the second table of the output the data have been arranged into a 2 × 2 contingency. The number of cases on which the forensic psychologist and the psychiatrist agree are shown in the diagonal cells of this table. They are 1 for the rating of 1, 0 for the rating of 2 and 8 for the rating of 3.

Psychologist * Psychiatrist Crosstabulation

Count

		Psychiatrist			
		1	2	3	Total
Psychologist	1	1	1	0	2
	2	0	0	2	2
	3	0	0	8	8
Total		1	1	10	12

In the third table kappa is shown as 0.400. Although kappa is statistically significant with $p = 0.046$, it indicates only moderate agreement.

Symmetric Measures

	Value	Asymp. Std. Error[a]	Approx. T[b]	Approx. Sig.
Measure of Agreement Kappa	.400	.219	2.000	.046
N of Valid Cases	12			

a. Not assuming the null hypothesis.
b. Using the asymptotic standard error assuming the null hypothesis.

Note that kappa allows for raters tending to use the same ratings most of the time. It is *not* a measure of percentage agreement.

30.9   Reporting the output

One way of reporting the results of this analysis is as follows: 'Kappa for the agreement between the ratings of the forensic psychologist and the psychiatrist was 0.40, which indicates only moderate agreement.'

31 Log-linear analysis

Overview

■ Log-linear analysis is used to analyse contingency tables consisting of three or more variables. It can therefore be regarded as an extension of the chi-square test discussed in Chapter 14.

■ Its purpose is to determine which of the variables and their interactions best explain (or reproduce) the observed frequencies in the table. Variables and their interactions on their own and in combination are known as models.

■ Goodness-of-fit test statistics are used to assess the degree of correspondence between the model and the data. Statistical significance indicates that the model being examined fails to account totally for the observed frequencies. Statistical non-significance means that the model being analysed fits the observed frequencies. If more than one model fits the data well, the model having the fewer or fewest variables and interactions is the simplest one and may be the preferred model. Likelihood ratio chi-square is employed as the test statistic.

The computation of a log-linear analysis is illustrated with the data in Table 31.1. This table shows the frequency of sexual and physical abuse in 140 female and 160 male psychiatric patients. To analyse a table of data like this one with SPSS we first have to input the data into the Data Editor and weight the cells by the frequencies of cases in them.

Table 31.1 A three-way contingency showing the relationship between sex, sexual abuse and physical abuse in a sample of psychiatric hospital patients

Sexual abuse	Physical abuse	Sex		Margin totals
		Female	Male	
Sexually abused	Physical abuse	20	30	50
	No physical	40	25	65
Not sexually abused	Physical abuse	35	55	90
	No physical	45	50	95
Margin totals		140	160	300

31.1 Log-linear analysis

Step 1:

Enter the data.
Weight the cases by 'Freq'.

	Sexual	Physical	Sex	Freq
1	1	1	1	20
2	1	1	2	30
3	1	2	1	40
4	1	2	2	25
5	2	1	1	35
6	2	1	2	55
7	2	2	1	45
8	2	2	2	50
9				

Step 2:

Select 'Analyze', 'Loglinear' and 'Model Selection...'.

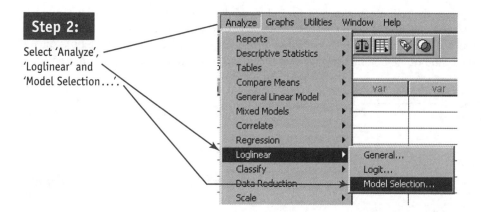

Analyze	Graphs	Utilities	Window	Help
Reports	▶			
Descriptive Statistics	▶			
Tables	▶			
Compare Means	▶		var	var
General Linear Model	▶			
Mixed Models	▶			
Correlate	▶			
Regression	▶			
Loglinear	▶	General...		
Classify	▶	Logit...		
Data Reduction	▶	Model Selection...		
Scale	▶			

Step 3:

Select singly or together 'Sexual', 'Physical' and 'Sex' and ▶ the button beside the 'Factor(s):' box to put them there.

Select 'Define Range'. As all three variables have the same range, they can be defined at the same time.

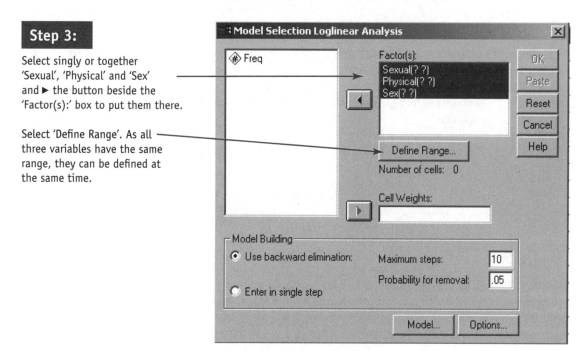

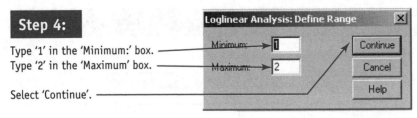

Step 4:

Type '1' in the 'Minimum:' box. ——

Type '2' in the 'Maximum' box. ——

Select 'Continue'. ——

Select 'OK' from the previous
screen, which reappears.

31.2 Interpreting the output

To display the full output shown below, click on the output in the Viewer window which
creates a frame around the output. The down-pointing arrow at the lower left corner of the
output indicates that there is more output to be viewed. Put the cursor on the little square
in the centre of the bottom fine and drag this line down until all the output is presented.

Click in the output away
from the margins to produce
the outline.

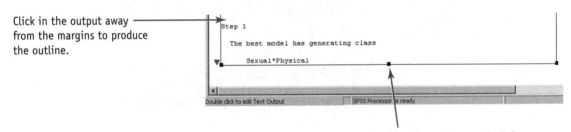

Move the cursor here, depress the left
key of the mouse and drag the line
downward until you reach the end of
the output. This takes a little practice.

Extensive output is revealed by this. Mostly it is best ignored. The final model is the most
important.

```
********** HIERARCHICAL LOG LINEAR **********
DATA    Information
          8 unweighted cases accepted.
          0 cases rejected because of out-of-range factor values.
          0 cases rejected because of missing data.
        300 weighted cases will be used in the analysis.
FACTOR    Information
    Factor    Level Label
    SEXUAL        2 Sexual abuse
    PHYSICAL      2 Physical abuse
    SEX           2 Sex
********** HIERARCHICAL LOG LINEAR **********
```

DESIGN 1 has generating class
   SEXUAL*PHYSICAL*SEX
  Note: For saturated models .500 has been added to all observed
  cells.
  This value may be changed by using the CRITERIA = DELTA subcommand.
The Iterative Proportional Fit algorithm converged at iteration 1.
The maximum difference between observed and fitted marginal totals is
.000 and the convergence criterion is .250

Observed, Expected Frequencies and Residuals.

Factor	Code	OBS count	EXP count	Residual	Std Resid
SEXUAL	Sexually				
PHYSICAL	Physical				
SEX	Females	20.5	20.5	.00	.00
SEX	Males	30.5	30.5	.00	.00
PHYSICAL	Not phys				
SEX	Females	40.5	40.5	.00	.00
SEX	Males	25.5	25.5	.00	.00
SEXUAL	Not sexu				
PHYSICAL	Physical				
SEX	Females	35.5	35.5	.00	.00
SEX	Males	55.5	55.5	.00	.00
PHYSICAL	Not phys				
SEX	Females	45.5	45.5	.00	.00
SEX	Males	50.5	50.5	.00	.00

Goodness-of-fit test statistics
 Likelihood ratio chi square =   .00000   DF = 0   P = 1.000
         Pearson chi square =   .00000   DF = 0   P = 1.000

*********** HIERARCHICAL LOG LINEAR ***********
Tests that K-way and higher order effects are zero.

K	DF	L.R. Chisq	Prob	Pearson Chisq	Prob	Iteration
3	1	1.185	.2764	1.181	.2772	3
2	4	9.680	.0462	10.013	.0402	2
1	7	28.834	.0002	28.000	.0002	0

Tests that K-way effects are zero.

K	DF	L.R. Chisq	Prob	Pearson Chisq	Prob	Iteration
1	3	19.154	.0003	17.987	.0004	0
2	3	8.495	.0368	8.833	.0316	0
3	1	1.185	.2764	1.181	.2772	0

*********** HIERARCHICAL LOG LINEAR **********
Backward Elimination (p = .050) for DESIGN 1 with generating class
   SEXUAL*PHYSICAL*SEX
 Likelihood ratio chi square =   .00000   DF = 0   P = 1.000

```
-----------------------------------------------------------------------
If Deleted Simple Effect is   DF    L.R. Chisq Change      Prob      Iter
  SEXUAL*PHYSICAL*SEX          1                 1.185     .2674        3
Step 1
 The best model has generating class
     SEXUAL*PHYSICAL
     SEXUAL*SEX
     PHYSICAL*SEX
Likelihood ratio chi square =    1.18471    DF = 1    P = .276
-----------------------------------------------------------------------
If Deleted Simple Effect is   DF    L.R. Chisq Change      Prob      Iter
  SEXUAL*PHYSICAL*SEX          1                  .454     .5005        2
  SEXUAL*SEX                   1                 1.963     .1612        2
  PHYSICAL*SEX                 1                 5.461     .0194        2
Step 2
 The best model has generating class
     SEXUAL*SEX
     PHYSICAL*SEX
Likelihood ratio chi square =    1.63849    DF = 2    P = .441
-----------------------------------------------------------------------
If Deleted Simple Effect is   DF    L.R. Chisq Change      Prob      Iter
  SEXUAL*SEX                   1                 2.272     .1317        2
  PHYSICAL*SEX                 1                 5.770     .0163        2
*********** HIERARCHICAL LOG LINEAR **********
Step 3
 The best model has generating class
     PHYSICAL*SEX
     SEXUAL
Likelihood ratio chi square =    3.91036    DF = 3    P = .271
-----------------------------------------------------------------------
```

```
┌──────────────────────────────────────────────────────────────┐
│ If Deleted Simple Effect is   DF    L.R. Chisq Change   Prob  │ Iter
│   PHYSICAL*SEX                 1                 5.770   .0163 │   2
│   SEXUAL                       1                16.485   .0000 │   2
└──────────────────────────────────────────────────────────────┘
```

```
 Step 4
 The best model has generating class
     PHYSICAL*SEX
     SEXUAL
Likelihood ratio chi square =    3.91036    DF = 3    P = .271
```

```
***********HIERARCHICAL LOG LINEAR ***********
The final model has generating class
    PHYSICAL*SEX
    SEXUAL
```

This is the final model. Below are the counts or frequencies for the data plus the expected frequencies under this model. The residuals are just the differences between the data and the data predicted by the model.

```
The Iterative Proportional Fit algorithm converged at iteration 0.
The maximum difference between observed and fitted marginal totals is
.000 and the convergence criterion is .250
```

Observed, Expected Frequencies and Residuals.

Factor	Code	OBS count	EXP count	Residual	Std Resid
SEXUAL	Sexually				
PHYSICAL	Physical				
SEX	Females	20.0	21.1	-1.08	-.24
SEX	Males	30.0	32.6	-2.58	-.45
PHYSICAL	Not phys				
SEX	Females	40.0	32.6	7.42	1.30
SEX	Males	25.0	28.8	-3.75	-.70
SEXUAL	Not sexu				
PHYSICAL	Physical				
SEX	Females	35.0	35.9	1.08	.19
SEX	Males	55.0	52.4	2.58	.36
PHYSICAL	Not phys				
SEX	Females	45.0	52.4	-7.42	-1.02
SEX	Males	50.0	46.3	3.75	.55

```
Goodness-of-fit test statistics
   Likelihood ratio chi square =    3.91036    DF = 3    P = .271
              Pearson chi square =    3.95320    DF = 3    P = .267
```

- There are two statistics used to test the goodness-of-fit of the various models. These are the likelihood ratio chi-square and Pearson chi-square. The likelihood ratio chi-square is the test more commonly used because it has the advantage of being linear so chi-square values may be added or subtracted.

- The likelihood ratio chi-square for the saturated or full model is presented first and is 0.00000 which has a probability of 1.000. In other words, the saturated model provides a perfect fit for the observed frequencies and so is non-significant. The saturated model in this case consists of the three main effects, three two-way interactions and one three-way interaction. In general, the saturated model includes all main effects and interactions.

- However, the saturated model includes *all* components whether or not they individually contribute to explaining the variation in the observed data. So it is necessary to eliminate components in turn to see whether this makes the model's fit worse. If it does, this component of the model is kept for the final model.

- SPSS begins with the full model and eliminates each effect in turn to determine which effects make the least significant change in the likelihood ratio chi-square.

■ The best-fitting model is presented last. In our example, this includes the interaction of physical abuse and sex and the main effect of sexual abuse. This model has a likelihood ratio chi-square of 3.91 (rounded to two decimal places), 2 degrees of freedom and a probability level of 0.271. In other words, it is not significant which means that the observed data can be reproduced with these two effects.

■ To interpret these two effects, we need to present the data in terms of a one-way table for sexual abuse and a two-way table for physical abuse and sex. We can do this using chi-square . . . for the one-way table and Crosstabs . . . for the two-way table. These two tables are shown below. The one-way table shows that more psychiatric patients have not been sexually abused than have been sexually abused. The two-way table indicates that males are more likely to be physically abused than females.

Physical abuse * Sex Crosstabulation

			Sex		Total
			Females	Males	
Physical abuse	Physically abused	Count	55	85	140
		Expected Count	65.3	74.7	140.0
		Residual	−10.3	10.3	
	Not physically abused	Count	85	75	160
		Expected Count	74.7	85.3	160.0
		Residual	10.3	−10.3	
Total		Count	140	160	300
		Expected Count	140.0	160.0	300.0

Sexual abuse

	Observed N	Expected N	Residual
Sexually abused	115	150.0	−35.0
Not sexually abused	185	150.0	35.0
Total	300		

■ It is possible to see the contribution of each component to the final model. Just before the final step (Step 4 in this example), there is a small table headed 'If Deleted Simple Effect is'. This contains a column called 'L.R. Chisq Change'. These entries essentially indicate the change (reduction) in the goodness-of-fit chi-square if each component is taken away. Thus 'PHYSICAL*SEX' has a L.R. Chi-Square Change of 5.770 which is significant (0.0163). 'SEXUAL' has a value of 16.485 which is very significant (0.0000). Obviously these two effects cannot be eliminated from the model because of their significant contribution.

■ In a hierarchical model, components of an interaction may be significant. Since 'PHYSICAL*SEX' has a significant contribution to the model, 'PHYSICAL' and 'SEX' may themselves be significant main effects. Select 'Model' in the 'Model' Selection Loglinear Analysis dialog box (Step 3 in Section 31.1). The window that appears will allow you to test these main effects by stipulating models containing only these particular main effects.

31.3   Reporting the results

One way of describing the results found here is as follows: 'A three-way frequency analysis was performed to develop a hierarchical linear model of physical and sexual abuse in female and male psychiatric patients. Backward elimination produced a model that included the main effect of sexual abuse and the interaction effect of physical abuse and sex. The model had a likelihood ratio $\chi^2(3) = 3.91$, $p = 0.27$, indicating a good fit between the observed frequencies and the expected frequencies generated by the model. About 38% of the psychiatric patients had been sexually abused. About 53% of the males had been physically abused compared with about 39% of the females.'

32 Multinomial logistic regression

Overview

- Logistic regression is a form of multiple regression (see Chapter 28). It identifies the variables which collectively distinguish cases which belong to different categories of a nominal (or category variable). For example, it could be used to identify the differentiating characteristics of psychology, sociology and physics students.

- Put another way, logistic regression identifies groups of variables that accurately classify people according to their membership of the different categories of a nominal variable.

- Binomial logistic regression is used if there are just two categories of the variable to be predicted. This is dealt with in Chapter 33. Multinomial logistic regression is used if there are three or more categories.

- The predictors (i.e. the independent variables) may be score variables, nominal (category or categorical) variables, or a mixture of both.

- The best predictors of which category a case belongs to have significant *b*-weights (or regression weights). This is much the same as for the more familiar multiple-regression procedures described in Chapter 28.

- The *b*-weights in logistic regression are actually applied to the natural logarithm of something termed the *odds ratio*, which is the ratio of the frequencies for two alternative outcomes. This logarithm is also known as the *logit*. Hence the term logistic regression. The odds ratio is simply the likelihood of being in one category rather than any of the other categories. There is little need for most researchers to calculate these values themselves so the logit is mainly of conceptual rather than practical importance.

- It is more important to understand the concept of *dummy variable*. This is a device by which a nominal variable may be dealt with numerically. If the nominal variable has just *two* categories then these may be coded numerically as 0 and 1.

- However, if the nominal category has *three* or more categories then the process is slightly more complex. Essentially, the data are coded for the presence or absence of each of the *three* (or more) categories. In effect, three (or more) new variables are created. So if the three categories are called A, B and C, three new variables are created:
  (i)   The individual is in Category A (or not).
  (ii) The individual is in Category B (or not).
  (iii) The individual is in Category C (or not).
  Each of these three variables is a different dummy variable.

■ However, one dummy variable from the set is always excluded from the analysis. It does not matter which one. The reason is that this dummy variable contains no new information which is not contained in the other dummy variables.

■ SPSS will generate dummy variables automatically for the dependent variable but needs to be informed which of the predictor variables are nominal (category variables).

■ Classification tables are generated by SPSS which indicate the prediction of category membership based on the predictor variables. This is a good indication of how good the prediction is because the number of correct classifications is indicated.

■ Logistic regression analyses contain numerous goodness-of-fit statistics based on chi-square. These serve a number of functions, but most importantly they indicate the improvement in fit of the predicted category membership to the actual category membership. A useful predictor should improve the fit of the predicted membership to the actual categories cases belong to.

■ Multinomial logistic regression must be used when there are three or more categories for the dependent (predicted or criterion) variable. If there are just *two* categories for the dependent variable, then binomial logistic regression is normally used (see Chapter 33).

The use of multinomial logistic regression can be illustrated using the data described in Table 32.1 (*ISP*, Table 36.2). These data are from a fictitious study of the differences

Table 32.1   Data for multinomial logistic regression

	Age	DAS	Mother hostile	Father hostile	Children's home	Physical abuse	Sexual abuse	Type of offence
1	younger	low	high	low	no	yes	no	rapist
2	younger	low	high	low	no	yes	yes	rapist
3	older	low	high	low	no	yes	yes	rapist
4	older	high	high	high	yes	no	no	incest
5	older	high	high	high	yes	yes	yes	rapist
6	younger	low	high	low	no	no	no	rapist
7	older	high	low	high	no	yes	yes	rapist
8	older	high	low	high	yes	no	no	incest
9	younger	low	low	high	yes	no	yes	incest
10	older	high	high	low	no	yes	yes	incest
11	older	high	low	low	yes	no	yes	incest
12	younger	high	low	high	no	yes	no	rapist
13	older	high	low	high	yes	no	yes	incest
14	older	high	high	low	yes	yes	yes	incest
15	older	low	high	high	no	yes	yes	incest
16	younger	high	high	low	yes	no	no	paedophile
17	older	high	low	high	yes	no	yes	paedophile
18	older	low	high	high	no	no	yes	paedophile
19	younger	high	low	high	yes	yes	yes	paedophile
20	older	low	low	high	yes	no	no	paedophile
etc.								

between rapists, incestuous sex offenders and paedophiles. This means that the categories of offender equate to a nominal or category variable with three different values. In this example all of the predictor variables – age, DAS (depression, anxiety and stress scale) mother hostile, father hostile, children's home, physical abuse and sexual abuse – are nominal (category) variables with just two different values in each case. It must be stressed that any type of variable may be used as a predictor in multinomial logistic regression. However, the researcher needs to indicate which are score variables in the analysis.

32.1 Entering the data

These data are entered into SPSS in the usual way with each variable being represented by a column. For learning purposes, the data have been repeated 10 times in order to have a realistic data set for the analysis, but to limit the labour of those who wish to reproduce the analysis exactly.

Enter the data.

Weight the cases with 'freq'.

	age	das	motherhs	fatherhs	childhom	physabus	sexualab	typoff	freq	var
1	1	1	2	1	2	1	2	1	10	
2	1	1	2	1	2	1	1	1	10	
3	2	1	2	1	2	1	1	1	10	
4	2	2	2	2	1	2	2	2	10	
5	2	2	2	2	1	1	1	1	10	
6	1	1	2	1	2	2	2	1	10	
7	2	2	1	2	2	1	1	1	10	
8	2	2	1	2	1	2	2	2	10	
9	1	1	1	2	1	2	1	2	10	
10	2	2	2	1	2	1	1	2	10	
11	2	2	1	1	1	2	1	2	10	
12	1	2	1	2	2	1	2	1	10	
13	2	2	1	2	1	2	1	2	10	
14	2	2	2	1	1	1	1	2	10	
15	2	1	2	2	2	1	1	2	10	
16	1	2	2	1	1	2	2	3	10	
17	2	2	1	2	1	2	1	3	10	
18	2	1	2	2	2	2	1	3	10	
19	1	2	1	2	1	1	1	3	10	
20	2	1	1	2	1	2	2	3	10	
21										

In *all* multinomial logistic regression analyses, dummy variables are created by SPSS. This is always the case for the predicted variable (offence type in this case), but there may be also nominal (category) predictor variables with more than two categories. If this is the case, SPSS generates new variables (dummy variables) for inclusion in the analysis. So do not be surprised to find variables reported in the output which were not part of the data input. SPSS does not show the dummy variables that it creates in the data spreadsheet – they are referred to in the output, however. SPSS creates appropriate dummy variables for the dependent (criterion) variable automatically based on the number of different values (categories) of that variable. The predictor or independent variables are also dummy coded if they are defined by the researcher as being nominal (category or categorical) variables. Dummy variables are discussed in the overview at the start of this chapter and also in the accompanying statistics text (*ISP*, Chapter 36).

Until Release 12 of SPSS, multinomial logistic regression was only available in a rather unsatisfactory number of options. However, from Release 12 onwards, SPSS includes a stepwise version in which variables are selected as predictors in order of their independent predictive powers. In this guide we will analyse the data using stepwise multinomial logistic regression. The findings are slightly different in detail from those of the accompanying statistics text (*ISP*), but not substantially so.

32.2 Stepwise multinomial logistic regression

Step 1:

Select 'Analyze', 'Regression' and 'Multinomial Logistic…'.

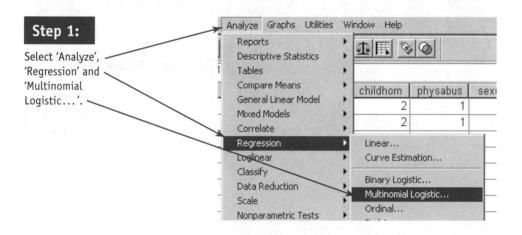

Step 2:

Select 'typoff' and the ▶ button beside the 'Dependent:' box to put it there.

Select the other seven variables either singly or together (excluding 'freq') and the ▶ button beside the 'Factor(s):' box to put them there.

Select 'Model:'.

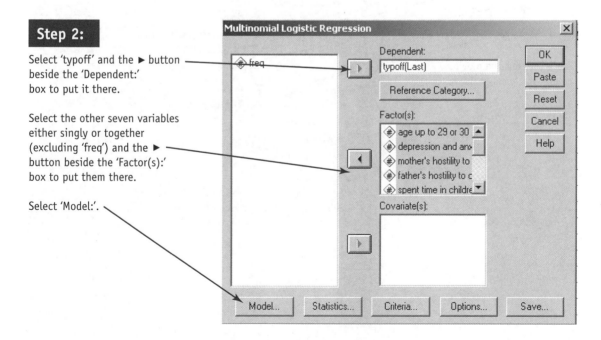

Step 3:

Select 'Custom/Stepwise'.
Select each of the seven
variables in turn and the ▶
button beside 'Stepwise
Terms:' to put them there.

Select 'Continue'.

Select 'Statistics...'
from the previous screen,
which will reappear.

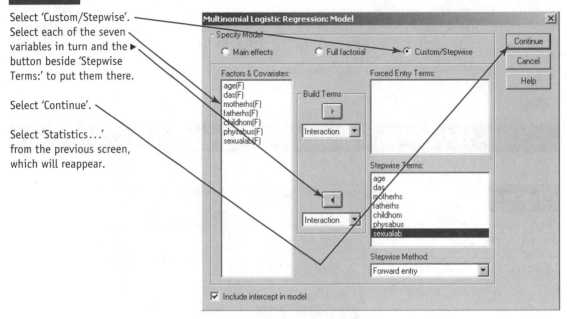

Step 4:

Select 'Cell probabilities',
'Classification table', and
'Goodness-of-fit'.

Select 'Continue'.

Select 'OK' from the previous
screen, which reappears.

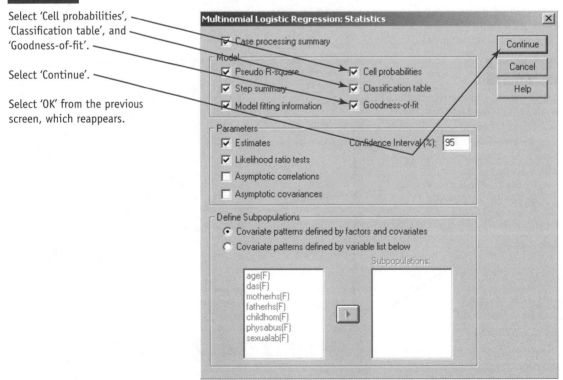

32.3 Interpreting the output

Nominal Regression

Warnings

There are 37 (64.9%) cells (i.e., dependent variable levels by subpopulations) with zero frequencies.
Stepwise procedure stopped because a numerical problem was encountered.
There is possibly a quasi-complete separation in the data. Either the maximum likelihood estimates do not exist or some parameter estimates are infinite.
The NOMREG procedure continues despite the above warning(s). Subsequent results shown are based on the last iteration of the last model fitted in stepwise procedure. Validity of the model fit is uncertain.

Case Processing Summary

		N	Marginal Percentage
type of offence	rapist	70	35.0%
	Incestuous child abuser	80	40.0%
	paedophile	50	25.0%
age up to 29 or 30 and above	younger	70	35.0%
	older	130	65.0%
depression and anxiety scale	low score	80	40.0%
	high score	120	60.0%
mother's hostility to offender as child	low hostility	90	45.0%
	high hostility	110	55.0%
father's hostility to offender as child	how hostility	80	40.0%
	high hostility	120	60.0%
spent time in children's home	yes	110	55.0%
	no	60	45.0%
physically abused as a child	yes	100	50.0%
	No	100	50.0%
Sexually abused as a child	yes	130	65.0%
	no	70	35.0%
Valid		200	100.0%
Missing		0	
Total		200	
Subpopulation		19[a]	

This table shows the distribution for each of the variables in the analysis. The offence distribution is circled.

a. The dependent variable has only one value observed in 18 (94.7%) subpopulations.

This table gives the order in which the predictor variables were selected.

The model at step 0 has no predictor variables. At step 1 the variable 'childhom' is entered. It is the best predictor available.

'Sexualab' is the last variable entered into the regression equation. The analysis proceeds no further after this in this example.

Step Summary

Model	Action	Effect(s)	−2 Log Likelihood	Chi-Square	df	Sig.
0	Entered	Intercept	407.957			
1	Entered	childhom	330.132	77.825	2	.000
2	Entered	age	300.651	29.481	2	.000
3	Entered	physabus	274.195	26.456	2	.000
4	Entered	sexualab[a]	258.708	15.487	2	.000

Stepwise Method: Forward Entry
a. Stepwise procedure stopped because a numerical problem was encountered.

Model Fitting Information

Model	−2 Log Likelihood	Chi-Square	df	Sig.
Intercept Only	407.957			
Final	258.708	149.250	8	.000

The 'Intercept Only' model includes *none* of the predictor variables. The 'Final' model is the one using the best set of predictors. Notice that there is a significant improvement in fit to the data by using the 'Final' model.

Goodness-of-Fit

	Chi-Square	df	Sig.
Pearson	240.587	28	.000
Deviance	255.236	28	.000

This table indicates how well the predicted data fit the actual data. There is a significant difference between the two – that is, the prediction is less than perfect.

Pseudo R-Square

Cox and Snell	.526
Nagelkerke	.594
McFadden	.345

This table gives three estimates of the 'multiple correlation' between the predictor variables and sex offender category membership. It is interpreted like a squared correlation coefficient. The values in this case are moderate (1.00 would indicate a perfect classification) confirming that the prediction is less than perfect.

This is a very important table which indicates whether removing each of the predictor variables from the prediction reduces significantly the fit of the prediction to the actual data. As can be seen, in this case removing any of the four predictors adversely affects the fit of the predicted data to the actual data.

Likelihood Ratio Tests

Effect	−2 Log Likelihood of Reduced Model	Chi-Square	df	Sig.
Intercept	258.708[a]	.000	0	.
age	275.878	17.170	2	.000
childhom	287.336	28.628	2	.000
physabus	298.372	39.664	2	.000
sexualab	274.195	15.487	2	.000

The chi-square statistic is the difference in −2 log-likelihoods between the final model and a reduced model. The reduced model is formed by omitting an effect from the final model. The null hypothesis is that all parameters of that effect are 0.
a. This reduced model is equivalent to the final model because omitting the effect does not increase the degrees of freedom.

This table gives the *b*-weights that the computer will use in making its predictions. The *b*-weights are useful to report, but a researcher would not need to actually do any calculations involving them.

Parameter Estimates

type of offence[a]		B	Std. Error	Wald	df	Sig.	Exp(B)	95% Confidence Interval for Exp(B) Lower Bound	Upper Bound
rapist	Intercept	.608	.660	.851	1	.356			
	[age=1]	.218	.559	.152	1	.697	1.243		
	[age=2]	0[b]	.	.	0	.	.	.416	3.718
	[childhom=1]	−2.252	.545	17.042	1	.000	.105		
	[childhom=2]	0[b]	.	.	0	.	.	.036	.306
	[physabus=1]	20.124[b]	.613	1077.1	1	.000	****		
	[physabus=2]	0	.	.	0	.	.	165110941.9	1826627708
	[sexualab=1]	−18.582	.000	.	1	.	.000		
	[sexualab=2]	0[b]	.	.	0	.	.	.000	.000
Incestuous child abuser	Intercept	.326	.565	.334	1	563			
	[age=1]	−1.533	.455	11.330	1	.001	.216		
	[age=2]	0[b]	.	.	0	.	.	.088	.527
	[childhom=1]	.122	.486	.063	1	.802	1.130		
	[childhom=2]	0[b]	.	.	0	.	.	.436	2.929
	[physabus=1]	.782	.496	2.485	1	.115	2.185		
	[physabus=2]	0[b]	.	.	0	.	.	.827	5.774
	[sexualab=1]	.299	.455	.431	1	.512	1.348		
	[sexualab=2]	0[b]	.	.	0	.	.	.552	3.291

a. The reference category is: paedophile.
b. This parameter is set to zero because it is redundant.

When interpreting the output the values of the variable should be carefully checked. The *b*-weight is −1.533 for the category 1.00 of the variable age – the other category is given a weight of 0.00. The value label 1.00 in this case means that the offender was younger. However, there is a negative value of *b*. This means that incestuous child abusers are partly distinguished from the other two groups by being older. This is a little confusing at first but is simply the way SPSS operates.

The standard error is 0.00 so the Wald value would be infinitely large. No significance level can actually be computed although this variable is highly statistically significant.

The classification table indicates in a simple form how good the prediction is. As can be seen, the predictors are very good at predicting rapists correctly (85.7% correct). The predictors do a poor job at predicting paedophiles (only 20% of paedophiles correctly identified).

Classification

Observed	Predicted rapist	Incestuous child abuser	paedophile	Percent Correct
rapist	60	10	0	85.7%
Incestuous child abuser	20	50	10	62.5%
paedophile	10	30	10	20.0%
Overall Percentage	45.0%	45.0%	10.0%	60.0%

This gives all possible combinations of the values of the predictor variables. As such, it can be used to trace the most likely predicted outcome for any combination of the predictor variables. That is, an individual offender's predictor pattern could be used to find the most likely prediction for that pattern.

Observed and Predicted Frequencies

Sexually abused as a child	physically abused as a child	spent time in children's home	father's hostility to offender as child	mother's hostility to offender as child	depression and anxiety scale	age up to 29 or 30 and above	type of offence	Frequency Observed	Predicted	Pearson Residual	Percentage Observed	Predicted
yes	yes	yes	low hostility	high hostility	high score	older	rapist	0	1.387	−1.269	.0%	13.9%
							Incestuous child abuser	10	7.078	2.032	100.0%	70.8%
							paedophile	0	1.535	−1.347	.0%	15.3%
			high hostility	low hostility	high score	younger	rapist	0	3.601	−2.372	.0%	36.0%
							Incestuous child abuser	0	3.192	−2.165	.0%	31.9%
							paedophile	10	3.207	4.603	100.0%	32.1%
				high hostility	high score	older	rapist	10	1.387	7.882	100.0%	13.9%
							Incestuous child abuser	0	7.078	−4.922	.0%	70.8%
							paedophile	0	1.535	−1.347	.0%	15.3%
		no	low hostility	high hostility	low score	younger	rapist	10	8.501	1.328	100.0%	85.0%
							Incestuous child abuser	0	.702	−.869	.0%	7.0%
							paedophile	0	.797	−.930	.0%	8.0%
						older	rapist	10	6.281	2.433	100.0%	62.8%
							Incestuous child abuser	0	2.987	−2.064	.0%	29.9%
							paedophile	0	.732	−.889	.0%	7.3%
					high score	older	rapist	0	6.281	−4.110	.0%	62.8%
							Incestuous child abuser	10	2.987	4.845	100.0%	29.9%
							paedophile	0	.732	−.889	.0%	7.3%
			high hostility	low hostility	high score	older	rapist	10	6.281	2.433	100.0%	62.8%
							Incestuous child abuser	0	2.987	−2.064	.0%	29.9%
							paedophile	0	.732	−.889	.0%	7.3%
				high hostility	low score	older	rapist	0	6.281	−4.110	.0%	62.8%
							Incestuous child abuser	10	2.987	4.845	100.0%	29.9%
							paedophile	0	.732	−.889	.0%	7.3%
	No	yes	low hostility	low hostility	high score	older	rapist	0	.000	.000	.0%	.0%
							Incestuous child abuser	10	6.785	2.177	100.0%	67.9%
							paedophile	0	3.215	−2.177	.0%	32.1%
			high hostility	low hostility	low score	younger	rapist	0	.000	.000	.0%	.0%
							Incestuous child abuser	10	3.130	4.685	100.0%	31.3%
							paedophile	0	6.870	−4.685	.0%	68.7%
					high score	older	rapist	0	.000	.000	.0%	.0%
							Incestuous child abuser	10	13.571	−1.710	50.0%	67.9%
							paedophile	10	6.429	1.710	50.0%	32.1%
		no	high hostility	high hostility	low score	older	rapist	0	.000	.000	.0%	.0%
							Incestuous child abuser	0	6.514	−4.323	.0%	65.1%
							paedophile	10	3.486	4.323	100.0%	34.9%
no	yes	no	low hostility	high hostility	low score	younger	rapist	10	10.000	.000	100.0%	100.0%
							Incestuous child abuser	0	.000	.000	.0%	.0%
							paedophile	0	.000	.000	.0%	.0%
			high hostility	low hostility	high score	younger	rapist	10	10.000	.000	100.0%	100.0%
							Incestuous child abuser	0	.000	.000	.0%	.0%
							paedophile	0	.000	.000	.0%	.0%
	No	yes	low hostility	high hostility	high score	younger	rapist	0	1.523	−1.340	.0%	15.2%
							Incestuous child abuser	0	2.141	−1.651	.0%	21.4%
							paedophile	10	6.336	2.405	100.0%	63.4%
			high hostility	low hostility	low score	older	rapist	0	.701	−.868	.0%	7.0%
							Incestuous child abuser	0	5.675	−3.622	.0%	56.7%
							paedophile	10	3.624	4.194	100.0%	36.2%
					high score	older	rapist	0	.701	−.868	.0%	7.0%
							Incestuous child abuser	10	5.675	2.761	100.0%	56.7%
							paedophile	0	3.624	−2.384	.0%	36.2%
				high hostility	high score	older	rapist	0	.701	−.868	.0%	7.0%
							Incestuous child abuser	10	5.675	2.761	100.0%	56.7%
							paedophile	0	3.624	−2.384	.0%	36.2%
		no	low hostility	high hostility	low score	younger	rapist	10	6.374	2.385	100.0%	63.7%
							Incestuous child abuser	0	.835	−.954	.0%	8.3%
							paedophile	0	2.791	−1.967	.0%	27.9%

The percentages are based on total observed frequencies in each subpopulation.

The output for multinomial logistic regression is quite substantial. Of course, it is possible to reduce the amount of output, but then you need to be clear just what aspects of the output are not necessary for your purposes. Since it is easier to ignore surplus tables than to redo the analysis then it is better to err on the side of too much output.

■ It is a useful reminder to examine the table entitled 'Case Processing Summary'. This provides a reminder of the distributions of the categories of each of the variables in the analysis. In our example all of the variables simply have two categories, and so no dummy variables need to be created. However, the predictor variables may have three or more categories in which case SPSS will create appropriate dummy variables for all but one of the categories of that variable. (This does not apply to variables defined as a covariate which are treated as score variables.) There are, however, three different values of the criterion variable of offence type – rapists, incestuous offenders and paedophiles, and SPSS will create two dummy variables from these three categories.

■ The 'Step Summary' table essentially gives the sequence of variables entered into the stepwise multiple regression. Remember that in stepwise analyses the predictors are selected in terms of their (distinct) predictive power. So the best predictor is selected first, adjustments made, and the remaining best predictor selected second, and so forth. There is a Step 0 which contains only the intercept of the regression line. Steps 1 to 4 in this example add in the strongest predictors in turn. The variable 'childhom' (children's home) is added in Step 1, 'age' in Step 2. 'physabus' (physical abuse) in Step 3 and 'sexualab' (sexual abuse) in Step 4. Each of these produces a significantly better fit of the predicted (modelled) data to the actual data. This can be seen from the lowering values of the −2 log likelihood values (which are chi-square values) given in the table. Each of these changes is significant in this example, meaning that none of the predictors may be dropped without worsening the accuracy of the classification.

■ The 'Model Fitting Information' table gives the value of the −2 log likelihood chi square for the fit of the model (i.e. the significant predictors plus the intercept). This value is significant in this case. It merely is an indication that the model (predictor variables) does not completely predict the actual data. In other words, the prediction is less than complete or partial. Clearly, there are other factors which need to be taken into account to achieve a perfect fit of the model to the data. This will normally be the case.

■ The table of the 'Pseudo R-Square' statistics merely confirms this. The R-square statistic gives the combined correlation of a set of predictors with the predicted variable for score data. The pseudo R-square is analogous to this in interpretation but is used when it is not possible to accurately compute the R-square statistic itself, as in the case of logistic regression. As can be seen, there are three different methods of calculation used. They are all indicators of the combined relationship of the predictors to the category variable. A value of zero means no multiple correlation, a value of 1.00 means a perfect multiple correlation. Values of around 0.5 are fairly satisfactory as they indicate an overall combined correlation of the predictor variables with the predicted variable of around 0.7. (This is obtained by taking the square root of 0.5.)

■ The table of the 'Likelihood Ratio Tests' tells us what happens to the model if we remove each of the predictor variables in turn. The model is merely the set of predictors which emerge in the analysis. In this case we have four predictors as already described. In each case there is a significant decrement in the fit of the predicted data to the actual data after dropping any of the predictors. In other words, each of the predictors is having a significant effect and normally should be retained. Of course, should the researcher have good reason then any predictor can be dropped, though it is recommended that inexperienced researchers do not do this.

■ The table of the 'Parameter Estimates' basically gives the intercept and the regression weights for this multinomial regression analysis. The intercept value is clear at 0.608 for rapists. But notice a number of things. The dependent variable (offence type) which has three categories has been turned into two dummy variables 'Rapists' (versus the other two groups) and 'Incestuous Child Molester' (versus the other two groups). Remember that the number of dummy variables is given by the number of categories minus one. There are three offender categories so two dummy variables. The dummy variables are created by taking one of the three offender categories and contrasting this with the remaining offender categories. In our example, we have:

rapists versus incestuous child molesters *and* paedophiles
incestuous child molesters versus rapists *and* paedophiles
paedophiles versus rapists *and* incestuous child molesters

The choice of which of the possible dummy variables to select is arbitrary and can be varied by selecting 'Custom/Stepwise' in Step 3 of Section 32.2. Also notice that the variables have been given two regression weights – a different one for each value. However, one of the pair is always zero, which essentially means that no contribution to the calculation is made by these values. The significance of each of these regression weights is given in one of the columns of the table. Significance is based on the Wald value which is given in another column. Don't worry too much if you do not understand this too clearly as one does not need to do any actual calculations. It is explained in more detail in our accompanying statistics text (*ISP*, Chapter 36).

■ The 'Classification' table is very important and gives the accuracy of the predictions based on the parameter estimates. This cross-tabulation table indicates what predictions would be made on the basis of the significant predictor variables and how accurate these predictions are. As can be seen, the predictions are very accurate for rape offenders and to a lesser degree for the incestuous child molesters. However, the classification is poor for paedophiles.

■ The 'Observed and Predicted Frequencies' table is probably most useful to those who have a practical situation in which they wish to make the best prediction of the category based on the predictor variables. The table gives every possible pattern of the predictor variables (SPSS calls them covariates) and the actual classifications in the data for each pattern plus the most likely outcome as predicted from that pattern. In other words, the table could be used to make predictions for individual cases with known individual patterns.

32.4 Reporting the findings

There is no conventional method of reporting the findings succinctly for a multinomial logistic regression. If the technique has been used for previous studies in the chosen area of research then the reporting methods used in those might be adopted.

For the data analysed in this chapter, it is clear that there is a set of predictors which work fairly effectively in part. One way of reporting these findings would be as follows: 'Multinomial logistic regression was performed to establish what characteristics distinguish the three different types of offender. Out of the seven predictor variables included in the analysis, four were shown to distinguish the different types of offender to a degree. Rapists were correctly identified as such in 85.7% of cases, incestuous child abusers were correctly identified in 62.5% of instances, but paedophiles were correctly identified in only 20.0% of instances. Paedophiles tended to be misclassified as incestuous child abusers very often. The predictors which distinguished rapists from others the best were time spent in a children's home ($b = -2.252$), physical abuse ($b = 20.124$) and sexual abuse ($b = -18.582$). The latter is not reported as significant as such in the table. No significance is given. However, paedophiles were best distinguished from the other two groups only by age ($b = -1.533$).'

33 Binomial logistic regression

Overview

■ Binomial logistic regression may be regarded as a special case of multinomial logistic regression, which was described in Chapter 32. The major difference is that it differentiates the characteristics of people in just *two* different groups.

■ SPSS has a much more extensive repertoire of regression techniques for binomial logistic regression although Releases 12 and 13 of SPSS have introduced a little more flexibility to its multinomial logistic regression procedures.

■ Binomial logistic regression is a form of multiple regression. It identifies patterns of variables which can effectively differentiate between the members of two different categories. That is, binomial logistic regression predicts category membership as opposed to a score as in the case of multivariate regression (Chapter 28). For example, one could use it to examine the pattern of variables which best differentiates male from female participants in a study of reasons for seeking medical advice. There may be a different pattern of reasons why men go to a doctor from the pattern or reasons why women go to a doctor.

■ Another way of putting this is that binomial logistic regression uses predictor variables to predict the most likely category of the dependent variable to which different individuals belong.

■ The binomial logistic regression procedure calculates *b*-weights (or regression weights) much as in multiple regression (Chapter 28). The big difference is that in binomial logistic regression these *b*-weights are *not* applied to predict scores. Instead they are applied to something called the logit which is the natural logarithm of the odds ratio. The odds ratio is rather like a probability. It is simply the ratio of the numbers in one category to the number of cases in the other category. The logit (and natural logarithms for that matter) generally are not crucial to a researcher's use of binomial logistic regression so do not require detailed understanding.

■ Although the categories are always a binomial (binary or two-value) category variable, the other variables in the analysis may be score variables, nominal (category or categorical) variables, or a mixture of both.

■ Any category variable which has more than two categories is automatically turned into a set of dummy variables by SPSS. Each dummy variable consists of one of the categories of the variable versus all of the rest of the categories. There are as many dummy variables as categories. For technical reasons, one of the possible dummy variables is arbitrarily omitted from the binomial logistic regression. This is because it contains no new information which is not already contained in the other dummy variables.

■ Binomial regression, for example, can proceed using stepwise procedures, forward entry of poor predictors, backward elimination of poor predictors and so forth. The choice of the type of model to use is often a rather subtle matter. Stepwise procedures gradually build up the model by selecting on a step-by-step basis variables which are good at differentiating between the members of the two categories of the dependent variable. Forward entry means that at each step the computer finds the best remaining variable for differentiating between the two categories. If it does not meet certain requirements in terms of predictive (or classificatory) power then it is not entered into the model. For many purposes, stepwise forward entry is a good choice in psychology.

■ Much of the binomial logistic regression output from SPSS consists of indicators of how well the modelled data (the category membership predicted by the predictor variables) fits the actual data (the actual category which the individual belongs to). These are based on chi-square for the most part. A useful predictor should improve the fit of the predicted membership to the actual categories cases belong to.

■ More directly understood are the classification tables generated by SPSS which indicate how well the predictions match the actual classifications.

The example we will be working with is a study of the variables which might be used to help assess whether a prisoner is likely to reoffend or not reoffend after leaving prison. Reoffending is known as recidivism. The data from the study are shown in Table 33.1 (*ISP*, Table 37.5). For pedagogical purposes and the convenience of those who wish to follow our steps on a computer, the 19 cases are reproduced five times. As can be seen, recidivism is a binomial category variable – in a given period of time, a prisoner either reoffends or does not. Since the purpose of our analysis is to find the pattern of variables which predict which of these two categories a prisoner will fall then this is an obvious set of data for the binomial logistic regression.

Any type of variable – scores or nominal (category) – may be used as the predictor variables in binomial logistic regression. However, in our example, we have used very simple variables such as age, previous imprisonment, treatment, contrition, marital status and whether or not the offender is a sex offender. All of these are binomial nominal variables. We can use score variables, which are defined as covariates in SPSS. We can also use nominal (category) variables with three or more different values (categories). In this case, SPSS recodes the variable into a number of dummy variables automatically. This means that the set of predictor variables is actually greater than the initial number of variables in the data. If we had a variable such as type of crime with the categories sex crime, violent crime and theft then, in theory, we could create three dummy variables. These would be:

Dummy variable 1 = sex crime or not
Dummy variable 2 = violent crime or not
Dummy variable 3 = theft or not

It really is as simple as that to create dummy variables. There is just one complication to note. One of the dummy variables actually contains no new information if we know a

Table 33.1   Data for the study of recidivism – the data from 19 cases is reproduced five times to give realistic sample sizes but only to facilitate explanation

	Recidivism	Age	Previous prison	Treatment	Contrite	Married	Sex offender
1	yes	younger	yes	no	no	no	yes
2	yes	older	yes	no	no	no	yes
3	yes	older	yes	yes	no	no	yes
4	yes	older	yes	yes	no	yes	no
5	yes	younger	yes	no	no	no	no
6	yes	younger	no	yes	yes	no	no
7	yes	older	no	yes	yes	yes	yes
8	yes	younger	yes	no	no	no	yes
9	yes	younger	no	no	no	yes	yes
10	yes	older	no	no	no	no	no
11	no	younger	no	yes	yes	no	no
12	no	older	no	yes	yes	no	no
13	no	older	yes	yes	yes	yes	yes
14	no	younger	no	yes	yes	yes	yes
15	no	younger	no	yes	yes	no	yes
16	no	younger	no	no	yes	yes	no
17	no	older	no	no	no	yes	no
18	no	older	yes	yes	yes	no	no
19	no	older	yes	yes	yes	no	no
etc.	yes	younger	yes	no	no	no	yes

person's values for the other two dummy variables. So, if we know that someone has not committed a sex crime and we know that they have not committed a violent crime then they must have committed a theft. Since they are *all* offenders, this is a simple logical assessment. Because always one of the dummy variables is repetitive and redundant, in logistic regression there is always one less than the maximum number of dummy variables. SPSS chooses this arbitrarily unless the user stipulates otherwise.

Table 33.2 demonstrates one way of coding the data ready for the computer analysis. It is best to enter data numerically into SPSS so each value of each variable is given a numerical code. 1s and 0s have been used in every case to indicate the presence or absence of a characteristic. The values would be given value labels in SPSS so as to make the output as clear as possible.

Binomial logistic regression in SPSS has a good variety of analysis options. Beginners will find the range a little bewildering and many of the options will be of no interest to many researchers. Choosing the appropriate options (what some would refer to as the appropriate model) depends very much on the purpose of one's analysis and only the researcher knows this. Generally speaking, if the sole purpose of the analysis is to obtain the best set of predictors to categorise people then it is sufficient to enter all of the predictors at the same time – SPSS merely takes the variables in the order they are listed. However, more typically the researcher is trying to build up a theoretical/conceptual explanation; e.g. of why some offenders reoffend in this example. In these circumstances, the researcher may wish to give some variables priority in the analysis. This involves

Table 33.2   Data from Table 33.1 coded in binary fashion as 0 and 1 for each variable

	Recidivism	Age	Previous prison	Treatment	Contrite	Married	Sex offender
1	1	0	1	0	0	0	1
2	1	1	1	0	0	0	1
3	1	1	1	1	0	0	1
4	1	1	1	1	0	1	0
5	1	0	1	0	0	0	0
6	1	0	0	1	1	0	0
7	1	1	0	1	1	1	1
8	1	0	1	0	0	0	1
9	1	0	0	0	0	1	1
10	1	1	0	0	0	0	0
11	0	0	0	1	1	0	0
12	0	1	0	1	1	0	0
13	0	1	1	1	1	1	1
14	0	0	0	1	1	1	1
15	0	0	0	1	1	0	1
16	0	0	0	0	1	1	0
17	0	1	0	0	0	1	0
18	0	1	1	1	1	0	0
19	0	1	1	1	1	0	0
etc.	1	0	1	0	0	0	1

entering the predictors hierarchically in blocks. Furthermore, one needs to identify the best predictors. The variables may be entered in step-by-step form, in which the best predictor is taken first, then the next remaining best predictor entered second (allowing for correlations between predictors), and so forth until no significant improvement in prediction is achieved.

An alternative is to enter all of the predictors initially, then drop predictors one by one. If dropping the weakest predictor significantly reduces the accuracy of the prediction then it should be retained. However, it can be eliminated *if* dropping it makes no change to the accuracy of the prediction. The process goes on step by step by examining the effect of removing the weakest predictor in the remaining set. There is only one complication of note – that is eliminated predictors can actually return to the set of predictors if the elimination of another variable results in the previously eliminated variable increasing its independent predictive power.

Finally, backwards elimination is *not* better than other approaches, it largely does the job in a different way. It does not necessarily give exactly the same findings as other methods either – it is simply one reasonable and appropriate approach to the data.

33.1 Binomial logistic regression

Step 1:

Enter the data. Weight the cases using 'freq'.

	recidivi	age	prepris	treatmen	contrite	married	sexoff	freq
1	1	1	1	1	1	1	0	5
2	1	0	1	1	1	1	0	5
3	1	0	1	0	1	1	0	5
4	1	0	1	0	1	0	1	5
5	1	1	1	1	1	1	1	5
6	1	1	0	0	0	1	1	5
7	1	0	0	0	0	0	1	5
8	1	1	1	1	1	1	0	5
9	1	1	0	1	1	0	0	5
10	0	0	0	1	1	1	0	5
11	0	1	0	0	0	1	0	5
12	0	0	0	0	0	1	1	5
13	0	0	1	0	0	0	1	5
14	0	1	0	0	0	0	1	5
15	0	1	0	0	0	1	0	5
16	0	1	0	1	0	0	0	5
17	0	0	0	1	1	0	0	5
18	0	0	0	0	0	1	1	5
19	0	0	1	0	0	1	1	5

Step 2:

Select 'Analyze', 'Regression' and 'Binary Logistic...'.

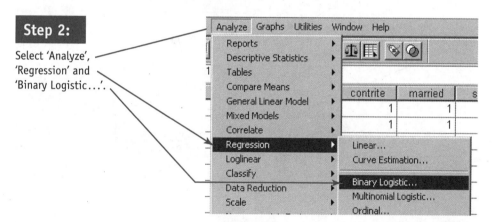

Step 3:

Select 'recidivi' and the ► button beside the 'Dependent:' box to put it there.

Select the other six variables (excluding 'freq') and the ► button beside the 'Covariates:' box to put them there.

Select 'Categorical...'.

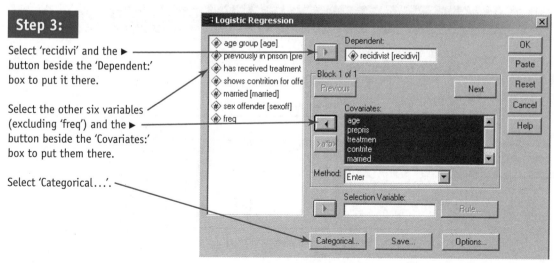

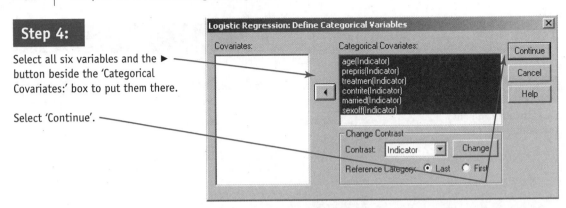

Step 4:

Select all six variables and the ► button beside the 'Categorical Covariates:' box to put them there.

Select 'Continue'.

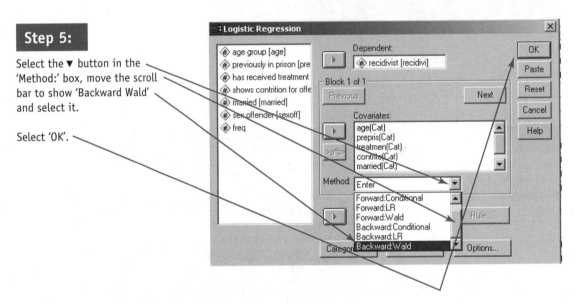

Step 5:

Select the ▼ button in the 'Method:' box, move the scroll bar to show 'Backward Wald' and select it.

Select 'OK'.

33.2 Interpreting the output

Logistic Regression

Case Processing Summary

Unweighted Cases[a]		N	Percent
Selected Cases	Included in Analysis	19	100.0
	Missing Cases	0	.0
	Total	19	100.0
Unselected Cases		0	.0
Total		19	100.0

a. If weight is in effect, see classification table for the total number of cases.

Dependent Variable Encoding

Original Value	Internal Value
No	0
yes	1

Check this table – it makes clear just how the dependent variable has been coded by SPSS (the 'Internal Value'). In this case they are the same as the values that we entered but it is well worth checking otherwise serious errors can be made.

Categorical Variables Codings

		Frequency	Paramete (1)
sex offender	sex offender	10	1.000
	not sex offender	9	.000
previously in prison	no previous	11	1.000
	previous prison	8	.000
has received treatment in prison	treated	11	1.000
	not treated	8	.000
shows contrition for offence	Contrite	10	1.000
	not contrite	9	.000
married	married	7	1.000
	not married	12	.000
age group	older (30 plus)	10	1.000
	younger	9	.000

This table breaks down each variable and gives numbers in each category. Thus there are 9 in the sample who are not sex offenders.

Block 0: Beginning Block

Block 0 is before any predictors have been taken into account. Generally you can skip this section.

Classification Table[a,b]

			Predicted		
			recidivist		Percentage
Observed			No	yes	Correct
Step 0	recidivist	No	50	0	100.0
		yes	45	0	.0
	Overall Percentage				52.6

a. Constant is included in the model.
b. The cut value is .500.

This table gives the actual numbers of recidivists and non-recidivists. There are 45 recidivists and 50 non-recidivists.

Variables in the Equation

		B	S.E.	Wald	df	Sig.	Exp(B)
Step 0	Constant	−.105	.205	.263	1	.608	.900

The constant is more or less the same as the intercept in multivariate regression.

Variables not in the Equation

			Score	df	Sig.
Step 0	Variables	age(1)	2.299	1	.129
		prepris(1)	21.159	1	.000
		treatmen(1)	6.345	1	.012
		contrite(1)	31.714	1	.000
		married(1)	.452	1	.501
		sexoff(1)	.293	1	.588
	Overall Statistics		50.804	6	.000

No predictors have been included at this stage so there cannot be any in the regression equation.

Block 1: Method = Backward Stepwise (Wald)

Block 1 contains the key tables.

Omnibus Tests of Model Coefficients

		Chi-square	df	Sig.
Step 1	Step	70.953	6	.000
	Block	70.953	6	.000
	Model	70.953	6	.000
Step 2[a]	Step	−3.825	1	.050
	Block	67.128	5	.000
	Model	67.128	5	.000
Step 3[a]	Step	−17.310	1	.000
	Block	49.818	4	.000
	Model	49.818	4	.000
Step 4[a]	Step	−.116	1	.733
	Block	49.702	3	.000
	Model	49.702	3	.000
Step 5	Step	16.968	1	.000
	Block	66.670	4	.000
	Model	66.670	4	.000

Step 1 includes all of the predictors.

Step 2 and the later steps below each involve the elimination of a variable – that is they are the backward elimination steps.

The 'Variables in the Equation' table (follows) indicates which predictors are in the model at each step.

a. A negative Chi-squares value indicates that the Chi-squares value has decreased from the previous step.

Model Summary

Step	−2 Log likelihood	Cox & Snell R Square	Nagelkerke R Square
1	60.482[a]	.526	.702
2	64.307[a]	.507	.676
3	81.617[b]	.408	.545
4	81.733[b]	.407	.544
5	64.765[a]	.504	.673

a. Estimation terminated at iteration number 20 because maximum iterations has been reached. Final solution cannot be found.

b. Estimation terminated at iteration number 6 because parameter estimates changed by less than .001.

These are indexes of the fit of the model to the actual data. The nearer the two (pseudo) R-square measures are to 1.0 the better the fit of the model at that step to the data. The smaller the −2 log likelihood value the better the fit of the model to the data.

Notice that the final model (Step 5) shows an improved fit – a variable has been allowed to re-enter the regression equation.

Classification Table[a]

	Observed		Predicted		
			recidivist		Percentage Correct
			No	yes	
Step 1	recidivist	No	45	5	90.0
		yes	5	40	88.9
	Overall Percentage				89.5
Step 2	recidivist	No	45	5	90.0
		yes	5	40	88.9
	Overall Percentage				89.5
Step 3	recidivist	No	50	0	100.0
		yes	10	35	77.8
	Overall Percentage				89.5
Step 4	recidivist	No	50	0	100.0
		yes	10	35	77.8
	Overall Percentage				89.5
Step 5	recidivist	No	45	5	90.0
		yes	5	40	88.9
	Overall Percentage				89.5

a. The cut value is .500.

This table indicates the accuracy of the classification at each step. The overall accuracy remains constant throughout – what changes is the relative proportions of recidivists and non-recidivists correctly identified. According to one's objectives, one of the earlier models may be more useful. For example, if it is more important to identify correctly those who will not reoffend, then the Step 3 or Step 4 models may be preferred since these more accurately identify non-reoffenders.

The least significant predictor in Step 1 is chosen for elimination in Step 2. 'treatmen' and 'sexoff' both have significances of 0.998 but 'treatmen' occurs first and is selected.

Variables in the Equation[c]

		B	S.E.	Wald	df	Sig.	Exp(B)
Step 1[a]	age(1)	−2.726	.736	13.702	1	.000	.065
	prepris(1)	−1.086	.730	2.215	1	.137	.337
	treatmen(1)	19.362	8901.292	.000	1	.998	2.6E+08
	contrite(1)	−41.459	11325.914	.000	1	.997	.000
	married(1)	−.307	.674	.208	1	.648	.735
	sexoff(1)	−20.641	7003.093	.000	1	.998	.000
	Constant	23.802	7003.093	.000	1	.997	2.2E+10
Step 2[a]	age(1)	−2.775	.787	12.417	1	.000	.062
	prepris(1)	−1.471	.717	4.210	1	.040	.230
	contrite(1)	−22.879	7449.317	.000	1	.998	.000
	married(1)	−.448	.667	.450	1	.502	.639
	sexoff(1)	−21.102	7449.317	.000	1	.998	.000
	Constant	24.926	7449.317	.000	1	.997	6.7E+10
Step 3[a]	age(1)	−1.919	.710	7.306	1	.007	.147
	prepris(1)	−2.115	.686	9.496	1	.002	.121
	contrite(1)	−2.510	.617	16.539	1	.000	.081
	married(1)	.191	.560	.116	1	.733	1.210
	Constant	3.465	.940	13.600	1	.000	31.989
Step 4[a]	age(1)	−1.913	.711	7.247	1	.007	.148
	prepris(1)	−2.089	.685	9.299	1	.002	.124
	contrite(1)	−2.517	.616	16.687	1	.000	.081
	Constant	3.535	.926	14.566	1	.000	34.285
Step 5[b]	age(1)	−2.731	.786	12.077	1	.001	.065
	prepris(1)	−1.571	.695	5.107	1	.024	.208
	contrite(1)	−22.765	7466.473	.000	1	.998	.000
	sexoff(1)	−20.951	7466.473	.000	1	.998	.000
	Constant	24.648	7466.473	.000	1	.997	5.1E+10

a. Variable(s) entered on step 1: age, prepris, treatmen, contrite, married, sexoff.
b. Variable(s) entered on step 5: sexoff.
c. Stepwise procedure stopped because removing the least significant variable result in a previously fitted model.

Although 'sexoff' was discarded as a part of the model by Step 3 and does not appear in Step 4, it has been allowed to re-enter at Step 5 simply because the dropping of 'married' after Step 3 has resulted in 'sexoff' having enough independent predictive power to meet the criterion for re-entry as a good predictor.

It is important to note that the regression weights are only applied to the value of the category variable coded as 1. So the negative regression weight for 'sexoff(1)' of −20.951 actually indicates that sex offenders are *less* likely to reoffend on release. Great care is needed to know what codings are given to the different values of variables. This is made worse because nominal variables not coded as 0 and 1 may be recoded by SPSS into those values.

Variables not in the Equation

			Score	df	Sig.
Step 2[a]	Variables	treatmen(1)	2.638	1	.104
	Overall Statistics		2.638	1	.104
Step 3[b]	Variables	treatmen(1)	6.160	1	.013
		sexoff(1)	13.026	1	.000
	Overall Statistics		14.017	2	.001
Step 4[c]	Variables	treatmen(1)	5.736	1	.017
		married(1)	.116	1	.733
		sexoff(1)	12.609	1	.000
	Overall Statistics		14.123	3	.003
Step 5[c]	Variables	treatmen(1)	2.809	1	.094
		married(1)	.453	1	.501
	Overall Statistics		2.994	2	.224

a. Variable(s) removed on step 2: treatmen.
b. Variable(s) removed on step 3: sexoff.
c. Variable(s) removed on step 4: married.

This table gives the significance of the variables not included in the model. See how significant 'sexoff' is at Step 4. Hence its reinclusion at Step 5.

33.3 Reporting the findings

One way of reporting the findings of this analysis is as follows: 'Using Wald's backward elimination model, characteristics differentiating prisoners who reoffend after release from those who do not reoffend were investigated. The final regression model indicated that younger offenders, those with a previous history of prison, those who were not contrite about their offences, and those who were not sex offenders were more likely to reoffend. Age and previous imprisonment were significant predictors at the 5% level. The Cox and Snell pseudo R-square was 0.50 indicating that the fit of the model to the data was only moderate. This model was almost equally accurate for reoffending (88.9% correct) as for non re-offending (90.0%).'

APPENDIX A
Confidence intervals

■ Confidence intervals are far from new in statistics but have recently been advocated as preferable to the sorts of point estimates commonly used in most statistical analyses. The mean of a sample can be used as an estimate of the mean of the population from which that sample was taken. This single estimate is a point estimate of the population mean since it is expressed as a single value such as 5.3. However, we know that this estimate, based on a sample, is merely the best one and that the actual population mean is likely to be different from this estimate.

■ In confidence intervals, the estimated mean is expressed in terms of a range of means within which the actual population mean is likely to lie. Thus the confidence interval for a mean may be from 4.2 to 6.4.

■ The confidence interval will vary according to the level of certainty required by the researcher. So, for the same data, the confidence interval that is 95% likely to include the population mean is narrower than the confidence interval that is 99% likely to include the population mean.

■ Earlier in this book we used confidence intervals when they seemed particularly useful. One of the difficulties with the confidence interval approach lies in the fact that any statistic theoretically has a confidence interval. Despite this, it is difficult to find the methods for calculating them in the statistical literature and textbooks. This limits the applicability of the confidence interval approach. More to the point here, SPSS in common with other computer programs only provides a limited number of confidence intervals.

Confidence intervals have been presented in the output for the following tests described in this book:

Regression B: see the table on page 67
Related t-test: see the table on page 86
Unrelated t-test: see the table on page 91
One-way unrelated ANOVA: see the table on page 133
Two-way unrelated ANOVA: see the tables on pages 143 to 144
Multiple-comparison tests: see the table on page 150
One-way ANCOVA: see the table on page 155

Confidence intervals can also be readily obtained for the following statistics:

One-sample t-test
One-way related ANOVA
Two-way mixed ANOVA
Regression – predicted score

APPENDIX B
Other statistics in SPSS

Other statistical tests provided by SPSS but not described in this book are shown below in terms of their options on the 'Analyze' menu, submenu and dialog box options.

Analyze menu	Analyze submenu	Dialog box
Descriptive Statistics	Crosstabs ...	Lambda
		Uncertainty coefficient
		Gamma
		Somers' d
		Kendall's tau-b
		Kendall's tau-c
		Risk
		Eta
Correlate	Bivariate ...	Kendall's tau-b
Regression	Curve Estimation ...	
	Binary Logistic ...	
	Multinomial Logistic ...	
	Ordinal ...	
	Probit ...	
	Nonlinear ...	
	Weight Estimation ...	
	2-Stage Least Squares ...	
	Optimal Scaling ...	
Loglinear	Logit ...	
Classify	TwoStep Cluster ...	
	K-Means Cluster ...	
	Hierarchical Cluster ...	
	Discriminant ...	
Data Reduction	Correspondence Analysis ...	
	Optimal Scaling ...	
Scale	Multidimensional Scaling ...	
	Multidimensional Scaling[PROXSCAL] ...	
	Multidimensional Scaling [ALSCAL]	
Nonparametric Tests	Binomial ...	
	Runs ...	
	1-Sample K-S ... (Kolmogorov–Smirnov)	
	2 Independent Samples ...	Kolmogorov–Smirnov Z
		Wald–Wolfowitz runs
		Moses extreme reactions

Analyze menu	Analyze submenu	Dialog box
	K Independent Samples . . .	Kruskal–Wallis H
		Jonckheere–Terpstra
		Median
	2 Related Samples . . .	Marginal Homogeneity
	K Related Samples . . .	Friedman
		Kendall's W
		Cochran's Q
Time Series	Exponential Smoothing . . .	
	Autoregression . . .	
	ARIMA . . .	
	Seasonal Decomposition . . .	
Survival	Life Tables . . .	
	Kaplan–Meier . . .	
	Cox Regression . . .	
	Cox w/ Time-Dep Cov . . .	

Index